Mixing it up

Integrated, Interdisciplinary, Intriguing Science in the Elementary Classroom

An NSTA Press Journals Collection

NSTApress®

NATIONAL SCIENCE TEACHERS ASSOCIATION

Arlington, Virginia

NATIONAL SCIENCE TEACHERS ASSOCIATION

Claire Reinburg, Director
J. Andrew Cocke, Associate Editor
Judy Cusick, Associate Editor
Betty Smith, Associate Editor

ART AND DESIGN Linda Olliver, Director
PERIODICALS PUBLISHING Shelley Carey, Director
PRINTING AND PRODUCTION Catherine Lorrain-Hale, Director
    Nguyet Tran, Assistant Production Manager
    Jack Parker, Desktop Publishing Specialist
MARKETING Holly Hemphill, Director
NSTA WEB Tim Weber, Webmaster
PERIODICALS PUBLISHING Shelley Carey, Director
PUBLICATIONS OPERATIONS, Hank Janowsky, Manager
sciLINKS Tyson Brown, Manager
        David Anderson, Web and Development Coordinator

NATIONAL SCIENCE TEACHERS ASSOCIATION
Gerald F. Wheeler, Executive Director
David Beacom, Publisher

Mixing It Up: Integrated, Interdisciplinary, Intriguing Science in the Elementary Classroom
NSTA Stock Number: PB175X
Printed in the USA by Victor Graphics. Printed on recycled paper.

05 04 03   4 3 2 1

Library of Congress Cataloging-in-Publication Data
Mixing it up: integrated, interdisciplinary, intriguing science in the elementary classroom: an NSTA Press journals collection.
    p. cm
Includes bibliographical references.
"NSTA stock number: PB175X"—T.p. verso.
ISBN 0-87355-231-8
1. Science—Study and Teaching (Elementary)—United States. 2. Interdisciplinary approach in education—United States. I. National Science Teachers Association.
LB1585.3.M59 2003   2003011673
372.3'5—dc21

NSTA is committed to publishing quality material that promotes the best in inquiry-based science education. However, conditions of actual use may vary and the safety procedures and practices described in this book are intended to serve only as a guide. Additional precautionary measures may be required. NSTA and the authors do not warrant or represent that the procedures and practices in this book meet any safety code or standard of federal, state, or local regulations. NSTA and the authors disclaim any liability for personal injury or damage to property arising out of or relating to the use of this book including any of the recommendations, instructions, or materials contained therein.

 Featuring sciLINKS®—a new way of connecting text and the Internet. Up-to-the minute online content, classroom ideas, and other materials are just a click away. Go to page xvii to learn more about this new educational resource.

Contents

Section 1   Helping Students Build Connections

A   Engaging and Exploring: Students and Inquiry

v

Section 2   School and Community Connections

A Schoolwide Themes

Introduction

The most recent educational reform that began with national standards in the various disciplines has now reached an age of greater accountability. Though the *National Science Education Standards* (NRC 1996) establishes the expectation that all children have access to quality science learning experiences throughout their school years, the language of "No Child Left Behind" shifts the instructional dynamic, especially in K–6 classrooms. No Child Left Behind is the federal education law that promises to reform K–12 education through increased testing and accountability, flexibility, and more parental choice.

Beginning in 2005, every student will be tested annually in reading and math in grades 3 to 8 and the scores from these tests will be used to hold the schools and states accountable for increased student achievement. The demand for accountability in reading and mathematics has the potential of placing the science instruction in many schools at risk. As a result, already minimal science instruction is even further diminished.

One way to enhance the quantity and quality of science instruction is through integrating content between and among disciplines. With time at a premium in the elementary classroom, integrated and interdisciplinary work increase the chances that science will be taught. Integration of content builds connections in the brain and to the world, a strategy that increases student understanding of science concepts.

This compendium of articles from *Science & Children,* the elementary school journal of the National Science Teachers Association, is aimed at helping teachers build those connections in their students' minds. The articles describe lessons and units that are interdisciplinary, both integrated and interdisciplinary, or thematic.

The language used to describe integration of content within and among disciplines is inconsistent and, as a result, promotes confusion. The terms "integration," "integrated," "interdisciplinary," and "thematic" are common but are used differently, even in the included articles. It is important to clarify the language used in developing this book so the reader understands the organization.

In the development of science lessons and units, "integrate" describes the process of combining concepts and processes within sciences or among disciplines. In this book, the integration of concepts and processes within sciences (such as physical and life sciences) is called "integrated science" while the integration of concepts and processes between or among disciplines (such as mathematics and science) is called "interdisciplinary." In both cases, the focus of learning is on engagement in and understanding of the disciplines.

The word "thematic," sometimes referred to as "multidisciplinary," views the curriculum through the lens of a discipline that includes content from other disciplines to increase relevance. Themes, when done well, are usually broad topics (rather than specific concepts and processes) to which multiple disciplines connect.

Each article is categorized according to the following:
• Interdisciplinary (ID), integrated and interdisciplinary (I-ID) or thematic (T)
• Appropriate grade level (K–2 or 3–6)
• Standards addressed

A quick-reference chart listing these categories for each article begins on page xv.

In addition, the book is divided into two sections—"Helping Students Build Connections" and "School and Community Connections"—based on specific ways in which this integrated and interdisciplinary work builds connections that advance science learning.

Section One, "Helping Students Build Connections," includes articles that build the connections in the brain necessary to making sense of science concepts. They demonstrate ways in which interdisciplinary work engages students in science and enhances teaching for understanding. This section includes three categories of interdisciplinary lessons, each aligned with portions of the 5E learning cycle instructional model. Though there are many learning cycle models, this model described by Rodger Bybee (1997) is increasingly referenced in the literature and in curriculum. It was selected to guide the organization of this book because teachers are increasingly familiar with it. The five parts of the cycle include:
• *Engagement* – Initiates the learning task, makes connections between past and present learning experiences, and organizes students' thinking toward the learning outcomes.
• *Exploration* – Provides students with common experiences around the concepts, processes, and skills identified to develop in the lesson.
• *Explanation* – Provides opportunities for students to demonstrate conceptual understanding, process skills, or behaviors. Gives teachers opportunities to introduce a concept, process, or skill.
• *Elaboration* – Challenges and extends students' conceptual understanding and skills.
• *Evaluation* – Encourages students to assess their understandings and skills. Provides teachers opportunities to evaluate student progress.

Each phase has a specific function and informs both teachers' orchestrated instruction and students' understandings of science knowledge, attitudes, and skills. The selected articles support use of strategies appropriate to various phases of the instructional model

- The first category in Section One includes articles about interdisciplinary lessons that use literature to *engage* students in inquiry. In "Leaders, Readers, & Science," Arlene G. Terrell discusses how use of a language arts unit on survival led to students' inquiry into properties of ice. Joy L. Lowe's and Kathryn I. Matthew's article, "Puppets & Prose," shares ideas on how to engage students in scientific inquiry and establish their prior knowledge through the use of trade books and puppets. Finally, "Habitat Sweet Habitat" (Roberta J. Aram, Sherry Whitson, and Rosemarie Dieckhoff) uses literature as a springboard to inquiry explorations that develop students' understandings of camouflage.

- The second category in Section One includes articles about interdisciplinary lessons that use the language arts and fine arts to process understanding and demonstrate critical skills to develop the minds-on aspect of hands-on learning—*explaining and elaborating*. In "Taking Science Dialogue by Storm," Jacqueline Leonard discusses ways to encourage and use emergent classroom discourse to stimulate student interaction around science concepts. Audrey C. Rule and Cynthia Rust share a Teaching with Analogies model in "A Bat Is Like a...," an interdisciplinary unit on bats. "Someone's in the Kitchen with Science," by Patricia K. Lowry and Judy Hale McCrary, uses literature and science journals to engage students in inquiry and to help them process information for understanding.

  In "The Sky's the Limit," Deborah Roberts again uses journals as children work with parents on a Moon journal and incorporate reading and writing into the process. Daniel P. Shepardson and Susan J. Britsch outline an analysis of students' science journals that include writing and drawing, as well as discuss how journals enhance students' abilities to think like scientists in "Analyzing Children's Science Journals." In the "The Nature of Haiku" Peter Rillero, JoAnn V. Cleland, and Karen A. Conzelman describe the use of haiku to improve students' observational skills as they learn about the natural world. Finally, in "Drawing on Student Understanding," Mary Stein, Shannan McNair, and Jan Butcher explore the use of art and drawing as a tool to deepen students' science understandings.

- The final category in Section One includes articles about interdisciplinary lessons that use mathematics to process understanding and demonstrate critical skills—again *explaining and elaborating*. Although each article points to other interdisciplinary connections, the primary focus is the use of mathematics to explain science. In Jennifer Hoffman's "Out of Sight," students use equipment and tools to collect data and extend their senses, as well as use data to construct explanations. They then apply this learning to ways scientists map the ocean floor.

David A. Wiley and Christine Anne Royce describe a similar application of mathematics that analyzes impacts from meteorites and craters in "Crash into Meteorite Learning." In "Convection Connections," Ann M. L. Cavallo uses mathematics and the learning cycle to help students relate the concept of convection to everyday life events. To close this segment, Katie Rommel-Esham and Christopher Souhrada share a classroom simulation in which students use scale models and statistics to study "populations" on Mars in "Mission to Mars: A Classroom Simulation."

While Section One focuses on lessons that develop connections in the brain, **Section Two,** "School and Community Connections," focuses on articles that demonstrate ways to build connections from science to school and community. The three categories in this section include schoolwide themes, project-based learning, and authentic projects in the community.

- The first category includes two articles on schoolwide themes, both related to water. "Diving into a Schoolwide Science Theme," by Michele Lee, Maria Lostoski, and Kathy Williams, is a schoolwide theme that connects all disciplines for all students to oceans. In "Testing the Waters," Roberta J. Aram, Mary Brake, David Smith, Gina Wood, and Pat Hamilton present another schoolwide theme with water as the central element, but this unit takes students out the schoolroom door and to the water for authentic inquiry.

- The second category in Section Two includes examples of project-based and interdisciplinary science units. Projects are natural ways to integrate concepts and processes from various disciplines because it is impossible to separate the disciplines during a project. In Elizabeth Lener's "Our Growing Planet," students use their study of human population growth and its impact on Earth to develop projects (including a play and a webpage) aimed at making positive changes in the local community. In "Curriculum with a Common Thread," Maureen M. McMahon, Susan P. O'Hara, William G. Holliday, Bernadette B. McCormack, and Elizabeth M. Gibson describe six thematic units in Project WRITE (World Resources for Integrated Thematic Education) in which science is at the heart of each unit, but literacy skills are essential to the outcome of each unit.

In Melissa DiGennaro King's "Rev Up Your Veggies!" students learn about force and motion as they build fruit and vegetable racing cars and a display at the school's entrance to spread the word. In the next article, "Project Reptile!" Deborah Diffily describes a project that results in student learning about reptiles and a museum space with an exhibit for family and friends. Finally, Lynn Astarita Gatto and Reeda Stamper Hart describe in "Box Up Your Habitat" how students use enviroboxes from other schools around the world—the project has students develop an envirobox and send it to other schools. Not only do they learn about their own area, but they also learn about environments around the globe.

- When projects are moved outdoors, teachers open the doors to environmental citizenship and authentic science. This third category focuses on projects that result in community impact during authentic science experiences and that lead to better understandings of how scientists work. In Susan Goethals's "Lessons from a Lake," students are engaged in an integrated and interdisciplinary unit that gives them insight into the history of their community, enhances their science knowledge and skills, and involves them in a study of a nearby lake. The next two articles find students gardening outside their urban school—Linda Keteyian's "A Garden Story"—and re-vegetating nearby Big Bend National Park—"Project FLORA," by Mary Nied Phillips, Melissa Forsythe, and DJ Sanders. In the final article, "http://World Wide Weather," Kay Berglund Newhouse describes GLOBE, a worldwide program that has students from kindergarten to the graduate level record scientific data that scientists can use to study the global environment.

Susan Koba, NSTA Director for Coordination & Supervision 01–04
Project Director, Banneker 2000: Community of Excellence in Mathematics and Science
Omaha Public Schools
May 2003

References

Bybee, Rodger W. 1997. *Achieving scientific literacy: From purposes to practices.* Portsmouth, NH: Heinemann.
National Research Council. 1996. *National science education standards.* Washington, DC: National Academy Press. Online version at *www.nap.edu/books/0309053269/html/index.html*

Quick-Reference Chart of Articles

Article	Standards[1]	Grades[2]	Category[3]
Leaders, Readers, & Science	See article, p. 4	5–6	ID
Puppets & Prose	Content Standard C (Life Science)	K–2	ID
Habitat Sweet Habitat	See article, p. 18	K–2	ID
Taking Science Dialogue by Storm	Content Standards A (Abilities to do Inquiry) and F (Natural Hazards)	5–6	ID
A Bat Is Like a...	Content Standard C (Life Science)	3–4	ID
Someone's in the Kitchen with Science	See article, p. 40	K–2	ID/I
The Sky's the Limit	Content Standard D (Earth & Space Science)	K–2	ID
Analyzing Children's Science Journals	K-4 Content Standard D (Earth & Space Science)	K–2	ID
The Nature of Haiku	See article, p. 60	K–4	ID
Drawing on Student Understanding	Content Standards A (Science as Inquiry) and C (Life Science)	K–6	ID
Out of Sight	Content Standards A (Science as Inquiry), E (Science & Technology), and C (Life Science)	K–4	ID/I
Crash into Meteorite Learning	5–8 Content Standard A (Inquiry - Models), Content Standard B (Motions and Forces), and Content Standard D (Earth & Space Science)	4–6	ID/I
Convection Connections	Content Standards A (Inquiry) and D (Earth & Space Science)	5–6	ID
Mission to Mars	See article, p. 96	4–6	ID/I

(continued next page)

(continued from previous page)

Article	Standards[1]	Grades[2]	Category[3]
Diving into a Schoolwide Science Theme	See article, p. 106	K–6	T
Testing the Waters	Content Standards A (Inquiry), D (Life), and F (Science and Technology)	K–6	T
Our Growing Planet	Content Standards C (Life) and F (Personal and Social Perspective)	K–6	ID
Curriculum with a Common Thread	See article, p. 128	5–6	ID/I
Rev Up Your Veggies!	See article, p. 138	4–5	I
Project Reptile!	See article, p. 146	K–4	ID
Box Up Your Habitat	See article, p. 154	K–6	ID/I
Lessons from a Lake	Content Standards A (Inquiry), B (Physical) and C (Life)	4–5	ID/I
A Garden Story	Content Standards C(Life), D(Earth), and E (Science and Technology)	K–6	ID/I
Project FLORA	Content Standards A (Inquiry), C (Life), E (Science and Technology), and F (Science in a Personal and Social Perspective)	4–6	ID
http://World Wide Weather	See article text, p. 180	K–6	ID/I

[1] National Research Council. 1996. *National Science Education Standards.* Washington, DC: National Academy Press.

[2] Many of the grade-specific articles can be adapted to other grades.

[3] The articles are classified by:

- ID for interdisciplinary
- I for integrated
- T for thematic.

How can you and your students avoid searching hundreds of science websites to locate the best sources of information on a given topic? SciLinks, created and maintained by the National Science Teachers Association (NSTA), has the answer.

In a SciLinked text, such as this one, you'll find a logo and keyword near a concept your class is studying, a URL (*www.scilinks.org*), and a keyword code. Simply go to the SciLinks website, type in the code, and receive an annotated listing of as many as 15 webpages—all of which have gone through an extensive review process conducted by a team of science educators. SciLinks is your best source of pertinent, trustworthy Internet links on subjects from astronomy to zoology.

Need more information? Take a tour—*http://www.scilinks.org/tour/*

Section

1

Helping Students
Build Connections

Leaders, Readers, & Science

By Arlene G. Terrell

A terrific interdisciplinary, cooperative-learning science experience grew out of my sixth-grade students' love of adventure. As an education specialist, I work with gifted students. During one project, sixth-grade students were exploring the importance of leadership skills as they simultaneously read two books. *Shipwreck at the Bottom of the World* (Armstrong 2000) describes the 1914 transAntarctic expedition led by Ernest Shackleton that went awry as ice engulfed and slowly crushed the ship, leaving the crew of 27 with three lifeboats and only the necessities for survival to endure storms, icebergs, and extreme cold before returning alive 19 months later in 1916. *Carry On, Mr. Bowditch* (Latham 1983) tells the story of Nathaniel Bowditch, an American mathematician and astronomer, who in 1802 wrote a navigation manual, *The New American Practical Navigator*, that led to safer sailing practices.

It was students' fascination with the television show *Survivor* that led me to incorporate these books into the curriculum. Every day, I teach a two-hour reading and English class. For four and a half weeks, students read the books both in class and at home, did hands-on activities, and kept journal entries related to their discoveries. Although the project began primarily as a language arts assignment to compare the leadership skills of two fascinating men, it grew to encompass an exploration of ice's properties and taught students important cooperative-group skills and science concepts.

Setting the Stage for Science

To begin, I introduced the assignment with a prereading activity: "Write a journal entry about the most dangerous situation you've ever endured. How did you deal with the situation, and what contributed to your survival?" The students shared their entries, noting common threads that made survival possible, such as remaining calm, assessing the situation, devising a plan of rescue, knowing first aid, and having good communication skills. After that, students explored the conditions of the Antarctic through "Danger on the Ice" by Peter Tyson, which students accessed on the Internet at *www.pbs.org/wgbh/nova/shackleton/surviving/danger.html*. We discussed what people would have to know, have, and be able to do in order to survive there. A competent leader was at the top of the list.

The list also included such items as knowledge of the Antarctic (weather, plants, animals, water, terrain, temperature); a plan; an understanding of the dangers and risks involved; monetary support to purchase supplies, boats, and equipment for cutting through the ice; navigation skills and equipment (navigation charts, compass, sextant); an able crew; a sense of anticipation and an ability to plan for the unexpected; and a means of communication.

Students began the study by reading *Shipwreck at the Bottom of the World*. As they read the book, students were asked to record examples of Shackleton's leadership skills in a packet I had created for them. The packet contained guided questions about the reading, as well as information about 10 key leadership skills I had paraphrased from *Leading at the Edge* (Perkins et al. 2000). According to this book, an effective leader will

- Set long- and short-term goals
- Provide distractions from problems
- Celebrate successes
- Maintain an optimistic outlook
- Take informed risks
- Deal with conflict head on
- Keep enemies close by
- Work in the trenches alongside those being led
- Lead by example with strong communication skills
- Find ways to deal with stress.

An Icy Experience

The challenge Shackleton faced in the Antarctic's icy climate inspired students to find out more about the Antarctic. Students wanted to know what it would be like to visit the Antarctic. They looked at various websites and read books and other materials I had gathered and

Students wanted to know what it would be like to visit the Antarctic. They looked at various websites and read books and other materials...

made available in the classroom (see Resources). The Antarctic is often associated with ice and extreme cold. My students first became intrigued with the ice as they read about how it slowly crushed the ship, leaving the crew at the mercy of the ice. Many types of ice were discussed and described in the book:

- *Firn*—compressed snow with the air squeezed out, making it dense, heavy ice (this is what makes the ice appear blue)
- *Nilas*—a layer of thin, flexible ice
- *Pancake*—nilas disturbed by the wind, forming rounded disks that look like white lily-pads with their edges turned up
- *Ice field*—pancakes packed together forming a single sheet.

The students' interest in ice led them to think about inquiry experiences to do with a block of ice. A few students wanted to hollow out an eggshell, label and name it, and test to see how much pressure or weight from the ice it would take to crush the eggshell just as Shackleton's ship *Endurance* was crushed. Other students wondered about different ways to melt ice. Would sea salt melt ice faster than table salt?

Since the class was reading about leadership skills, the group activity was a chance to put some of the ideas they were reading about in action.

Would vinegar melt ice faster than ammonia?

To explore some properties of ice, students conducted an observation laboratory (an opportunity for students to gather preliminary information prior to an organized investigation of a problem) with ice cubes using a variety of materials (wool cloth, salt, wooden rods, wood, and nails). In this activity, students observed physical and chemical properties of the ice as they tested the effect of different materials and treatments of the ice.

After the introductory exploration, I challenged students to come up with their own investigation with a larger, 12 cm by 15 cm block of ice using a variety of materials and tools, including different types of salt; different types of cloth to test effects of friction; materials to make an electrical circuit; acids (vinegar) and bases (ammonia); different types of metal; and dials made of wood, plastic, and Teflon. Students were also allowed to bring in items from home with teacher approval.

Since the class was reading about leadership skills, the group activity was a chance to put some of the ideas they were reading about in action. Each student chose one person he or she wanted to work with, and then, if possible, I paired teams of two males and two females to form cooperative groups of four. Once the groups were formed, each student wrote a brief paper stating why he or she should be the leader of their group; I chose a leader for each group based on these papers. Students used the "four-question strategy" (Cothron, Giese, and Rezba 1989) to identify independent and dependent variables needed to come up with questions to investigate:

1) What materials are available for conducting experiments on ice? (ice, substances, or conditions that can change or alter the ice block)
2) What does ice do? (melts, changes states, is cold, wet, hard)
3) How could we change any of the materials used to change the ice to affect what ice does? (ice: size, pH of liquid, thickness, texture, weight, state of matter; changeable applications: temperature, amount of pressure, metals, acids and bases, length of time, salts) These are independent variables.
4) How could we measure or describe the response of the ice to the change? (the amount of time it takes to completely dissolve the ice; the time it takes to bore a hole through the ice; the "weight" of ice needed to crush an eggshell) These are dependent variables.

Let the Investigations Begin!

Each student came up with a question to investigate, and the group voted on which one to tackle.

One group investigated the question, "What effect does the number of D-cell batteries have on the time it takes wire to slice through the block of ice?" This group hypothesized the greater the number of batteries, the quicker the wire will slice through the ice.

In this experiment, the leader assigned two students to set up the circuit, one student to create a chart on which to record the data, and a third student to record with the stopwatch the time it takes the wire to melt the ice. As the teacher/facilitator watched, the students, wearing thick gloves and safety glasses, set up the circuit using six D-cell batteries, a battery holder, uninsulated copper wire, and alligator clips. Students recorded their observations in their journals. They observed that the wire melted the ice faster when a greater number of batteries was in use. Initially, these students used insulated copper wire before realizing that the ice might melt quicker if they removed the insulation from the wire. They were able to conclude that the stripped copper wire melted the ice faster than the insulated wire, but the insulated wire did give off enough heat to slowly melt the ice. Students in this group generated the following questions for further study: "What effect does the kind of wire have on the time that it takes the wire to slice through the block?" and "What effect do different types of batteries have on the time that it takes the wire to slice through the ice?"

Another group of students investigated the question, "Which substance will melt ice quicker, vinegar or ammonia?" The group hypothesized that vinegar, an acid, would melt the ice faster than the same amount of ammonia. Wearing gloves and safety goggles and using measuring cups, students conducted their activity. Students placed two blocks of ice in identical containers, labeling one container A (ammonia) and the other one B (vinegar). Next, they poured 480 mL of ammonia in container A and the same amount of vinegar in container B. The students recorded their observations for each container of ice every 30 minutes and measured the amount

Connecting to the Standards

This article relates to the following National Science Education Standards:

Content Standard A

- All students should develop abilities necessary to do scientific inquiry.
- All students should develop understandings about scientific inquiry.

Content Standard B

- All students should develop an understanding of properties and changes of properties in matter.

of liquid in each container, recording that figure in a data chart. When they were done with their measurements, students returned the liquids to containers A and B to continue the process. They continued this process until the class ended. Students observed that the ammonia melted the ice faster than the same amount of vinegar. Since the liquids covered about 2/3 of the ice blocks, the 2/3 were affected by the chemicals changing their shape. At the end of one hour, approximately 1/3 of the block using ammonia was melted and the block using vinegar was approximately 1/4 melted. Students were surprised to find that the ammonia melted the ice faster than the vinegar. One group member wondered, "How can this be, when I thought acid 'ate through' things?"

Their questions for further research included: "What effects do different amounts of vinegar and ammonia have on the time it takes to completely melt a block of ice?" and "What effect do different acids or bases have on the dissolving rate of a block of ice?"

Figure 1. Students' rubric to assess cooperative-learning group skills.

5—Exceptional (few of these)
4—Outstanding
3—Very Good
2—Good
1—Needs Improvement

Leader

1. Maintained an optimistic perspective.
2. Promoted cooperation and team spirit.
3. Used knowledge of each member of the group to keep everyone on task; dealt with conflict head on; and avoided power struggles.
4. Facilitated the experimental design, completion of the investigation, and the lab report.
5. Was realistic and focused the group on a long-term goal and several short-term goals.
6. Used "quiet" humor and/or courtesy to resolve conflict.
7. Maintained a respectful noise level.

Group Members

1. Maintained a positive perspective.
2. Was a cooperative and respectful member of the group and exhibited team spirit.
3. Followed the directions of the leader.
4. Completed his or her fair share of the work.
5. Applied knowledge of the content and contributed to the goal setting.
6. Completed the long-term goal and the short-term goals.
7. Spoke courteously and was mindful of the noise level.

A third group of students investigated the question, "What effect does the size of the ice block (or container) have on the pressure needed to crush the hollow eggshell?" These students brought in hollow eggshells from home.

The night before class, students obtained two plastic containers of different sizes but made of the same plastic material. They labeled one 12 cm by 15 cm container *A*, and the other 24 cm by 30 cm container *B*. Next, they made a clay stand for the eggshells at the bottom of each container, placing a hollowed eggshell on each one. Then they filled each container with tap water, leaving 1 cm at the top for expansion, and put both containers in a freezer for the same length of time.

The next day, students recorded qualitative (descriptive) observations about the condition of each eggshell every 30 minutes until the end of class. They also assigned a quantitative (numerical) value to the qualitative observations to be recorded in a chart and graphed: 0—no dent or smashing; 1—small dent; 2—1/4 of shell dented or smashed; 3—1/2 of shell dented or smashed; 4—eggshell completely smashed in.

Students were surprised that neither of the eggshells were dented or smashed. They inferred that a lot more ice pressure (larger containers) was needed to dent or smash the eggshells.

Analyzing the Experiences

When students had completed their investigations, the class discussed the data and their group experiences.

Students used a rubric (Figure 1) to assess their cooperative-learning skills. Students recognized there were members of the group who also possessed leadership skills, and that one never knows when he or she might have to help or assume a leadership role. Some comments about their experiments included

- I wonder if we should have used salt water instead of tap water to make the experience more realistic like ocean water? (These students referred to the information in the reading that salt water freezes at a lower temperature than fresh water. They wondered if this made a difference in the melting rate of the blocks of ice.)
- We didn't realize how much pressure was necessary to crush the eggshell; the ice pressure must have been *massive* to crush Shackleton's ship.
- The size of the granules of salt as well as the

placement of the salt affected the melting rate of the block of ice.
- Ice can stick to your skin and be dangerous.
- Different chemicals affect the melting rate of the ice differently.

Some comments on their group dynamics included

- I thought that I did a good job encouraging people, but I had a difficult time dividing the jobs equally.
- I liked how our group passed the lab report around and we all completed different parts of it.
- We enjoyed celebrating one another's good ideas.

Through their investigations, students developed a clearer understanding of what constituted a good leader. While learning about the various properties of ice, students discovered for themselves that there is usually one main leader and secondary leaders who play a key role in a group's success. They also learned that an understanding of what makes a group functional for all is equally important.

Although I conducted the investigations with advanced students who were able to design their own experiments, variations on the ice-block investigation could be adapted for students of different learning levels. For example, rather than having students design their own investigation, cooperative groups might compete to see which group could melt the ice the quickest. The challenge for the students would be to choose the materials and procedures they feel will melt the ice the quickest and solve the problem.

Another Leader, More to Learn

To further learning, students also read *Carry On, Mr. Bowditch*, which describes the life of Nathaniel Bowditch, whose *The New*

American Practical Navigator is still used on ships today. This book also lent itself to hands-on investigations.

For example, Bowditch took *lunars* (a way to find latitude using the stars) to find his locations at sea. Navigators used lunars to determine their position in the ocean. Regular and predictable paths of the moon were recorded in almanacs. Bowditch figured out a new way to take lunars by taking the position of the moon in relation to three stars instead of waiting for the moon to cover one star, which was the way it had been done. A navigator, using a sextant, can measure the height of a star above the horizon. The measurement of a star's height or altitude and the use of proper almanacs or tables will give navigators their latitude. Chronometers were used to find longitude. Students used star charts in class to help them understand this process and to see its value.

This unit was a memorable one for my students and me. Through their reading and hands-on investigations, students learned about the properties of ice. They also learned the importance of a good leader and the need to practice cooperative-group skills. The study was fun, engaging, and informative. Students' fascination with the extraordinary lives of two men resulted in a newfound respect for life and an appreciation of the importance of a work ethic, goal setting, problem solving, taking informed risks, working in a group, and communicating effectively. That's a lot of learning from a block of ice!

Arlene Terrell is a sixth-grade gifted education specialist at Walker Upper Elementary School in Charlottesville, VA.

References

Armstrong, J. 2000. *Shipwreck at the bottom of the world*. New York: Random House/Crown Books for Young Readers.

Cothron, J., R. N. Giese, and R. J. Rezba. 1989. *Students and research*. Dubuque, IA: Kendall/Hunt.

Latham, J. L. 1983. *Carry on, Mr. Bowditch*. New York: Houghton Mifflin.

Perkins, D. N. J., M. Holtman, P. Kessler, and C. McCarthy. 2000. *Leading at the edge*. Washington, DC: American Management Association.

Resources

Print

Alexander, C. 1998. *The Endurance: Shackleton's legendary Antarctic expedition*. NewYork: Alfred A. Knopf.

Kostyal, K.M. 1999. *Trial by ice: A photobiography of Sir Ernest Shackleton*. New York: Scholastic.

Lansing, A. 1999. *Endurance: Shackleton's incredible voyage*. New York: Carroll and Graf.

Lerangis, P. 2000. *Antarctica: Journey to the pole*. New York: Scholastic.

Svensson, S. 1998. *The lore of ships*. New York: Barnes and Noble.

Internet

Tyson, P. NOVA Online/Shackleton's Antarctic Odyssey/Danger on the Ice. August 2, 2000. *www.pbs.org/wgbh/nova/shackleton/surviving/danger.html*

Live from Antarctic *quest.arc.nasa.gov/Antarctica*

Puppets & Prose

By Joy L. Lowe and Kathryn I. Matthew

Children are fascinated by and relate to puppets, books, animals, and insects. They view puppets as toys, and toys equal fun. Adding puppets and children's literature to the science classroom makes learning entertaining and motivating. Realistic puppets hold children's attention and engage their natural curiosity as they learn about animals and insects. The puppets bring imaginations to life as students recreate stories and learn the parts of the animals while using the puppets.

Bridges Between Trade Books and Science

Walpole (1999) highlights the importance of building bridges between science textbooks and children's prior knowledge to foster comprehension of science content. Using science trade books can help build these bridges by extending and enhancing the science concepts presented in textbooks (see NSTA's website at *www.nsta.org/elementaryschool* for lists of "Outstanding Science Trade Books for Children"). These informational books often present material in a different format than the textbook and on a variety of reading levels. The colorful illustrations in trade books, their photographs, diagrams, charts, and short blocks of text can make science concepts more understandable and easier to read than in textbooks. Additionally, science trade books help students see science as part of their everyday lives (Stiffler 1992).

Dixey and Baird (1996) contend that using children's literature to teach science can enliven instruction, stimulate children's learning, and excite them about learning. Further, Dreher (1999) stresses the importance of engaging children in reading a diverse selection of fiction and nonfiction books to enhance their reading achievement.

Some books contain incorrect science concepts, both explicit and implicit (Rice and Rainsford 1996, Rice and Snipes 1997). These inaccuracies are often found in trade books and realistic fiction. Teachers must be aware of possible inaccuracies in books and the negative impact these books have on student learning.

To identify books with incorrect science concepts, teachers must be familiar with the science content presented in the books. By becoming familiar with the authors of children's books, teachers can learn which authors are noted for writing accurately about science concepts. Such authors as Gail Gibbons, Jean Craighead George, and Dorothy Hinshaw Patent write science books for children and are known for thorough research and attention to detail. Reading reviews of science trade books is another way for teachers to become familiar with books that contain accurate science concepts. Recently published books are more likely than older books to have science concepts presented accurately.

Puppets and Stories

Piazza (1999) suggests using realistic puppets as props to narrate stories, try out ideas, and examine curriculum content. Puppets encourage children to try out ideas and investigate on their own. Seeing a video of chickens hatching from eggs or watching chickens hatch in the classroom provides students with opportunities to observe this natural phenomenon. However,

putting a hand inside an egg puppet and pushing a chick through the hole to make it hatch enables children to experience this idea again and again as they seek understanding.

Puppets encourage children to examine curriculum content in ways not possible with live animals. For example, the sideways or rectilinear movements of snakes can be explored through the use of puppets. Explaining to students about endangered animals and the need to preserve their environments can be made more personal by the introduction of realistic puppets. Students can more easily relate to the animals if they can hold, touch, and snuggle with a realistic puppet of the animal.

Colorful characters in storybooks come to life when teachers use puppets as they retell favorite stories in their own words. Storytelling does

Integrating Science and Literature

Caterpillars wiggle and crawl and tickle your hand as they move. They also eat lots of leaves. This is what children will tell you when you show them a caterpillar puppet and ask them what they know about caterpillars. They have often observed caterpillars and investigated them in their own backyards.

Prior to reading *Creepy, Crawly Caterpillars,* explain to students that they are going to hear a story about caterpillars and ask them what they think the caterpillars will eat. Hold up poster-board cutouts of the different foods a caterpillar eats. Ask the students to name the foods. Students bring the food up to the caterpillar puppet manipulated by the teacher. As the story is told, the storyteller turns the puppet inside out to change it from a caterpillar to a butterfly.

Elicit comments from the children about what happened to the caterpillar. Ask if they have ever eaten a big meal and then fallen asleep. Are they changed when they wake up? Why did the caterpillar change?

This story serves as an introduction to metamorphosis and addresses science Content Standard C: Life cycles of organisms (National Research Council, 1996). Encourage students to think about and then discuss which foods a caterpillar would eat. Have a bulletin board divided into three sections: 1) foods a caterpillar would eat 2) foods a caterpillar would not eat and 3) foods a caterpillar might eat. The class decides together where to place the cardboard cutouts of the foods. As the students continue their investigation of caterpillars, they return to the bulletin board to move the foods into the correct categories. This activity addresses Content Standard A as students develop their abilities to do scientific inquiry.

not require memorization of the story; storytellers read the story several times to become familiar with it and remember the sequence of events. Once familiar with the story, they practice retelling the story in their own words using puppets, gestures, expressions, and voice inflections to entrance their listeners. Storytelling with puppets is not a puppet show with a puppet for each character; rather, storytellers manipulate a puppet of the main character and one or two lesser characters.

Favorite books such as Facklam's (1996) *Creepy, Crawly Caterpillars* can be accompanied by a caterpillar puppet and used to introduce students to the cycle of metamorphosis. Listening to a familiar story stimulates children's prior knowledge, encourages them to participate in the storytelling, and provides them with a basis for learning new content. A realistic puppet encourages children to make connections with the science concept and their personal life experiences. In this story, children move from the familiar to the unfamiliar as they learn more details about metamorphosis.

Realistic animal puppets can be used to introduce children to a variety of animals and encourage them to learn more about real animals. In any given classroom students will be reading on different levels, so a variety of books have been included. Once the teacher has shared the puppets and books with the students, both puppets and books should be placed in a science center for students' independent explorations. Therefore it is imperative that every book used in this activity contains accurate science.

Where to Get Realistic Puppets

Internet sites provide access to an array of realistic animal puppets and ideas for using them. The award-winning, realistic Folkmanis puppets (1219 Park Ave., Emeryville, CA 94608) come in a variety of sizes and include finger and glove puppets. On their website, at *www.folkmanis.com/nearyou.htm*, is a map of the United States showing local retailers who carry the puppets. The Acorn Naturalists site (17821 East 17th St., #103, Tustin, CA 92780), *www.acorn-group.com/p1417.htm*, sells animal puppets and has information on using the puppets to teach animal diversity, the food chain, anatomy, and the care of live animals. Another online source for animal puppets is Chuckles' Emporium of Puppets (3138 South 3200 West, Salt Lake City, UT 84119), which categorizes the puppets for easy selection, *www.aros.net/~chuckles/index.htm*.

Puppets hold a magical attraction for children. Students' eyes grow wide and they become entranced when stories are told with puppets. Puppets are nonthreatening, approachable objects that come to life through the skillful manipulations of a puppeteer. The animation holds children's attention and appeals to their sense of wonder. The puppets help students relate to their world and examine animals they might not otherwise be able to approach.

Articulate children respond animatedly to puppets, and quiet children are emboldened by the puppets. After finishing a storytelling session an author was approached by a very quiet child in the class. The storyteller placed the puppet on the child's hand, and the child began talking to the puppet. She asked why the puppet was not responding, and the storyteller told her that she had to respond for the puppet. So the child began conversing with the puppet, providing both voices. Realistic puppets provide children a creative way to interact with and investigate their world.

Joy L. Lowe, a former associate professor in the College of Education at Louisiana Tech University, Ruston, is now a fulltime author. Kathryn I. Matthew is an assistant professor in the College of Education at Louisiana Tech.

Recommended Books

Alligators

Arnosky, J. 1994. *All about alligators*. New York: Scholastic. 32pp. 0-590-46788-3. $14.95. Recommended for Grades K–3.
Limited text and large, detailed drawings introduce young readers to the fascinating world of alligators. Readers are invited to the swamp for a close-up look at alligators.

Bats

Arnold, C. 1996. *Bat*. New York: William Morrow. 48pp. 0-688-13726-1. $15.93. Grades 1–3.
This photo essay of the life and behavior of bats dispels superstitions about bats and provides interesting information. Because bats spend most of their lives upside down, their bodies are adapted to this position. These nocturnal mammals use their large ears and their keen sense of hearing to locate prey.

Stuart, D. 1994. *Bats: Mysterious flyers of the night*. Minneapolis, MN: Carolrhoda Books. 47pp. 0-87614-814-3. $19.95. Grades 2–5.
These shy, gentle mammals are vital to our environment because they pollinate flowers, disperse seeds, and control the insect population. Color photographs capture the fascinating variety of ears, noses, and wings found on bats. The book covers bats' remarkable navigation system, their protective coloring, their benefits to man, and the superstitions surrounding them.

Bears

Murphy, J. 1993. *Backyard bear*. New York: Scholastic. 0-590-44375-5. $15.95. Grades 2–4.
As older bears force younger bears out of their territory, the younger bears show up in backyards across America looking for food. On his search, a young bear makes his way through a sleeping neighborhood. The bear's scary journey is seen through his eyes and the eyes of the families he awakens.

Patent, D. H. 1994. *Looking at bears*. New York: Holiday House. 40pp. 0-8234-1139-7. $15.95. Grades 1–3.
Bears are powerful, intriguing animals. The evolution of bears; physical characteristics; habitats; and behaviors, including hibernation, are presented in this book.

Caterpillars

Facklam, M. 1996. *Creepy, crawly caterpillars*. Boston: Little, Brown. 32pp. 0-316-27391-0. $4.95. Grades 2–4.
Detailed colorful drawings portray metamorphosis and show which caterpillars become moths and butterflies. Caterpillars spend much of their short lives eating and growing. Their appearance, habits, habitats, and food preferences are discussed.

Foxes

Arnold, C. 1996. *Fox*. New York: Morrow Junior Books. 48pp. 0-688-13728-8. $16. Grades 2–5.
With their sharp senses, quick reflexes, and innate cunning, foxes are one of the most successful predators in the world. They are also among the most adaptable—living in habitats from the arid deserts of North Africa to the frozen tundra of the Arctic Circle. This book focuses on the tiny kit fox found in the United States.

George, J. C. 1992. *The Moon of the Fox Pups*. New York: Harper Collins. 48pp. 0-06-022859-8. $14.89. Grades 3–7.

June is the "growing up" moon, when fox pups emerge from the safety of their den and begin to explore the world. This is when adult foxes teach their pups everything from the mysteries of a box turtle to the wily ploys of a woodchuck to the unexpected behavior of the bullfrog.

Frogs

Gibbons, G. 1993. *Frogs*. New York: Holiday House. 32pp. 0-8234-1052-8. $15.95. Grades PreK–3.

There are more than 38,000 types of frogs. This book describes how their bodies change as they grow from tadpoles into frogs, how they make sounds that mean different things, how they hibernate, and how they differ from toads.

Owls

Arnosky, J. 1995. *All about owls*. New York: Scholastic. 32pp. 0-590-46790-5. $14.95. Grades K–3.

These nocturnal birds use their superb night vision and acute sense of smell to keep the insect and rodent population under control. There are owl calls to practice and detailed illustrations depicting owl anatomy.

Sattler, H. 1995. *The book of North American owls*. New York: Clarion Books. 64pp. 0-395-60524-5. $15.95. Grades 4–7.

Colorful illustrations of owls and their body parts accompany informative text. A glossary includes drawings of different owls, facts about owls, and maps showing where they live in the United States.

Yolen, J. 1988. *Owl moon*. New York: Philomel. 32pp. 0-399-21457-7. $16.95. Grades PreK–1.

This Caldecott Medal winner describes a very special winter evening of quiet, cold, and companionship as a father and child go "owling."

This search for the elusive owl is filled with anticipation and excitement.

Penguins

Paladino, C. 1991. *Pomona: The birth of a penguin*. Danbury, CT: Franklin Watts. 32pp. 0-531-15212-X. $19.60. Grades 2–4.

Follow the early life of a blackfooted penguin at the New England Aquarium as it is hatched from an egg and raised by scientists. Interspersed in the text and accompanying photographs is information about the habits and habitats of penguins. The plight of penguins in the wild is described at the end of the book.

Patent, D. H. 1993. *Looking at penguins*. New York: Holiday House. 40pp. 0-8234-1037-4. $15.95. Grades 2–4.

Rather than fly through the air, these birds are "underwater flyers." Striking photographs provide a close-up look at these fascinating animals. This book describes penguins' hunting patterns, feeding habits, and breeding rituals.

Snakes

Ling, M., and Atkinson, M. 1997. *The snake book*. New York: Dorling Kindersley. 32pp. 0-7894-1526-7. $12.95. Grades 1 and up.

Two- and four-page spreads of color photographs make these snakes seem as though they will slither off the pages. Intertwined with the snakes is text that describes what the snakes eat, how they kill their prey, and where they live.

Souza, D. 1992. *Slinky snakes*. Minneapolis, MN: Carolrhoda Books. 40pp. 0-87614-711-2. $19.95. Grades 1–4.

The easy-to-read text with bold keywords and definitions accompanied by photographs and illustrations make this a reader-friendly book. Young readers can relate to the text with passages such as the one comparing snakes shedding their skins to pulling off socks. Illustrations of snakes' movements—including undulation, sideways, concertina, and rectilinear—will have students wanting to imitate them.

Resources

Dixey, B. P., and Baird, K. A. 1996. December. *Students' entry into science through literature.* Paper presented at the Global Summit on Science and Science Education, San Francisco, CA. (ERIC Document Reproduction Service No. ED 408 159)

Dreher, M. J. 1999. Motivating children to read more nonfiction. *The Reading Teacher, 52*(4), 414–415, 417.

National Research Council. 1996. *National Science Education Standards.* Washington, DC: National Academy Press.

Piazza, C. L. 1999. *Multiple forms of literacy: Teaching literacy and the arts.* Upper Saddle River, NJ: Prentice-Hall.

Rice, D. C., and Rainsford, A. D. 1996, April. *Using Children's Tradebooks to Teach Science: Boon or Boondoggle?* Paper presented at the annual meeting of the National Association for Research in Science Teaching, St. Louis, MO. (ERIC Document Reproduction Service No. ED 393 700)

Rice, D. C., and Snipes, C. 1997, March. *Children's Trade Books: Do They Affect the Development of Science Concepts?* Paper presented at the annual meeting of the National Association for Research in Science Teaching, Oak Brook, IL. (ERIC Document Reproduction Service No. ED 406 170)

Stiffler, L. A. 1992. A solution in the shelves. *Science & Children, 29*(6), 17, 46.

Walpole, S. 1999. Changing texts, changing thinking: Comprehension demands of new science textbooks. *The Reading Teacher, 52*(4), 358–369.

Habitat Sweet Habitat

By Roberta J. Aram, Sherry Whitson, and Rosemarie Dieckhoff

Reading and communication arts are essential elements of instruction in grades K–3, but so is science content. To achieve these important goals, many primary teachers use literature—including trade books and basal reading texts—as a principal way to provide science content instruction and efficiently use time in a crowded school schedule. Although reading and writing about science concepts are excellent communication arts strategies, literature can also be used as a springboard for hands-on science inquiry explorations crucial for full development of science literacy. With careful development, inquiry experiences can create a simple, cohesive path between ideas discussed in a story or poem and fundamental science understandings.

Primary-grade students often need to be taught how to learn in an inquiry-rich environment. Although the ideal may be to provide young students with hands-on experiences with living organisms in their natural habitats, this is not always possible in the classroom. Alternatively, many teachers use simulations and models to help children develop explanations of interactions of animals and their environment.

We devised a successful simulation that explores animal camouflage and the fundamental idea that organisms depend on their environment. Though we used a story from a basal reader as a springboard for students' learning, the activity could easily be adapted to other science trade books that teachers use to enhance children's construction of science ideas.

Butterfly Habitat Inquiry

This activity was part of a "habitats and migration" unit in which students studied butterflies and other animals that migrate.

Driving questions included "Where do birds and butterflies go when they leave?" and "Why do they go somewhere else?" When we reached the story about the butterfly in the arboretum in the basal reading series, we integrated both science and social studies while expanding the meaning of the story.

For this activity, students needed

- one cloth "habitat" per team of students (one square yard of fabric in forest, desert, beach, vegetation, or other habitat motif) plus one square yard of solid black fabric and one square yard of solid white fabric
- large labels identifying the name of each

habitat (we used plain pieces of paper pinned onto the fabric)

- masking tape
- one butterfly diagram (5–7.5 cm wingspan) per student (photocopy the template)
- one set of six to eight crayons, colored pencils, or markers matched to the colors in each fabric "habitat" for each team
- one data collection sheet per student

Before class, we labeled and hung the cloth habitats around the classroom and prepared the crayon sets (about four to six crayons each) to match the colors of the fabric in each different habitat. Fabric can be purchased at any fabric or craft store that carries bolts of fabric for about $2 to $8 per yard. We recommend using a cotton or cotton-polyester blend that is washable. The fabric doesn't have to be expensive, just durable and colorful and include "lifelike" patterns.

When students arrived, we did not call attention to the habitats. To begin the activity, we read the story "The Plant Castle" (Mora 2000), though another story of your choosing would also work. The children in this story learn about various animal habitats by visiting an arboretum and observing a butterfly as it flies through desert, forest, vegetation, and beach environments. At first the students were not impressed with this story because they didn't understand it. They didn't know what an arboretum was, so we used the Internet to locate information on arboretums. We "Asked Jeeves" and found several sites about arboretums and printed some pictures from the sites. Students also visited the school library for information. We found butterfly books that we brought back to the classroom. At this point an arboretum was as familiar as the idea of habitat and students were ready for the activity.

Figure 1. Photocopy and cut out the template below for students to color.

Immediately after reading the story, we divided the class into cooperative learning teams of four students each and gave each team a set of crayons and butterfly diagrams (see Figure 1) for each child to color. Students colored the butterflies, but we didn't comment on the colors that were in their set of crayons. When everyone was finished coloring, we brought the class together for a group discussion.

We explained that in the story students observe there are different kinds of places, or habitats, where plants and animals live. We asked students to describe the habitats mentioned in the story.

Typically, students shared their ideas of desert and rainforest habitats from the perspective of the butterfly. Students remembered that the butterfly is first spotted among orchids as it flits from room to room. The desert room is always dry and hot, even when it's snowing outside. It is sunny and full of cacti. The rainforest

Figure 2. Butterfly camouflage activity student data sheet.

Habitat Sweet Habitat Data Sheet

Prediction: I think my butterfly will be safest in the _____Forest_____ habitat.
(habitat number)

Data: I observe that the butterfly is hard to see in the

1. Beach Habitat	2. Sunflower Field	3. Garden Habitat	4. Forest Habitat	5. Night Habitat	6. Tropical Habitat	7. Desert Habitat
			 ☺			

Conclusion: I found out that my butterfly was safest in the _____Forest_____ habitat because _____the
(habitat number)
leaves hide it. It is the same color.

is filled with tall green trees and vines, and the air feels heavy and wet. This discussion led students to consider the relationship between an animal's coloration and its environment and how its coloration can help protect the animal from harm.

To further learning, we asked a series of questions to assess students' prior knowledge and guide their thinking. "What does an animal need to survive?" (air, water, shelter, food, and space), "What does a shelter provide that animals need to survive?" (A shelter is something that provides protection), and "What kinds of shelter are there?" "Did you know that some animals do not live in closed shelters like the houses we live in?" "Did you know that some animals are sheltered 'in the open,' like in trees and on other plants or on the ground?" Children typically provided the answers in the parentheses above. Rather than using the word *protection*, children usually suggested that a shelter keeps animals safe from harm. A shelter also keeps an animal from being seen, caught, and eaten by a bigger animal. Children mentioned houses, caves, holes, and trees as types of shelters in which animals can find safety.

By the end of the discussion many students naturally began to wonder, "How can an animal that lives out in the open keep safe from being seen and eaten by other animals?" At this point it is easy to make a connection between this question and the butterfly in the story and the diagram they have colored—the students are ready to begin collecting data.

Collecting Data

As the discussion concluded, students' attention was drawn to the labeled fabric habitats displayed around the room. We then distributed a data sheet to each child (see Figure 2). The data sheet was designed to guide students in making predictions, collecting data, analyzing data, drawing conclusions, and providing evidence for their conclusions.

At their seats students examined the butterflies they colored and the habitats displayed around the room and predicted the habitat in which their butterfly would be safest. Students recorded on their data sheets the name and number of the habitat.

After making their predictions, students tested their predictions with their group. To do this, students in each group moved from habitat to

Science Inquiry Starters

These book suggestions can be used for developing habitat and other science-inquiry activities for young children. For additional titles, check out the NSTA Recommends site (www.nsta.org/recommends) and the list of Outstanding Science Trade Books for Children on *Science & Children's* website at www.nsta.org/elementaryschool.

Brust, B. 1990. *Butterflies.* Mankato, MN: Creative Education.

Cassie, B., and Pallotta, J. 1995. *The butterfly alphabet book.* Watertown: Charlesbridge.

Gibbons, G. 1990. *Monarch butterfly.* New York: Holiday House.

Goor, N., and Goor, R. 1990. *Insect metamorphosis from egg to adult.* New York: Silver Burdett Ginn.

Heiligman, D. 1996. *From caterpillar to butterfly.* New York: HarperCollins.

Heller, R. 1992. *How to hide a butterfly and other insects.* New York: Grosset and Dunlop.

Heller, R. 1992. *How to hide a crocodile and other reptiles.* New York: Grosset and Dunlop.

Heller, R. 1992. *How to hide a meadow frog and other amphibians.* New York: Grosset and Dunlop.

Heller, R. 1992. *How to hide a parakeet and other birds.* New York: Grosset and Dunlop.

Heller, R. 1992. *How to hide a polar bear and other mammals.* New York: Grosset and Dunlop.

Heller, R. 1992. *How to hide an octopus and other sea creatures.* New York: Grosset and Dunlop.

Howe, J. 1997. *I wish I were a butterfly.* San Diego: Voyager.

Kaner, E. 1999. *Animal defenses: How animals protect themselves.* Niagara Falls, NY: Kids Can Press.

Rotter, C. 1993. *Monarch butterflies.* Chicago: The Child's World.

Ryder, J. 1989. *Where butterflies grow.* New York: E.P. Dutton.

Settel, J. 1999. *Exploding ants: Amazing facts about how animals adapt.* New York: Atheneum.

Saintsing, D. 1987. *Where animals live: The world of butterflies.* Milwaukee: Gareth Stevens.

Simon, N. 1976. *Why am I different?* Morton Grove: Albert Whitman.

habitat, taping the butterfly to the habitat fabric and evaluating how well they could see their butterfly.

Students recorded their findings on the data sheet by marking an "X" on the square under the name of the habitat in which their butterfly was the most difficult to see—the safest spot for the butterfly. Students were encouraged to revisit the habitats as often as needed to confirm their choice. When students were satisfied with their conclusion, they drew a "happy face" under the name of the appropriate habitat on the data sheet.

Processing Data and Drawing Conclusions

After students visited all habitats and recorded their findings, we guided them through data analysis. Students placed their butterfly over the happy face marking the habitat that best protected their butterfly. Team members compared their findings and discussed differences. Typically, students pointed out the habitat they chose and how well the butterfly "blended in." Students realized the habitat they chose might be safe but not the safest one available. Again, students were encouraged to visit the habitats to come to a consensus of the safest butterfly habitats.

Finally, the teams identified factors that made their butterfly difficult to see and recorded their conclusions on individual data sheets. Typically, students identified color first, then shape and pattern of the butterfly markings.

Most of the children determined that, because of the butterfly's color, shape, and pattern, the butterfly was hidden in the habitat background material. The students finally realized these factors made the butterfly hardest to find and thus safest. Children who didn't quite understand this concept at first usually made the connection

between animal coloring and background when they placed their butterflies on the solid color habitats.

Communicating the Findings

When all the students completed their individual data sheets, they got together as a class and shared the findings. Each team explained its conclusion and provided evidence by showing its butterfly on the habitat and telling what made its butterflies difficult to see and therefore kept them safest.

Students were guided in identifying patterns in the evidence, such as the recurrence of the idea of color, size, or shape as characteristics that help butterflies survive in their environment. At this point we introduced the word *camouflage*, defined as "the word we use to describe how an animal's protective coloration allows it to blend with its environment and helps to keep it safe."

Assessment

Students conducted various activities that teachers used to assess learning. For example, students answered such questions as "What did you learn about butterflies and their habitats?" and "What surprised you about butterflies and their habitats?" Typically, students' comments included, "butterflies live in an area that looks like them" and "butterflies go where there is color like their wings" and "butterflies find places that match their colors."

In addition, students created a drawing of a camouflaged butterfly or other insect with characteristics that would keep it safe in the classroom or school yard and included with their picture a written explanation of "things about the butterfly/insect that protect it from harm." Finally, students created stories, poems, plays,

National Science Education Standards

This article addresses the following *National Science Education Standards* (National Research Council, 1996) at the K–4 level by describing an opportunity for children and their teacher to extend the idea presented in a basal reader text. Learners are encouraged to articulate the idea presented in the story, formulate a hypothesis based on the idea, test the hypothesis using a simulation and draw conclusions based on evidence from the simulation.

Science as Inquiry Content Standard A— As a result of the activities in grades K–4, all students should develop inquiry skills as they are presented with a scientific question and use their observations to construct explanations.

Life Science Content Standard C— As a result of the activities in grades K–4, all students should develop an understanding of a relationship between the physical characteristics of an organism and its environments.

Roberta Aram is an associate professor in an elementary teacher preparation program and teaches science methods courses at Southwest Missouri State University in Springfield. Sherry Whitson is a lecturer in the School of Teacher Education at Southwest Missouri State University in Springfield. Rosemarie Dieckhoff retired as a teacher in a multi-age kindergarten and first-grade classroom at McGregor Elementary School in Springfield, MO.

Resources

Print

Mora, P. 2000. The plant castle. *Scholastic literacy place: Information finders.* New York: Scholastic.

National Research Council. 1996. *National Science Education Standards.* Washington, DC: National Academy Press.

Outstanding Science Trade Books for Children for 2000. *Science and Children, 37*(6), 19–25.

Internet

www.monarchwatch.org/tagmig/index.htm
www.teachers.net/lessons/posts/372.html
www.vbe.com
mgfx.com/Butterfly/index.htm

songs, puzzles, and riddles involving animals with protective characteristics. Students' data sheets, journal pages, assessment work, and other materials were also kept in a portfolio to document students' progress in acquiring science content knowledge and inquiry skills.

The camouflage activity was a simple experiment that used everyday materials and helped young students develop important science inquiry skills. It demonstrated that with creativity teachers can go beyond the typical literature-response activity in helping children build their own science knowledge.

B

Explaining and Elaborating: Language and Fine Arts

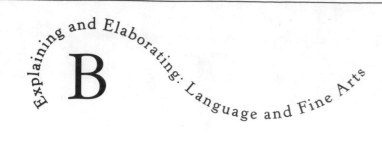
Taking Science Dialogue by Storm

By Jacqueline Leonard

The variability of discourse is part of what keeps teachers on their toes and students interested in learning. Classroom discourse—otherwise known as the ways in which students and teachers think, develop knowledge, and express themselves (Ball 1991)—has always been a fascinating aspect of science learning. Typically, discourse involves a teacher-question and student-response scenario.

Another type of discourse, however, *emergent classroom discourse*, does not follow the traditional pattern. This kind of discourse is more of a dialogue and results from relaxed social norms. Students spontaneously respond to questions from anyone in the class.

Facilitating emergent classroom discourse during science lessons is particularly important because

- It allows teachers to listen to students as they gain knowledge.
- Teachers become aware of students' knowledge deficits and misconceptions.
- Lessons become exciting and motivating as students engage in conversations about science content that is relevant to their lives.

In this article, I discuss the discourse of my sixth-grade students as they take part in an integrated science and mathematics unit on natural catastrophes.

Tornadoes Are It!

Catastrophic events such as tornadoes, hurricanes, and blizzards are discrepant events to the extent that no one expects them to happen; they provide a context for teachers and students to share prior knowledge, expose misconceptions, and engage in scientific inquiry (Thomas 1998).

Studying discrepant events also allows teachers to integrate science and mathematics. Lehman (1994) suggests that teachers integrate science and mathematics because "science can provide students with concrete examples of abstract mathematical ideas that can improve the learning of mathematics concepts," and "mathematics can enable students to achieve a deeper understanding of science concepts by providing ways to quantify and explain science relationships."

I began the unit on natural catastrophes by initiating a classroom discussion about various types of storms. The resources for these lessons

Topic: natural disasters
Go to: www.scilinks.org
Code: MIX26

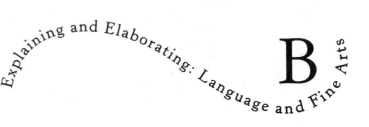
included *Weatherschool* (Yaros 1991) and *Exploring Data* (Landwehr and Watkins 1995). *Weatherschool* provides numerous simple experiments that students can do, such as measuring classroom temperatures at different elevations, humidity, and outdoor wind speed; *Exploring Data* provides such interesting data sets as the number of people visiting amusement parks and the number of thunderstorms in U.S. cities during a given year.

To my surprise, the students immediately preferred to discuss tornadoes, claiming they already had a tremendous amount of background knowledge on tornadoes. This interest in tornadoes was encouraging, for following the class discussion on weather I planned to have the students experiment with making a tornado in a jar.

Developing Dialogue

The following text shows the discourse that developed during the class discussion on storms:

Teacher:	Who can tell me something about tornadoes?
Student A:	*Twister!* [referring to the movie]
Student B:	I know how they start.
Teacher:	How do they start?
B:	Okay. What happens is that up in the clouds they start to build up, and they start turning black. Then they come down from the sky, and they eat up everything…
Class:	[Laughs]
B:	That's not funny. And it gets bigger and bigger, and it's a funnel. It gets bigger and bigger and some of it eats houses and cars. Then it goes back up in the sky and builds up again.
C:	When a tornado starts to form… It's all because of the wind and how the funnel starts to spin.
Teacher:	What do we call a really bad tornado?
C:	A number 4.
Class:	No!
D:	It's an F5. It eats up lots of stuff. That's how they classify them.
E:	You can actually see it forming in the clouds.
B:	In the movie, they said an F5 was the "finger of God."
Teacher:	I heard that, too. In order to have a tornado, what has to occur?
C:	Tornadoes start when warm air hits cold air.
D:	To get a tornado, you have to have warm and cold fronts.
Teacher:	Thank you for these explanations.

The foregoing discussion provides an example of emergent classroom discourse. Students began to respond spontaneously because the topic was of interest to them, and some students had background knowledge about tornadoes. Allowing students to share their knowledge with the class creates a student-centered environment that empowers them to learn even more about a given topic. Because the students themselves explained what they knew about how tornadoes are formed, they will most likely retain that information.

Science at the Movies

Teachers can use media, such as television programs and movies, as a springboard for classroom discourse in science. The students' discussion and comments suggested to me that they absorbed a great deal from such media as the movie *Twister*. I also discovered that the tornado activity generated a lot of questions and that student interest in catastrophic events increased. "How do you know when a tornado will happen?" "Where is tornado alley?" "Can you live through an F5 tornado?" (Tornadoes are classified on a scale from F1 to F5, with F5 being the most dangerous.)

Since the students seemed to have gathered most of their preexisting knowledge on natural disasters from film, I showed them a video on Pompeii to illustrate the ramifications that occur when volcanoes erupt. Students were particularly moved by images of people and animals covered with lava and ash. (The movies *Volcano* and *Deep Impact* could also stir classroom discourse.) Teachers can use these media to discuss the use of special effects and scientific error in movies and how they reinforce the misconceptions some people have about the Earth and space science.

One of the misconceptions that students had after watching the movie *Twister,* for example, was that tornadoes are strong enough to lift cows and 18-wheelers in the air like feathers. Although animals, humans, and property are blown around and sometimes destroyed in a tornado, the images in the movie were exaggerated by special effects. I addressed this issue by showing scientific film footage about tornadoes and discussing students' personal experiences or the stories shared by grandparents and parents who had lived through tornadoes.

On to Fact Finding

I also had students browse websites for factual information on natural catastrophes. We browsed mostly *www.msnbc.com* and *www.noaa.gov*: The MSNBC homepage has a weather link, and the National Oceanic and At-mospheric Administration website has many links on hurricanes and tornadoes for students. I suggested they learn as much as they could about hurricanes and tornadoes since hurricanes sometimes occurred in our area of the country (Maryland).

From these sites, students learned that hurricanes are also called *cyclones* and occur over the Atlantic, Caribbean, Gulf of Mexico, and Eastern Pacific. They learned that tornadoes occur most often in "tornado alley": Nebraska, Kansas, Iowa, Illinois, Indiana, Missouri, Arkansas, Mississippi, Ohio, Oklahoma, and Texas. One student shared his finding that the deadliest tornado, known as the Tri-State Tornado, occurred in 1925, killing 689 people.

Miniature Tornadoes

After numerous class discussions on weather patterns and natural catastrophes, students made their own miniature tornado in groups of three. They needed

- One glass jar for each group (At the beginning of the year I asked students to save jars from food products for use in classroom projects.)
- 5 mL of salt
- One drop of liquid dishwashing detergent
- Two to three drops of food coloring.

I instructed students to fill the jars to the top with water, add the rest of the materials, put the lid on the jar, and then swirl the water in the tightened jar in a clockwise or counterclockwise motion. The students responded with many "Oohs!" as they observed a funnel cloud spinning in the water. I explained how the soap and salt caused the water to foam up and how the food coloring made the funnel visible. Whenever the jar was swirled, a small funnel started at the bottom of the jar and worked its way up to the top.

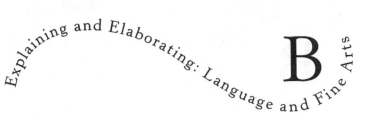
Talking About Tornadoes

Students were eager to talk about their experience making the tornado. They learned that the harder they swirled the water in the jar, the larger the funnel cloud and the longer it lasted. Students tried to articulate the strength and intensity of the tornado in the jar. I observed how these students were gradually learning to use the language of science and how to communicate it to others.

The following dialogue took place among three students. Their discourse involved asking for information, giving information and directions, and making an evaluation.

Student A: You want to shake it, or do you want me to shake it?

Student B: Let me shake it.

A: Here. I'll do some, and you can do some.

Student C: Hey, somebody didn't put my lid on tight.

A: [Records observations] Here. Shake it up. Shake it up.

B: [Shakes jar]

Teacher: What do you see?

C: [To A] Write down what we see. It's fuzzy at the top.

A: [Takes the jar from B] Hey, let me do it one more time because I want to see it. [Shakes jar and sees the tornado] Cool!

Using their tornado models as a guide, the class discussed how a real tornado might look and act as it rotates to form a cloud of dust and debris. Some described their funnel in the jar as an F5 if it was able to last more than a few seconds.

From previous Internet research students had learned that the more intense the tornado is and the longer it stays on the ground, the more damage it can cause. However, just like the funnel in the jar, a real tornado has to dissipate sooner or later.

Mathematic Storm Trackers

To continue the storm exploration and to link to mathematics learning, students investigated which U.S. cities had the most thunderstorms. I gave each group a list of 81 cities and the number of thunderstorms that occurred in each city. (This data were obtained from *Exploring Data*.) The data were divided up among the group members—each student tackled a specific region (West, Central, South, or Northeast).

Students were to find the *mean, median,* and *mode* for the number of thunderstorms that occurred in a specific region of the country. (Students were familiar with these concepts because they had worked with them in fifth grade as well as earlier in the year.)

For example, one student was assigned to the South with the following data: Atlanta 50 thunderstorms per year, Biloxi 80, Birmingham 65, Dallas 41, Houston 59, Little Rock 56, Memphis 50, Orlando 85, and Raleigh 45. He used a calculator to add the data and divide by nine to find the *mean* (59). He then ordered the numbers to find the middle number for the *median* (56). Finally, after perusing the data, he found the *mode,* or number that was most common, (50). From these averages he could describe the thunderstorm activity for the entire region.

Each student also made stem and leaf plots (a particular kind of graph that splits the data into two pieces) of the data for his or her particular region (Figure 1). These tasks allowed the students to use their prior knowledge about mean, median, and mode to record the data and complete the graph.

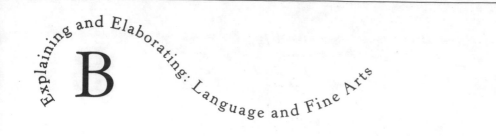

Figure 1.

Stem + Leaf plot for South

Mean = 52	0
Mode = 52	1
Median = 52	2
	3	2,5,6,6,7
	4	0,1,5
	5	0,0,2,2,2,6,8,8,9
There are about	6	3,5
52 storms in the	7	1,3
South each year.	8	0,0,5,6
	9	1

To conclude the unit, we looked at the general data patterns for each region and discussed how the number of thunderstorms in a given region is related to the number of its tornadoes. Students could now understand why certain regions of the country were vulnerable to tornado activity—these cities also had a high number of thunderstorms.

Benefits for All

Based on my experience, I believe event-based science and media, including movies, television shows, books, and the Internet, encourage emergent classroom discourse and resulting student interaction. The students in my classroom combined previous scientific knowledge with what they learned from the popular movie *Twister* to describe how tornadoes form, how they behave once they touch the ground, and how meteorologists classify them.

Generating genuine student excitement about science requires teachers to think outside of the box. While all content cannot be connected to an event or the movies, facilitating classroom discourse around weather-related events is a good start!

Jacqueline Leonard is an associate professor of mathematics education in the Department of Curriculum, Instruction, and Technology at Temple University in Philadelphia, PA.

Resources

Ball, D. L. 1991. Improving, not standardizing, teaching. *Arithmetic Teacher,* 39 (1): 18–22.

Cazden, C. B. 1998. *Classroom discourse: The language of teaching and learning.* Portsmouth, NH: Heinemann.

Cochran-Smith, M., and S. L. Lytle. 1990. Research on teaching and teacher research: The issues that divide. *Educational Researcher,* 19 (2): 2–11.

Jegede, O. J., and J. O. Olajide. 1995. Wait-time, classroom discourse, and the influence of sociocultural factors in science teaching. *Science Education,* 79 (3): 233–249.

Landwehr, J. M., and A. E. Watkins. 1995. *Exploring data.* Palo Alto, CA: Dale Seymour.

Lehman, J. R. 1994. Integrating science and mathematics: Perceptions of preservice and practicing elementary teachers. *School Science and Mathematics,* 94 (2): 58–64.

Longo, P. 1993. National mathematics standards and communicative competence: A sociolinguistic analysis of institutionalized and emergent forms of classroom discourse. Dissertation Abstracts International, A:55/11. 3440.

Mulryan, C. M. 1995. Fifth and sixth graders' involvement and participation in cooperative small groups in mathematics. *The Elementary School Journal,* 95 (4): 297–310.

National Middle School Association. 1995. *This we believe: Developmentally responsive middle level schools.* Columbus, OH: J. Leonard.

National Research Council. 1996. *National Science Education Standards.* Washington, DC: National Academy Press.

Thomas, G. C. 1998. Classroom volcanology: Using constructivism to teach students about volcanoes and the factors that influence eruptions. *The Science Teacher,* 65 (5): 28–31.

Yaros, R. A. 1991. *Weatherschool: Teacher research guide.* T. Roberson (Ed.). Chesterfield, MO: Yaros.

B

A Bat Is Like a ...

By Audrey C. Rule and Cynthia Rust

Analogies, or comparisons based on similarities between things that are otherwise dissimilar, can greatly enhance science learning for children. Analogous reasoning "is a central component of human cognition. It is involved in classification and in learning, it provides a tool for thought and explanation, and it is important for discovery and creative thinking" (Goswami 1992).

As teachers, you probably have already used analogies to explain basic science concepts. The DNA molecule as a ladder, the heart as a pump, and the eye as a camera are just a few of the most common analogies used in science classrooms. This article explains how one third-grade teacher incorporated analogy-based activities into an interdisciplinary lesson on bats.

The teacher followed the Teaching with Analogies (TWA) model (Glynn 1985), a six-point technique on how to examine relationships through analogies. In this model, ideas are transferred from a familiar concept, termed *analog*, to an unfamiliar one, termed *target*. Analogies are made when the analog and target share some similar features, and these features can be depicted graphically by *mapping*. The six operations of the TWA model are

1. Introduce the target concept.
2. Review the analog concept.
3. Identify relevant features of target and analog.
4. Map similarities.
5. Indicate where the analog breaks down.
6. Draw conclusions.

Many inventions have been inspired by creative analogy with plants or animals (Swenson 2000). For example, Pringles Potato Chips, packed as a stack of processed, uniform chips, were inspired by a comparison to wet leaves that pack together snugly without breaking. Eli Whitney was inspired to invent the cotton gin after watching a cat attempt to catch a chicken through a fence. Georges de Mestral discovered Velcro after noticing burrs that adhered to his clothing.

Bats Are the Target

The teacher chose to use bats as the target concept for several reasons. She had learned about the TWA model in her science methods course during her teacher preparation program and was eager to use it. The study of bats aligned with Idaho's third-grade science curriculum, which asks students to "examine inherited attributes of living things" and "describe how

Topic: bats
Go to: www.scilinks.org
Code: MIX32

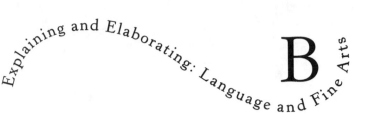

various organisms satisfy their needs within the environment" (Idaho State Department of Education 2001). These curriculum objectives were based on Life Science Content Standard C of the *National Science Education Standards* (National Research Council 1996).

Another reason the teacher chose bats was that several species of bats were native to the arid Southwestern Idaho area. Students expressed an interest in learning about bats because of their unusual habits and characteristics, particularly their nocturnal lifestyle, mammalian flight, and echolocation (a sensory system in which bats emit high-pitched sounds and interpret their echoes to determine the direction and distance of objects).

The teacher introduced the target concept by reading aloud age-appropriate information books on bats and bat lifestyles. After each book, students added facts they remembered from the book to a chart of bat adaptations on the chalkboard. This chart included such bat features as claws for gripping cave ceilings and tree branches, fur to insulate the body, and echolocation for travel and insect capture in the dark.

Reviewing the Analogs

The second step of the TWA model calls for students to review the analogs—the objects that students would compare to the bat features. To do this, the teacher assembled a box of 8 to 12 familiar items that had forms and functions analogous to bat features. Among the items in the box were a sweater, stethoscope bell, hair clip, dust cloth, an empty aspirin bottle, an old autofocus camera, and a long-handled dishwashing sponge. A toy parachute, hang glider, satellite dish, and papoose board were also included. When a real item was too large or dangerous to be handled by students, a toy or miniature replica of the item was used. The advantage of using actual objects rather than pictures is that students can examine the physical forms (color, shape, texture, flexibility, and so on) of the objects, which provides multisensory information to connect more strongly new and existing learning.

The teacher chose which items to place in the box based on their corresponding forms and functions to bats. For example, bat fur is composed of hairs and fibers that trap heat next to the skin to insulate the body. Similarly, a sweater consists of a network of twisted fibers that covers the body to trap heat next to the skin. Both the bat fur and sweater share a similar form (fibrous material) and function (insulate the body).

In the same box, the teacher placed a corresponding set of cards she had made that listed the bat part's form and function on the front and the matching item's form and function on the back. These cards served as a memory prompt for the teacher when she first presented the lesson to students. One card, for instance, might read on the front, "Bat fur is a fibrous covering that traps heat next to the skin to insulate the body, keeping it warm," and, on the back, "A sweater consists of fibrous material that covers the body, trapping heat next to the skin. It insulates the body to keep it warm in cool weather."

Exploring Form and Function

The students sat on the floor in a circle around the teacher. "Today we are going to look at some objects in this box and describe them," she said. "Physical characteristics like shape, texture, and color of things designed by people are carefully chosen so that these items can better serve a purpose." She took the toy parachute out of the box and held it up so that everyone could see it. "An example of this is the parachute. The fabric of the parachute must be airtight, lightweight, thin, and flexible, yet tough enough so that it doesn't rip. This form allows parachutes to be folded and resist being torn apart as the person glides down to Earth. If a parachute were made of velvet instead of nylon, it would be too heavy and bulky to fit comfortably on a person's back. Also, velvet is not as strong or airtight as nylon. It might tear or allow air to pass through it—a disastrous situation for the person using the parachute!"

Next, the teacher took the long-handled dishwashing sponge out of the box and said, "The long handle allows the sponge to reach deep into bottles for cleaning. So as you can see, form is frequently related to its use." As she removed each item from the box, she asked students to identify and describe them as she had done.

She then introduced how animal and human bodies also have forms that help those body parts serve a purpose. For example, human fingers have many joints so that a person's hand can close around an object to securely grasp it. Many animals, such as monkeys and squirrels, have jointed fingers for grasping. Since the focus of the lesson was on bats, the teacher prompted students to name some ways that a bat's body is designed to help the bat survive. "What parts of a bat's body help it obtain food, move from place to place, protect it from enemies, or take care of its young?" she asked. Students remembered the information from books they had read and suggested that bats use echolocation to find insects, have fur to keep warm, have wings to fly, and use claws to hang onto cave ceilings or tree branches.

Relationships Revealed

The teacher connected the items to bats by explaining that each item had a form and function similar to a form and function of a bat's body. She picked up the parachute and let it fall to the floor, showing students how the air resistance of the parachute allowed the toy figure to glide through the air. She asked them, "What part of a bat's body allows the bat to glide through the air?" Students immediately replied, "The wings." The teacher added, "Remember how we said that the parachute must be thin, lightweight, and tough? Do you think that the skin on a bat's wings would have the same form—would it be thin, lightweight, and tough?"

The teacher then asked students to look at the items she had taken out of the box and displayed on a desk and see if any of the items were similar to bat body parts in form and function. One student immediately commented that the sweater was like bat fur because both were "woolly" and kept people and bats warm. Another student pointed to the hair clip, saying, "That hair clip has fingers that grab hair and hold it in place just like a bat has claws to hold onto the cave ceiling to roost." The teacher told students that these types of connections were called *analogies*: "You are making analogies, which means finding ways that two different things, in this case bats and items, are the same."

Making Analogies

The teacher went through the box a second time, choosing items students had not yet mentioned and asking students to freely make connections between the displayed object and bats. For example, after taking the stethoscope bell out of the box, she asked, "What does this bell have in common with bats?" One student responded, "A doctor listens to your heart with it, and bats use their ears to hear." "Why are both the stethoscope bell and bat ears cup-shaped?" the teacher asked. "Maybe it helps them hear

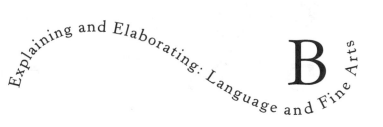
better," suggested a student. "Let's try it," invited the teacher as she demonstrated cupping her hand over her ear. "Listen to me with your hand cupped around your ear and see if you can hear better." Students tried it and enthusiastically agreed they could indeed hear better. The teacher then explained how the cup shape gathers sound waves and directs them into the ear canal or along the stethoscope cable.

There were some items in the box for which the students could not suggest an analogy. The teacher set these items aside until all ideas were exhausted. She referred to her cards, reading a fact from the front of one of the cards to the students and asking them to match the card with one of the remaining objects that had the same form and function. In the case of the papoose board, she read from her card: "Adult bats leave young bats hanging in caves or trees with other bats to keep the young safe and warm." She asked the class, "Is there any object here that allows a baby to be suspended in a safe place?" Students pointed to the miniature papoose board. The teacher then read from the back of the card: "Some Native American mothers place their babies on papoose boards hanging from the mother's back, which keeps the baby safe and warm. Similarly, adult bats leave their young hanging in colonies in caves and other protected areas to keep them safe and warm."

She asked students to put in their own words the way a papoose board can be compared to a bat. One student replied, "Baby bats are left hanging in a safe place, and a papoose [board] allows a child to be hung on a person's back like a backpack so that the child is safe."

Multiple Analogs

After explaining the analogous relationship between the objects and bats, the teacher asked,

"Can you think of any other objects that have something in common with bats?" One student described how a bat's tail acts like a spoon to scoop insects to its mouth for eating and how bat fur acts like a camouflage jacket because it blends in with trees and rocks when the bat hides.

Constructing several analogies for the same concept can help students see the target idea from different perspectives, for each analogy has its own strengths and limitations.

For example, bats leave their young hanging from cave ceilings to keep them safe while they find food. The analog of a papoose board works well because an infant is suspended on the back for safety. However, other analogs exist. One student, for example, switched categories from babies to food and suggested that suspending food high in a tree at night while camping to keep it safe from bears is similar to mother bats' leaving their young suspended from cave ceilings. In this example, the analogy extends to the idea of keeping both camping food items and bat young safe from animals. Another student said that hanging clothes in a closet to keep them from getting dirty, wrinkled, damaged, or lost could be another analogy. This analogy highlights the concept of keeping things in order and knowing where they are—the mother bat knowing where her young rest is similar to a person knowing the location of clothing.

Students also thought of other objects that, like bat wings, are folded to allow a large surface area to fit into a compact space when not in use. Recalling the parachute examined earlier, one student suggested a collapsible handheld fan that also pushes air. Several students thought of an umbrella. (An umbrella protects people from getting wet. This idea sparked the connection to bat wings shielding a roosting bat's body from rain and cold.) Another student, who was very interested in spacecraft, described how satellites unfold in space to allow their solar arrays to gather sunlight. Students wondered if bats might spread their wings in the daytime to gather sunlight and warm themselves. "Do bats ever fan their wings to cool off?" asked another student.

The teacher was elated at such a question! Scientists often use analogies to help them think of questions for investigation, which is exactly what was happening in her classroom.

Map It!

According to the TWA model, the next step in learning from analogies is to map them. *Mapping* is the systematic comparison of the target (bats) and analog (items). Graphic mapping of the relationship between target and analog can help young learners form mental images of the analogy and make more connections. The teacher chose to have the class compare skin on a bat's wing to a baseball glove for the first map. She wrote, "Skin on Bat's Wing" as a caption on the left side of the chalkboard and wrote, "Baseball Glove" on the right side. She titled the middle column, "Similar Form or Function." The teacher asked, "How is the skin on a bat's wing like a baseball glove?" Students replied that the wing and glove were both made of skin (which the teacher wrote in the middle column) because a bat's wing is skin (written on the left side) and a baseball glove is leather (written on the right side). "How else are they alike?" "They are both used to catch something," suggested a student. "Bat wings help catch insects, and baseball gloves catch balls." The teacher asked about shape. A student replied that a baseball glove was somewhat cup-shaped, and sometimes bats held their wings in a cupped shape. Those ideas

were added to the chart. Another student suggested that both bat wings and leather gloves had skin stretched between finger bones. Finally, a student mentioned how a baseball glove was tough and didn't tear, similar to a bat's wing. See Figure 1 for the completed chart.

Teachers of younger students may want to have students "map" bat analogies by drawing pictures instead of making charts.

Limits to the Analogy

The teacher asked students to think of ways bat wings and leather gloves were different. These were the *limits* of the analogy. "Sometimes similarities don't go very far," she explained. "In analogies, there are limits to the similarities between two things, otherwise the two things would be exactly the same."

She drew a line across the columns on the chart and labeled the bottom of the chart, "Limits of the Analogy." One student remarked how a bat's wing was living, but a leather glove was not alive. Another pointed out that a baseball glove is usually the same shape, but a bat can fold and open its wings to change their shape. These ideas were added to the chart. Another student observed that they catch different things—insects versus baseballs. Finally, a student suggested that baseball glove was for fun and play, but bat wings helped the bat survive. These limits are also included on the chart in Figure 1.

Analogies and Inventions

Older students (grades five and up) may enjoy applying what they learned about bat analogies to a challenging activity that uses the Scamper technique (Eberle 1972). SCAMPER is an acronym for seven different methods—Substitute, Combine, Adapt, Modify-minimize-maximize,

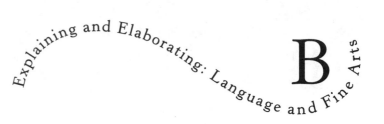

Figure 1. Mapping of an Analogy.

Target—Skin on Bat's Wing	Similar Form or Function	Analog—Baseball Glove
Made of bat skin	Skin material	Made of leather
Skin stretched between finger bones	Configuration	Leather stretched between fingers
Tough, elastic bat skin	Tenacity	Tough, stretched cowhide
Catching flying insects	Function	Catching flying baseballs
Held in cupped position	Shape	Cupped shape
	Limits of Analogy	
Living tissue	Material	Preserved cowhide
Bat can fold wings against body	Shape when not in use	Glove is generally same shape all the time
Insects	Items being caught	Baseballs or softballs
Helps bat survive	Purpose	Used for recreational game

Put to another use, Eliminate, and Rearrange—of changing an item to improve it. The Scamper technique can be combined with ideas from bat forms and functions and applied to commonplace objects to create product improvements or inventions.

For example, one teacher asked her middle level students to improve a paper plate by applying the Scamper technique to bat adaptation ideas. Students found the concept of using bat characteristics to improve a human product motivating because of its novelty. One student thought the plate should be edible similar to a tortilla bowl or ice cream cone (Scamper: Eliminate trash by consuming the plate). This idea was sparked by analogy to bats eating whole insects rather than select parts.

Another student suggested that plates have claw-like extensions to grip a person's lap similar to the way a bat attaches itself to roost (Scamper: Adapt plate for greater stability). Considering the way a bat scoops insects with its wings, a student suggested a hidden catch-all compartment below the plate into which people could scoop unwanted food (Scamper: Combine catchall with plate). The concept of bat skin resisting water led to the idea of a waterproof coating on the plate to prevent soak-through of saucy foods (Scamper: Modify plate material to make waterproof). The activity caused such a buzz of excitement that students began a discussion on how to patent their ideas!

Thinking Benefits

Incorporating analogy-based activities into science lessons boosts students' creativity, and creative-thinking processes can help solve problems in both daily activities and science. Yager (2000), in his vision for science education for a new millennium, emphasizes the need for more creative thinking to be purposefully incorporated into science programs. Practice in using analogies in the school setting can transfer to everyday life and vice versa (Silkebakken and Camp 1993).

For example, a person repairing a loose chair leg might fill the joint with epoxy to tighten it by recalling how gum grows around a tooth. Similarly, a student placing a damp towel over rising dough to retain the moisture may reason that soil moisture may be preserved with a blanket of mulch.

The teacher featured in this article used bats, a fascinating topic for many young children, to solidify a lesson on animal adaptations and lifestyles, as well as to build a foundation for new thinking skills. Other themes, such as endangered animals, forms and functions of body systems, and plants, work just as well. We encourage you to use creative analogy with the science topics in your classroom!

Audrey C. Rule is an associate professor in the Department of Curriculum and Instruction at SUNY Oswego in Oswego, NY. Cynthia Rust earned a master's degree from Boise State University in Boise, ID, and is a volunteer and substitute teacher at primary and secondary schools and with church youth groups.

Resources

Alexander, P. A., V. L. Wilson, C. S. White, and J. D. Fuqua. 1987a. Analogical reasoning in young children. *Journal of Educational Psychology*, 79: 401–408.

Alexander, P. A., V. L. Wilson, C. S. White, V. L. Wilson, M. K. Tallent, and R. E. Shur. 1987b. Effects of teacher training on children's analogical reasoning performance. *Teaching and Teacher Education*, 3: 275–285.

Alexander, P. A., V. L Wilson, C. S. White, J. D. Fuqua, G. D. Clark, A. F. Wilson, and J. M. Kulikowich. 1989. Development of analogical reasoning in four- and five-year-old children. *Cognitive Development*, 4: 65–88.

Eberle, R. F. 1972. Developing imagination through Scamper. *Journal of Creative Behavior*, 6(3): 199–203.

Glynn, S. 1995. Conceptual bridges: Using analogies to explain scientific concepts. *The Science Teacher*, 62(9): 25–27.

Glynn, S., and R. Duit, eds. 1995. *Learning Science in the Schools: Research Reforming Practice*. Mahwah, N.: Lawrence Erlbaum.

Goswami, U. 1991. Analogical reasoning: What develops? A review of research and theory. *Child Development*, 62(1): 1–22.

Goswami, U. 1992. *Analogical Reasoning*. Hove, UK: Lawrence Erlbaum.

Hadi-Tabassum, S. 1997. The invention convention: Mind meets simple machines. *Science and Children*, 34(7): 24–27, 47.

National Research Council. 1996. *National Science Education Standards*. Washington, DC: National Academy Press.

Nippold, M. A., and M. P. Sullivan. 1987. Verbal and perceptual analogical reasoning and proportional metaphor comprehension in young children. *Journal of Speech and Hearing Research*, 30: 367–376.

Silkebakken, G., and D. Camp. 1993. A five-step strategy for teaching analogous reasoning to middle school students. *Middle School Journal*, 24(4): 47–50.

Yager, R. E. 2000. A vision for what science education should be like for the first 25 years of a new millennium. *School Science and Mathematics*, 100(6): 327–341.

Websites

Swenson, D. X. 2000. Innovations and Inventions. *www.css.edu/users/dswenson/web/INNOVAT.HTM*
Idaho State Department of Education. 2001. *www.sde.state.id.us/instruct/Curriculum*

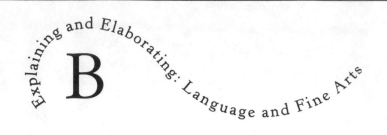

Someone's in the Kitchen with Science

By Patricia K. Lowry and Judy Hale McCrary

The kitchen is a natural source of science exploration and a great place for young children to develop and practice their science process skills. As professors of early childhood and elementary education who work directly with many children and their classroom teachers, we'd like to share a few of our favorite kitchen science activities we've conducted with students.

These easy-to-do activities require few materials, address the National Science Education Standards (See box), and introduce basic science processes, covering topics such as simple chemistry and healthy eating habits. They also incorporate the use of science journals and provide art and literature connections. Although we did the activities in the classroom, they also work well as home science for parents to do with their children.

Mix It Up!

The book *Mouse Paint* by Ellen Stall Walsh (1995) led one kindergarten class to explore col-

ors. In this story, three white mice climb into jars of red, yellow, and blue paint. After the mice realize they have changed to the paint color in the jar, they drip puddles of paint onto white paper. As they step into other paint puddles, the mice change colors again. After hearing the story read aloud, the students asked how the mice could have changed into a new color, noticing that combining two colors can create a new color.

Because the children were so enthusiastic about the book, their teacher decided to have them investigate primary and secondary colors to help the kindergarten students learn some art fundamentals as well as science—the concept of mixing two substances together to form a new substance.

The teacher first organized the class into small groups and gave each student three small sealable plastic bags, each filled with three spoonfuls (about 15 mL) of red, yellow, or blue colored gelatin (such as Jello) that had previously been made and chilled. She told the class that these three colors are called *primary colors*.

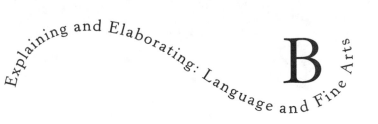
"Primary colors are the three basic colors. When you mix these three colors, new colors emerge. Primary colors can be observed all around us." She discussed with the children that the sun appears red, the sky looks blue, a lemon is yellow, and these colors can even be seen in a rainbow.

The teacher then added three spoonfuls of another color gelatin to each child's bag, making sure that all of the bags were sealed completely. She asked, "What do you think will happen when the two different colors are blended together?" Some students predicted that the colors would remain primary colors, while other children thought orange, green, and purple would result.

The teacher instructed the students to gently squeeze the contents of the bag for one minute to mix the colors. They had fun "squishing" the colors together and recorded their observations in a science journal (a notebook or folder with paper in it). They observed that mixing red and yellow formed orange, mixing yellow and blue made green, and mixing red and blue made purple.

Science Journals for Us

Although many teachers use science journals in upper elementary grades, we find journals appropriate even for very young learners. By writing in science journals on a regular basis, primary grade children learn to communicate their observations (Shepardson and Britsch 2000) and ideas while reinforcing their understanding of key science concepts. Kindergartners can make journal entries by drawing pictures, graphs, and charts of their observations (Ajello 2000).

Students repeated the mixing procedure for each bag, drawing their predictions and observations in their journals each time. After all the colors had been mixed, the teacher explained that the blended colors are called *secondary col-*

ors. "These secondary colors include orange, green, and purple," she continued. "Secondary colors can be seen in many familiar objects. A common fruit, the orange, is the same color as the new color formed by mixing red and yellow. The green of a frog is the color created by combining blue and yellow."

To extend learning from the color-mixing activity, students and the teacher read the book *Colors* by Gallimard Jeunesse and Pascale de Bourgoing (1991) and then conducted another activity with the gelatin. Using a clean, sealable plastic bag with red gelatin inside, students added to the bag green gelatin made in the previous activity. Based on their earlier experiences with the gelatin, most students predicted the color would change to blue or purple. When students gently squeezed the bag to mix the gelatins, they observed that the newly created color was brown. Thus they noted in their journals that mixing a primary color with a secondary color will always create brown.

Fruit and Vegetable Prints

We came up with another kitchen activity while working with third-grade students who were studying seeds, fruits, and vegetables for a unit on plants. In this unit, students learned about the main parts of the plant and that the fruit is an important part of plants because fruit contains the seeds. They had learned that many vegetables, such as bell peppers, squash, and tomatoes, are scientifically identified as fruits. Other vegetables, such as the potato and carrot, are roots of the plant.

To wrap up this unit, students conducted a science/art activity that allowed them to observe the insides of various fruits and vegetables and, at the same time, create beautiful artwork.

Before school one day, the teacher prepared

the classroom for small groups of students to make prints with cut fruits and vegetables and paints. The teacher

- Cut an assortment of apples, okra, potatoes, carrots, bell peppers, and mushrooms in half. For each group of four students, we recommend placing halves from four different fruits and vegetables on the table. For a group of 20 students, the cost is relatively inexpensive because only three whole apples, three whole potatoes, etc. are needed for this activity.
- Covered student worktables with newspapers and placed sheets of colored construction paper on top.
- Poured tempera paint—finger paint also works—onto paper plates or pie tins, setting various colors at each table.

Students wore smocks or men's button-up shirts (buttoned in the back) and brought their science journals.

When the students arrived in class, their faces lit up with excitement and they wondered what they would be doing. Before beginning the activity, however, they read *Eating the Alphabet: Fruits and Vegetables from A to Z* by Lois Ehlert (1989) and discussed fruits and vegetables to review what they had learned in class. Students discussed the difference between fleshy and dry fruits: They considered the peach, strawberry, and plum fleshy because they are soft when ripe. They recognized that other plants produce fruit that is dry when ripe, such as nuts.

The teacher explained how they would be making prints to help them remember some of the things they had learned about fruits and vegetables. In small groups, students examined the cut fruits and vegetables and wrote down their observations in their journals. For example, while looking at an apple cut in half horizon-

tally, one group observed a "star" inside the apple, counted the seeds (a fully developed apple has 10 seeds), and recorded the number of apple seeds in the journal.

To make a print, students carefully dipped the flat surface of the fruit or vegetable into the paint and then pressed it for about 10 seconds onto construction paper. The prints were then placed on a shelf for several hours, either during the day or overnight. Students observed the formation of the inside of the fruit or vegetable and a repetitious pattern if the print was made more than once.

When the prints were dry, students again compared the insides of the vegetables and fruits and counted the number of seeds inside some of the fruits. Later, students wrote the name of the vegetable or fruit at the top of the prints and added the pictures to their science journals. We also displayed the artwork around the classroom.

Let's Eat Right!

The following activity came about during a first-grade lesson on healthy eating habits. The children and their teacher read *The Edible Pyramid: Good Eating Every Day* by Loreen Leedy (1994) and discussed the various foods they had eaten earlier in the day at breakfast and lunch. The teacher introduced *The Food Pyramid for Children* (American Dietetic Association 2000), explaining that the food pyramid is a guide used by people to evaluate eating habits to discover if all nutrients needed by the body are obtained during one day. The food pyramid provides the recommended servings per day for the following food groups: bread, cereal, grains, and pasta; vegetables; fruits; milk, yogurt, and cheese; meat, poultry, fish, dry beans, eggs, and nuts; and fats, oils, and sweets. The pyramid can be

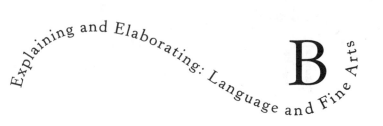
downloaded from *www.usda.gov/cnpp/KidsPyra*.

Several students wondered whether the foods they ate that day were on the food pyramid and whether they had followed the "rules" for healthy eating. The teacher gave each child a photocopy of the food pyramid and challenged students to figure out the categories of the foods they ate at either breakfast or lunch. The teacher also provided scrap magazines, scissors, crayons, markers, and paper and asked students to cut out or draw a picture of the foods they ate and place them in the appropriate position on the food pyramid.

As the students worked on their personal food pyramids, they observed how many servings from each group they had eaten during the day. They discovered their eating habits provided food items that were found in many of the levels of the pyramid and that much of what they ate belonged in the top level of the pyramid, "Fats/Oils/Sweets." (The United States Department of Agriculture recommends eating only a few portions from this level in the daily diet.) Only a few students were eating the recommended servings per day from all levels of the pyramid. The teacher explained the importance of using the pyramid as a guide to develop healthy eating habits and that the size of servings and the number of calories needed each day depends on an individual's size, age, health, and lifestyle.

To reinforce learning, the teacher asked students to make a day's food journal with their parents at home by either cutting-and-pasting pictures or drawing illustrations of foods eaten in one day. Using the food pyramid as a guide, students and their parents assessed the day's food journal, and students wrote in their journals what changes to make to fulfill the food requirements for that day. Finally, students created a "perfect day" food journal with foods they liked that fulfilled the necessary food groups. After sharing their "perfect day" food pyramids in class the next day, students planned a party with favorite foods from the food pyramid for later in the week. For the party fare, students brought in select items from home that represented each of the food groups, such as pizza (grains, vegetable, milk, and fat), ice cream (milk and fat), and dry cereal (grains). At the end of the party, students chose their favorite food and wrote about its taste in their journals. Sample journal entries included, "I like pizza because it can have so many different things on top of it. Cheese is my favorite topping!" "Vanilla ice cream is my favorite dessert because it makes me feel cool all over" and "I like the crunching sound when you eat different types of cereal."

Berry Exciting Fabrics

During class one day, a second-grade student was excitedly talking about a recent berry-picking experience. He was surprised at how hard it was to wash the berry juice off his hands. This conversation led the teacher to ask the class, "If it's hard to wash juice from your hands, do you think berry juice will stay on clothes or change a fabric's color?"

Students were skeptical about berries changing the color of fabric. To let them see for themselves, the teacher decided to have them try dyeing old handkerchiefs. (Old handkerchiefs can be brought to school from home or teachers/parents can cut muslin scraps.)

Students worked in small groups to "dye" the handkerchiefs. They chose raspberries and blackberries, but blueberries and strawberries work just as well. Wearing smocks to protect their clothing and plastic gloves to protect their

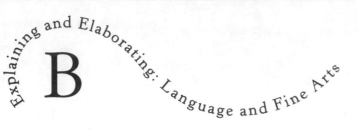

hands, they placed a handful of berries on a handkerchief—some tried to create a pattern, and others tried to cover the entire cloth with berries.

The next day, students washed the cloths (they had dried overnight) by rinsing them under a stream of water. Alas! They discovered the berry juice had stained the handkerchiefs! Stu-

dents were amazed at the individual patterns created by the berry stains. Comparing different colors and designs, they commented that rinsing the fabric longer created lighter colors. They also discussed how they might use their creation as a bandana, scarf, head wrap, or flag. Students recorded the changes they observed by drawing a picture of the handkerchief and describing the new color in their science journals.

National Science Education Standards

This article addresses the *National Science Education Standards* (National Research Council 1996) at the K–4 level.

Science as Inquiry Content Standard A

As a result of activities in grades K–4, all students should develop inquiry skills when presented with a scientific question, use different kinds of investigations depending on the type of question, develop explanations using observations and what they already know about the world, and describe the results in ways that enable others to repeat the investigations.

Physical Science Content Standard B

As a result of the activities in grades K–4, all students should develop an understanding of the properties of objects and materials as they react with other substances.

Science in Personal Perspectives Content Standard F

As a result of the activities in grades K–4, all students should develop an understanding of personal health issues, such as the basic need for healthy food and nutrients in the body.

Nature of Science Content Standard G

As a result of activities in grades K–4, all students should develop an understanding of science as a human endeavor through the experiences of investigating and thinking about written explanations.

Home Experiments

For further exploration, the teacher sent home a newsletter to parents that contained suggestions for additional fabric-dyeing experiments—for example, both onion skins (yellow and red) and mustard dye fabric (Harrell 2001). The letter began: "We have been discovering how to use products from the kitchen to dye fabrics. Two activities that your child and you may enjoy doing at home are explained in this letter. A word of caution—one activity involves boiling water and the other uses warm water from the sink. Be sure to supervise your child closely during these activities."

To make an onion skin dye, we outlined the following steps:

1. Pull the skins off onions in a three-pound bag of either yellow or red onions.
2. Add the skins to 9.5 L of water and 475 mL of vinegar in a large, nonreactive (stainless steel) pot.
3. Simmer the mixture over low heat for about an hour.
4. Strain the onion skins, leaving only the dye bath.
5. Add an old handkerchief to the pot and leave fabric in simmering water for about 30 minutes or until the fabric is a couple of shades darker than you want.
6. Rinse the fabric under running water until the water runs clear.

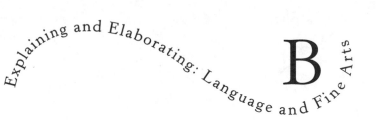

7. Let the fabric dry for a few hours or overnight.

Typically students who did these activities at home observed that red onions created a darker color than the yellow ones, which produced a golden color. They were also surprised to observe how intricate the design could become.

For the mustard dye, we outlined the following steps in the newsletter:

1. Shake the mustard in the jar or squeeze bottle and apply it directly to another piece of fabric.
2. Let the mustard set for about 30 minutes until it is nearly dry.
3. Rinse the cloth with a water spray of warm water until the mustard is dislodged and the water runs clear.
4. Immerse the cloth in 9.5 L of warm water and 234 mL of vinegar, allowing as much mustard as possible to loosen.
5. Seal the wet fabric inside a microwave-safe plastic bag and heat on 50 percent power for about five minutes. Watch it closely.
6. Hang the fabric up to dry.
7. Press with an iron to further set the design.

Students who did these activities at home commented it was a lot easier to create a design on paper by using the mustard in a squeeze bottle.

Science in the Kitchen

Kitchen-based activities allow teachers, students, and parents to use science in an exciting way. Especially with curious young children, even a simple classroom experience can generate enough excitement for children to continue science exploration at home. Through these activities children can practice the science process skills. As young students—and their parents—participate in each activity, their science skills and confidence grow, building a foundation for success in more challenging science explorations in the future.

Patricia K. Lowry is a professor and head of the Department of Curriculum and Instruction, and Judy Hale McCrary is an associate professor, both in the Department of Curriculum and Instruction at Jacksonville State University in Alabama.

References

Ajello, T. 2000. Science journals: Writing, drawing and learning. *Teaching K–8*, 30(5): 56–57.

Gillis, J. S. 1993. *An apple a day*. New York: Trumpet Club.

Harrell, G. 2001. Pantry dyes. *Better Homes and Gardens*, 79(2): 46–52.

Heddle, R. 1992. *Science in the kitchen*. London: Usborne.

Kepler, L. 1998. Journals of science. *Instructor*, 108(3): 82–83.

National Research Council. 1996. *National Science Education Standards*. Washington, DC: National Academy Press.

Shepardson, D. P., and S. J. Britsch. 2000. Analyzing children's science journals. *Science and Children*, 38(3): 29–33.

Victor, E., and R. D. Kellough. 2000. *Science for the elementary and middle school*. Upper Saddle River, N.J.: Prentice-Hall.

Children's Literature

Ehlert, L. 1989. *Eating the alphabet: Fruits and vegetables from A to Z*. New York: Trumpet Club.

Jeunesse, G., and P. de Bourgoing. 1991. *Colors*. New York: Scholastic.

Leedy, L. 1994. *The edible pyramid: Good eating every day*. New York: Trumpet Club.

Walsh, E. S. 1995. *Mouse paint*. New York: Harcourt Brace.

Internet

The American Dietetic Association. 2000. *Food Guide for Young Children*. *www.usda.gov/cnpp/KidsPyra*

B

The Sky's the Limit

By Deborah Roberts

Recently, I had a wonderful—though unexpected—experience while teaching first grade. I invited my students to participate in a study of the sky and the Moon. For their homework each day after school, students went outside to observe the sky and record their observations in their moon journals. On the mornings following the observations, students brought their moon journals to class and discussed what they had seen. The unexpected surprise was the involvement and reactions of students' parents.

This journal activity provided opportunities for parents and children to spend time together without pressure and share a common experience of learning about the Moon. It allowed parents to be involved in their child's school world and share cultural traditions. This activity also gave me an easy way to integrate literature and motivated students to write creatively in their daily moon journals.

Connecting to the *Standards*

Having primary students observe the sky and the Moon is advocated in the *National Science Education Standards* (NRC 1996) and the *Benchmarks for Science Literacy* (AAAS 1993). *Benchmarks* states that students in kindergarten through second grade should notice and de-scribe what the sky looks like to them at different times and observe how the Moon appears to change shape.

In the *Standards,* Earth and Space Science Content Standard D states that students in kindergarten through fourth grade should develop an understanding of objects in the sky and changes in the Earth and sky. The *Standards* even suggests that children draw the Moon's shape daily and determine the pattern in the shapes over several weeks. Providing opportunities and encouragement for children to share their observations with each other provides a richer observation for all (Brandou 1997).

The *Standards* also states that parents must work with teachers to foster their children's science education. If this is true, then teachers should help by providing opportunities for parents to be involved in their child's science education. I did not realize this was exactly what I was doing when I began this project.

Moon Journals

To start, I gave each student a moon journal filled with Moon-watching sheets (see figures). I did not specify a time they should make their observations since the Moon is often visible during daylight hours.

When students went home for the first night of Moon watching, I sent a note to parents ex-

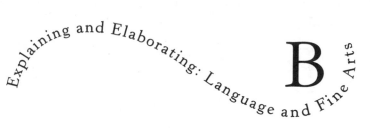
plaining the moon journals. I wanted the parents, an adult family member, or another responsible adult to go with the student to observe the Moon for a variety of reasons, the most important being security. I also hoped that parents would help children remember to record their observations in their moon journals.

The moon journal task encouraged students to make daily observations of the sky and record them both pictorially and verbally. In the journal, students drew what they saw in the sky, recorded what they thought about what they saw, and described what they wondered about their experience.

Students' thoughts could be creative, scientific, realistic, or poetic. One child wrote, "I think the Moon is asleep." Another wrote, "I think it is beautiful and it looks like a banana." After writing their thoughts, students recorded their "wonderings." Several children had the same question: "I wonder if I will ever get to the Moon?" One child asked, "Can the Moon hear me?" Each day, I invited students to share their observations, thoughts, and wonderings with the rest of the class. Each was eager to hear other students' observations.

The moon journaling task became a cooperative effort among students. They learned by sharing the responsibility of learning. For example, if one child drew a picture of a waxing Moon and

another drew a waning Moon, their classmates asked questions and compared the drawings. Questions like "What side of the house were you on?" "Are you sure it was pointing that way?" and "But look at the picture from yesterday; how come it's going backward today?" would usually get students to take a closer look.

Students began to notice the patterns of the changes of the Moon in a short period of time, partially because they were comparing and learning from their classmates. Those students who had some prior knowledge on the subject shared what they knew with the others.

Parent Involvement

Moon watching gave parents an opportunity to help with their child's homework and hear about what was said during classroom discussion. Many children and parents found this time to be wonderful as the students shared with their parents what they had learned in class.

Often during class discussion, students shared family beliefs or myths. One student said that

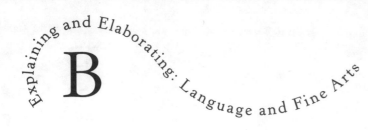

Day **2**

Date **11/3/97**

Day of the Week **Jueves**

Time of Day **8:00**

What I saw: **No vi la luna**

What I think: **ce me caye la noche**

What I Wonder: **¿Como lo hicieron todo en el cielo?**

moon journal assignment because they did not need to have a lot of science knowledge to help their children with this assignment. One parent shared with me, "In the United States, the way you teach things is different from my country. It's been a long time since I went to school, so looking at the Moon and writing about it is a way for me to feel comfort-

her grandmother went with her to look at the Moon and told her never to marry a man she met on the night of a full Moon. Her grandmother said if she did, the marriage would be full of problems. Some students responded by saying that when they got big, they were not going on dates if the Moon was full. "I'll just stay in with my mom," one girl explained. "We don't need any more problems."

Another child shared the story his father told him about werewolves that come out on the night of the full Moon. Many students had heard this before. Other students said, "That's just a cartoon, and your dad is making it up." The students didn't believe the myths, but they liked hearing them. We had read about and discussed myths and legends and how they were used to explain events that people did not understand.

Several parents told me that they liked the

able helping my son." Another parent said, "I don't have to read the assignment to my child, and I don't have to ask, 'What did the teacher say about this in school today?' because my child knows she only has to look at the Moon. It gives us a chance to talk about school and do homework without any tension."

Some parents also said they liked having an excuse to leave the daily routine for a few minutes to go out and look at the Moon. Another parent mentioned that, "Before we start the whole bedtime routine, we take all the children out with us to do the homework and look at the Moon. All of the children are interested in looking at the sky."

This activity allowed parents to share in the learning experience with their children. Many parents admitted not having studied the Moon when they were in school, or if they had, not re-

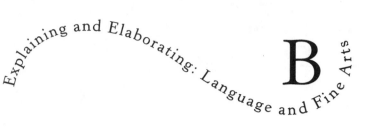
membering much about it. Other parents said it was a time for them to make their own observations about the changes in the sky and the Moon and to ponder them. A few parents made predictions with their child about what might be seen the next time.

More than half of my class is enrolled in a bilingual program that is part of the English for Speakers of Other Languages (ESOL) program in our school; many students wrote their moon journals in Spanish. Parents helped with spelling, and some wrote what their child dictated. Parents felt successful in helping their children in their native language whether it was English or Spanish, and children felt successful in observing the Moon.

Spanish-speaking students felt confident when sharing their journal with the class. The English speakers were also learning some Spanish; everyone knew *luna* meant moon and *noche* meant night. So when someone shared their picture and their entry, *anoche yo vi la Luna así* (last night I saw the Moon like this), many non-Spanish speakers understood part of the entry before they saw the picture. Sometimes a Spanish-speaking child would teach the class how to say what he or she wrote.

Literature Connections

After we began the moon journals, a number of students asked the school's media specialist about books on the Moon. As a class, we researched the Moon on the computer and compiled a list of books—fiction and nonfiction—in the library. We brought some of the books to the classroom for students to read in their free time.

Many of the books by Frank Asch became favorite fiction stories. Students even asked for these books to be read at the end of the day when we traditionally read stories together be-

Moon Books

Asch, F. 1993. *Moondance*. New York: Scholastic.

Branley, F. M. 1987. *The Moon Seems to Change*. New York: Crowell.

Brown, M. W. 1991. *Goodnight Moon*. New York: HarperCollins.

Davison, K. 1994. *Moon Magic: Stories from Asia*. Minneapolis, MN: Carolrhoda Books.

Fowler, S. G. 1994. *I'll See You When the Moon Is Full*. New York: Greenwillow Books.

Mizumura, K. 1977. *Flower, Moon, Snow: A Book of Haiku*. New York: Crowell.

Serwer-Berntein, B. 1970. *Let's Steal the Moon: Jewish Tales, Ancient and Recent*. Boston, MA: Little, Brown.

fore dismissal. The children brought books from home and from public libraries—they seemed very motivated and interested in reading about the Moon. It was exciting to use science to help teach reading!

Children were also adding moon-related words to their sight word vocabulary. Even children who struggled with reading had a variety of moon words they recognized and could read. *Moon, part, full, sky, phase, stars, dark, time,* and *sun* are just a few examples. Students used these words in their writing, and after using the words in their moon journal writing several times, they were soon spelling these words independently.

As the students arrived at the beginning of each day, I asked them to write in another daily journal. This was unrestricted writing—I provided no prompts, ideas, or directions for the writing and was happily surprised when several students wrote about the Moon.

One student wrote, "I went to outer space last night with my family. We landed on the Moon and we were looking around. Did you see us?" Another wrote, "I went to the Moon last night with Beetle Borg. We saw a big monster so we left." Not a bad integration of science, even though it is quite creative. The parents enjoyed reading some of these entries during parent-teacher conferences, and even became involved in informal conversations about the activity.

Insights into the Activity

This reflective researching has led me to several interesting insights. One of the most unexpected, but most exciting to me, was the level of family involvement. Parents felt comfortable helping their children with the moon journals, and children enjoyed observing nature with their parents. And by helping their child with homework, parents reinforced classroom instruction while modeling that they value education.

Families were able to share the school world through this activity—in an at-home setting, parent and child participated in "direct observations, activities that emphasize seeing the daily changes of the moon phases, including the angle in the sky, position in the sky, and the time of day or night" (Foster, 1996).

Did the children maximize their learning as a result of parental involvement? I cannot really answer the "maximize" part of that question, but I do feel that their learning was enhanced. I believe in a strong home/school connection, and this project seemed to result in a stronger connection for many of the parents.

When parents—and children—are given an opportunity to communicate in their own language, they feel valued and respected. And when parents feel valued and respected, they are more involved in their child's schooling.

I believe also that the participation level of parents who spoke Spanish was significant. My experience with Spanish-speaking parents has been that they want very much to be a part of their child's learning experience—especially through homework—but at times, language can make this difficult.

Much of the content is similar to what these parents encountered as children but is often presented in a different way. Even as an English-speaking parent, I have noticed many changes in teaching since I was a child. Looking at the Moon was a straightforward activity; Spanish-speaking parents were excited about helping their children write in Spanish because they want their children to become proficient in both languages.

This activity also shows how reading and writing can be taught through science. We read many books about the Moon during our daily reading/literacy activities. Reading time was exciting for many students because they wanted to read about the Moon.

For some students, writing in daily moon journals and sharing those entries was more motivating than reading. When the children who wrote about the Moon shared their journal entries with the class, they were always barraged with questions. "How did you get to the Moon? Did you build a spaceship? What did it look like on the Moon?" Many journal entries relate to "moon talk," as did some of our creative writing.

Moon Madness

When teachers encourage parental involvement, learning is a richer experience for students. The children came to school asking when sharing time would be, and sometimes brought their parents to school to participate. Moon madness had invaded the classroom. It seemed as if we didn't get through a single hour without mentioning the Moon. The art teacher noticed an abundance of moons in the art projects, and students asked the music teacher about moon songs.

"Moon and sun observations can encourage families to engage in a learning experience that can help develop habits of the mind that will serve the child throughout her or his life. And it can help establish strong links between adults, children, and education" (Brandou, 1997). With this much enthusiasm for learning about the Moon, what teacher or family can resist?

Deborah Roberts is a first-grade teacher at Oak View Elementary School in Silver Spring, MD.

Resources

American Association for the Advancement of Science. 1993. *Benchmarks for science literacy.* New York: Oxford University Press.

Bernhard, J., and Pacini, V. March 1998. *Latino parents' perspectives on the interactions between home and school in a Canadian setting.* Paper presented at the 19th Annual Ethnography in Education Research Forum, Philadelphia, PA.

Brandou, B. 1997. Backyard astronomy: Observing moon phases. *Science and Children, 43*(8), 18–21, 48.

Foster, G.W. 1996. Look to the moon: Students learn about the phases of the moon from an "Earth-centered" viewpoint. *Science and Children, 34*(3), 30–33.

Kasting, A. 1994. Respect, responsibility, and reciprocity—The 3 R's of parent involvement. *Childhood Education, 70*(3), 146–150.

National Research Council. 1996. *National Science Education Standards.* Washington, DC: National Academy Press.

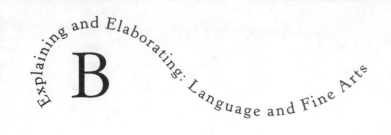

Analyzing Children's Science Journals

By Daniel P. Shepardson and Susan J. Britsch

The value of children's drawing and writing in science lies in its potential to assist children in making observations, remembering events, and communicating understandings. By creating their own journal pages, children are able to depict their ways of seeing and understanding the science phenomena, constructing or reconstructing the phenomena through their own lens of experience (Shepardson 1997). Elementary educators typically use children's journals in language arts activities (Tompkins and Hoskisson 1991), but children's journals can also be an important part of science learning. Children's science journals can serve the teacher as a guide to children's understandings (Elstgeest, Harlen, and Symington 1985) and as a diagnostic tool for informing practice. Students convey their science understandings through writing and drawing, so journals provide a window for viewing these understandings (Doris 1991).

For the past several years, the authors have been studying children's journals and what they can tell us about what children are learning. We also want to explore how journals can best be used in the elementary classroom. In February 1997, the *Science & Children* article "Children's Science Journals: Tools for Teaching, Learning, and Assessing" examined the ways in which children's science journals serve as a tool for teaching, learning, and assessing.

Here, we describe our experience using science journals with a group of nine first-grade students and seven second-grade students as part of a lesson exploring earth materials. We then discuss what can be inferred about some of the students' learning based on their journals' contents. This article focuses on one instructional sequence, but our work exploring the use of children's science journals spans all elementary grades and science topics and the points and issues described are applicable to other grades and topics.

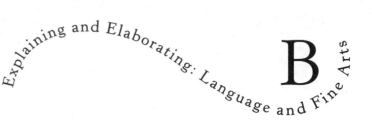
Overview

The lesson followed this sequence:

- On Day One, students explored the physical attributes and properties of five materials—clay, silt, sand, pebbles, and gravel. The children then described in their journals the properties and characteristics of the five materials they had observed.
- On Day Two, the children mixed pebbles and sand. Each child placed sand in a vial, added pebbles, and then shook the vial to mix the substances.
- On Day Three, the children used a sieve to separate the sand and pebbles.

In all three activities the children were encouraged to draw and/or write in their science journals, but were not given specific instructions about how or what to draw or write in their journals. Our purpose for not providing children with specific instructions was to observe how they would use their science journals without particular content or organizational requirements imposed by the researchers. We discuss the children's journal entries about these activities in terms of their implications to teaching, learning, and assessing.

Instructional Sequence Plays a Role

The order in which children received the materials influenced how they represented the materials on the journal page. When students received the gravel first and pebbles second, they apparently saw a contrast with the larger pieces of gravel. This observation was reflected in their journal entries. Some children used more specific labels for the pebbles, such as "little rocks" or "small rocks" (see Figure 1), while other students erased their labels, indicating that they had relabeled the gravel as "big rocks" or "gravel"

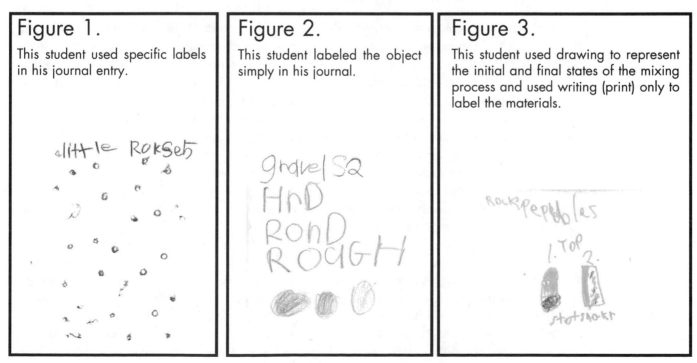

Figure 1.
This student used specific labels in his journal entry.

Figure 2.
This student labeled the object simply in his journal.

Figure 3.
This student used drawing to represent the initial and final states of the mixing process and used writing (print) only to label the materials.

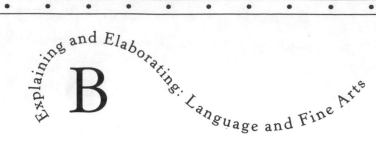
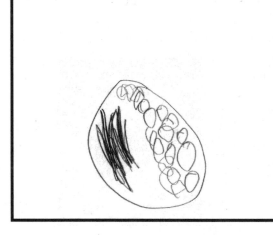

Figure 4.

This student used drawing only to represent the final state of separating the earth materials. Children predominantly represented the separation activity with one drawing, and as a single state.

Figure 5.

This student used "elaborate print" as an "analogy to characterize" the sand-pebble mixture.

to differentiate the pebbles from gravel. When children received the pebbles first, no contrast was noted in their labels (see Figure 2).

We also found that the children shifted from primarily labeling and describing (43 percent of the journal entries) the materials on Day One to representing the immediately observed science activity and simply labeling the materials in the mixing activity on Day Two (see Figure 3). On Day Three, the children predominantly depicted the immediately observed result of the separation activity (see Figure 4). In other words, the children's journal pages neither chronicled nor explained the mixing and separating processes, although the children may have chronicled their process while carrying out the science activity.

Graphic contexts describe the ways in which children use writing and drawing to represent their understandings on the journal page. The graphic contexts of children's journal pages from this activity are shown in Table 1. The nature of the instructional activity—exploring earth materials—invited children to use descriptive language and labeling to detail the attributes of the materials, whereas the mixing and separating activity emphasized processes. Thus, the science activity itself influenced the ways in which young children used their science journal to represent their understandings of the activity and the science.

Journals Don't Say It All

We also observed that the children's writing and drawing for the mixing and separating activity reflected the initial and/or final states of the mixing and separating processes, but did not depict the transformation of the materials. As shown in Figure 3, the child represented the initial state of the mixing activity, labeled "1," where the sand and pebbles were layered but then separated in the vial and represented the ending state of the mixing activity, labeled "2," where the sand and pebbles were commingled. Likewise, the child's journal page for the separating activity shown in Figure 4 represented only the final state of the separation activity—sand and pebbles drawn separated on the plate. Neither example illustrates the transition of the initial state to the final state. This finding is similar to Piaget and Inhelder's theory (1969) that young children's drawings tend to be static in nature and that it is not until around seven or eight years old that children's drawings begin to represent movement and transformations.

As the instructional sequence became more complex, the children's use of print declined. In the exploring earth materials activity, all children used a combination of print and drawing to represent their understandings. In the mixing activity 11 children (74 percent) used print, while in the separation activity only 5 children (23 percent) used print. Children overwhelmingly relied on drawing alone to represent the

---

Table 1. Graphic contexts describe the ways in which students use writing and drawing to represent their understandings.

Category	Description
Place-holding	The drawing or writing has value as a page-filler. Each page simply contains a marking. No concrete or imaginary referent or quality can be associated with the markings on the page.
Gestural activity	The graphic product has value as a motoric or physical activity that represents the quality of an object, event, or phenomenon. The context lies in the movement of the marker or pencil on that page.
Identifying or labeling	The child only labels or names the earth material or indicates what it is, implicitly distinguishing it from other substances by designating it as a separate referent.
Describing	The child elaborates one or more physical detail(s) about the earth material.
Characterizing use or manipulability	The child indicates a way(s) in which a human can use or handle the material; for example, a child may draw a person squeezing a ball of clay or building a castle of sand.
Indicating the immediately observed activity	The child uses drawing or writing to contextualize the earth material by surrounding it with people, materials, or processes drawn from the immediately observed classroom or from the science activity in which the child has engaged.
Specifying a natural environment	The child uses drawing or writing to contextualize the natural location of an earth substance; for example, the child may draw a field or show a layer of clay.
Creating an imaginary context	The child uses writing or drawing to contextualize the earth material by including it in an environment or scene not immediately observed by the child (e.g., the child has experimented with clay but draws cookies or a pizza).

separating activity. The increasing complexity of the mixing and separating activities did result in a more elaborate use (beyond single words) of print by those children who used print (See Table 2 for a list of the print categories or the grammatical structures we found in the children's journals). Children used more elaborate print to represent the mixing (20 percent) and separating (33 percent) activities compared to the exploring activity (0 percent).

For example, in the mixing activity, one second-grade student elaborated his labeling with an analogy to characterize the sand-pebble mixture (Figure 5). At the bottom of the page he used a metaphor that placed the final state of the substances in an imaginary context: "pebbles and sand, the rockes grave." Only one child used multiple sentences in combination with her drawings to characterize the separation activity. Her drawings depicted the pebbles trapped on the sieve and the sand on the plate. "They were separate," she wrote. "Some Gravels and Sand but the sand was on the plate. The pebbles were on the sieve."

Although the use of print was at its lowest on the day of the separation activity, it was then that we saw the highest use of descriptive phrases to characterize the separation process. As the science activity became more complex, the children struggled with using written language to represent their understandings. Many students

Table 2. Elaborated print categories describe the kinds of grammatical structures that students use in their journal entries.

Category	Description
Descriptive phrase	A phrase that tells what something is like, usually containing one or more adjectives followed by a noun.
Analogy	A simile or metaphor likening one thing to another.
Noun chaining	A series of nouns usually linked by a connective such as *and*.
Sentence chaining	A series of independent clauses linked by connectives such as *and* or *but*.

used drawing alone to represent their understanding on the journal page.

Analyzing the Journal's Content

Although all of the children used drawings to represent the materials on Day One, they used print primarily to either label or describe the substances in the activity. For example, the adjectives *little* and *hard* predominated; *little* was used in seven instances and *hard* was used nine times. To identify the materials, the children overwhelmingly used the term *rock(s)* to label both pebbles (60 percent of the time) and gravel (80 percent of the time). The word *rock* seemed to be applied generically to materials that were jagged (rough) and hard. Of the remaining materials, *sand* was used in 10 of 11 instances to represent sand. Seven children used the word *clay* to represent the clay, while four used "Playdoh." None of the children labeled silt as *silt*, although three used *dust*, five used *dirt*, one used *chalk*, one used *baking soda*, and one used *sand*. Thus, in order to identify an apparently unfamiliar earth material such as silt, these children used the names of more familiar sub-

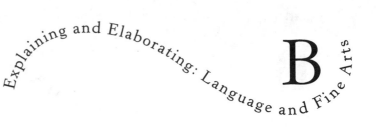
stances. Children used common everyday language to represent the earth materials, not understanding that the terms for earth materials, *gravel*, *pebbles*, *sand*, *silt*, and *clay* have specific scientific meaning related to size. This result is similar to Vygotsky's (1978) finding that young children name and designate more than represent the details or characteristics of phenomena.

In the mixing and separating activities the journals do not indicate that these children understood the science behind the mixing and separating process; that is, that the size of the earth materials allowed the pebbles and sand to be mixed and separated. The sand filled the space between the pebbles, and the sieve allowed the sand to pass through while trapping the pebbles. For example, one child's journal entry for the mixing activity represents only the initial state of the activity with the sand drawn at the bottom of the "stotshakr" (start shaker) and pebbles on top. The final state of the mixing activity is represented with the drawing labeled "2"—that depicts the sand and pebbles layered sideways in the vial.

The journal example for the separating activity represents only the final state of the activity: sand and pebbles drawn separate on the plate (see Figure 4).

In both examples children gave no indication on the journal page that they understood why sand and pebbles could be mixed and separated, perhaps showing that it happened but not why it happened. The children's journal pages for mixing and separating suggest that the children learned the science activity, but not that they learned the science. As teachers we must be careful to employ multiple modes of assessment in order not to confuse learning the activity with learning the science.

Strategies for Using Journals More Effectively

We need to understand that the ways in which we structure science activities will influence the ways children use their science journals to draw and write their understandings. This in turn influences the ways in which children come to understand the science activity and phenomenon. By analyzing students' journal pages, we can inform our teaching and assessment of students' observations. In this example we can focus children's observations of earth materials on the relationship between particle size and the mixing/separating processes. Because the journal entries reflected either a beginning or ending state in the mixing and separating activities, we could guide children's observations, drawing, and writing to focus on the initial, middle, and final states of the mixing and separating activities, recording these in their journals. This encourages children to chronicle a dynamic process versus a single state.

Using Journals to Assess Science Knowledge

From an assessment perspective, it is important to differentiate whether children are representing the science *activity* or the science *understanding* in their journals. For example, the journal entries for mixing and separating depicted only the states within the activity, not an understanding related to the size of the particles that make up the materials. Based on students' journal entries, we must be cautious about inferring that these children understand *why* mixing and separating occur. Generally, in assessing children's science journals we must:

- Carefully examine the drawings and writing to determine if students are representing the science activity or an understanding about a science process.

Table 3. Assessment logs like this one can be used to monitor children's progress in journal writing and drawing skills.

Science Activity: Mixing Earth Materials

Child's Name	Graphic Context	Process/Activity	Medium	Print Elaboration
Child 1 (Figure 2)	Labeling	Activity	Print	Adj. + Adj. + Noun
Child 2 (Figure 5)	Immediately observed	Activity	Drawing and print	Analogy

- Look at the language the children use and what it may tell about children's conceptual science understandings.
- Look for differences between content understanding and science processes.
- Note which medium the child primarily uses—drawing or print—in connection with each activity represented in the journal.
- Look for details that indicate the child's understandings about characteristics of objects or phenomena.
- Look at the words and language used to describe the objects or phenomena.
- Look at the ways in which the graphic context of the journal page indicates the ways in which children understand the science and provides insight into their developmental level.
- Look at the drawings for actions, movement, or transitions to gain insight into the developmental level of the child.
- Note the grammatical complexity of the print being used.

One way of documenting young children's journal writing and drawing—an assessment log—is illustrated in Table 3. The use of such assessment logs allows the teacher to profile each student's progress over several science activities throughout the school year and communicates to children that their journaling is an important and valued part of their science learning.

Closing Thoughts

The children in this classroom used their science journals to represent either the earth materials or the science activity itself. Alternatively, their understanding was characterized by a simple recording of what happened in the activity. Because these activities represented unfamiliar types of science experiences for these children, they need new ways of identifying what is important in a given science situation. The teacher's task is to provide children with opportunities to decide what is salient from the scientist's point of view. This means developing new ways of seeing, acting, and thinking about the science activity and the materials, and the representation of children's understanding on the journal page in new ways.

Daniel P. Shepardson is a professor of science education, and Susan J. Britsch is an associate professor of literacy and language education, both at the department of curriculum and instruction at Purdue University in West Lafayette, IN.

Resources

Dana, T. M., Lorsbach, A. W., Hook, K., and Briscoe, C. 1991. Students showing what they know: A look at alternative assessments. In G. Kulm and S. M. Malcom, Eds., *Science Assessment in the Service of Reform*. Washington, DC: Association for the Advancement of Science.

Doris, E. 1991. *Doing what scientists do: Children learn to investigate their world*. Portsmouth, NH: Heinemann.

Elstgeest, J., Harlen, W., and Symington, D. 1985. Children communicate. In W. Harlen Ed., *Primary science: Taking the plunge*. Portsmouth, NH: Heinemann.

Patton, M. Q. 1990. *Qualitative evaluation and research methods*. Newbury Park, CA: Sage Publications.

Piaget, J., and Inhelder, B. 1969. *The psychology of the child*. New York: Basic Books.

Shepardson, D. P. 1997. Of butterflies and beetles: First graders' ways of seeing and talking about insect life cycles. *Journal of Research in Science Teaching, 34*(9), 873–889.

Shepardson, D. P., and Britsch, S. J. 1997. Children's science journals: Tools for teaching, learning, and assessing. *Science and Children, 34*(5), 13–17, 46–47.

Tompkins, G. E., and Hoskisson, K. 1991. *Language arts: Content and teaching strategies*. New York: Macmillan.

Vygotsky, L. S. 1978. *Mind in society: The development of higher psychological processes*. Cambridge, MA: Harvard.

The Nature of Haiku

By Peter Rillero, JoAnn V. Cleland, and Karen A. Conzelman

Would you like your students to learn about nature and improve their observational abilities? Incorporating haiku into your curriculum can help meet these science goals and give children a positive writing experience as they learn about the world around them. We have helped fourth- and seventh-grade students understand nature through writing haiku.

Haiku is a succinct form of writing that originated in Japan in the seventeenth century. It focuses on nature and requires keen observation. Many U.S. elementary teachers know about haiku and may even have their students write haiku. In our opinion, however, many teachers have seized upon one feature of haiku—the 5-7-5-syllable pattern of the three lines—as the only significant characteristic. This singular focus may obscure the beauty and power of describing nature with an economy of words.

There are two reasons why the 5-7-5-syllable pattern should not be the emphasis in haiku writing. First, substance matters more than form. In haiku, the succinct description of nature is far more important than the number of syllables. Second, Japanese and English have different language structures. Use of the 5-7-5-syl-lable pattern in English produces wordy haiku that diminish the intensity effected through conciseness (Higginson 1985). For these reasons, 5-7-5 has ceased to be a fundamental criterion; haiku are best described as concisely written observations of nature.

Benefits of Haiku Writing

Haiku takes advantage of children's curiosity and interest in nature. The open-ended nature of haiku writing is motivational and student centered. Also, the simplicity of haiku allows children to have successful writing experiences.

At the same time, haiku writing advances many goals of elementary science education. Science and haiku both focus on the natural world, and looking more closely at nature helps students learn about nature. Their observations of nature may bring to mind previous learning, incite curiosity, encourage reading, or create interest in an upcoming lesson. Haiku is a vehicle for encouraging children to observe and reflect upon the natural world.

We believe observation is the most critical science process skill because other process skills are dependent on it. Haiku writing helps children develop this skill. Children learn to differentiate observation and inferences in some classrooms. With haiku, however, not only is there a

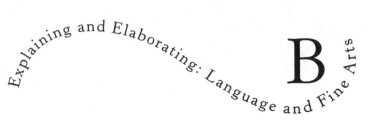
reason to learn the difference but also there is an immediate application that reinforces learning.

Other skills important in science and life are developed through haiku. Figure 1 on page 18 lists *National Science Education Standards* (NRC 1996) content standards that the haiku writing process meets. Students also learn concise writing, sequencing, and evaluation. In science publishing and haiku writing, communication with an economy of words is valued. To write effective haiku, children need to evaluate their observations, judge those that are most interesting, and sequence their observations in a logical order.

Children Writing Haiku

Children seem to have an easier time writing haiku than many adults. Curious about the world, most children are eager to observe nature closely and describe what they have observed. Simple haiku are the most powerful, and children are neither confused by nor afraid of this simplicity. Nevertheless, a methodical approach to teaching about haiku can facilitate haiku-writing experiences and develop keen observation skills. After reading haiku to children and helping them recognize the common features, we recommend the following seven-step approach to help children write haiku.

1. Stay with Observations. Three key things to remember in writing haiku are observation, observation, and observation. The power of haiku comes from careful observation and artful reporting of these observations in each line. The following tips may help children stay with their observations.

Children should differentiate observations and inferences. People gain information about an object, a scene, or an event through their senses. These are observations. Inferences are statements that seek to explain observations. A

Figure 1. Haiku writing and the *National Science Education Standards* (National Research Council, 1996).

Haiku assignments can advance the following *National Science Education Standards'* content standards. (Letters indicate content standards)

As a result of activities in grades K–4, all students should develop abilities

- necessary to do scientific inquiry (A)
- to distinguish between natural objects and objects made by humans (E)

As a result of activities in grades K–4, all students should develop an understanding of

- properties of objects and materials (B)
- position and motion of objects (B)
- characteristics of organisms (C)
- life cycles of organisms (C)
- organisms and environments (C)
- properties of Earth materials (D)
- objects in the sky (D)
- changes in Earth and sky (D)
- types of resources (F)
- changes in environments (F)

girl observes a deer running. She infers that the deer is afraid. Haiku stays with the observations.

In most forms of writing (including haiku), it is better to show rather than tell. Authors usually do not write, "it is a scary night"; instead, they describe aspects of the night—it is dark, the wind howls, a cat shrieks—so readers feel the frightening scene. A child may look at a flower and be tempted to write "it was beautiful" or "I feel wonderful." In haiku, however, he or she should describe the flower so readers can experience its beauty and their own sense of wonder.

Some types of writing value flowery metaphors such as "the path unfolded ahead like a garter snake moving through grass." Although this might help the reader visualize aspects of what the writer observes, it also puts a picture of a snake in the grass in the reader's mind. Haiku on the other hand describes a single scene in nature. Because metaphors transport readers to different scenes, they are a distraction to avoid.

Another lure when observing is the use of personification—giving human characteristics and feelings to nonhuman organisms or objects. The "sad, wilting plant" and "happy, singing birds" are examples of personification. The tendency to personify is powerful—children often overgeneralize their experiences of the world to other living things. Personification should and can be avoided by reminding students to stay with their observations.

2. Setting in Nature. Interesting haiku come from interesting observations. Taking children to places where they can make interesting observations improves haiku writing. These places can be on or off school grounds. Trips to exotic places, such as rain forests, are not necessary for children to discover fascinating intricacies of nature. The beauty of haiku writing lies in its helping children observe the ordinary and see extraordinary things.

As children are increasingly surrounded by the world of people, we believe it is important to move their observations to nature. Providing a few examples of the natural world along with things that don't belong to the natural world is a quick method of encouraging children to discover fascinating details in nature.

3. Observation Lists. In a natural setting, students can work in pairs and record observations. The observations should not be limited to vision—smells, sounds, and textures can produce

wonderful haiku. For safety reasons, the sense of taste should not be used.

When children write their observations, it is best to use present rather than past tense. For example, there is more immediacy to "the grasshopper jumps" than "the grasshopper jumped." The writer should also focus on one entity, which could be as narrow as a flower or as wide as a landscape.

Having students remain quiet prevents chatter from interfering with observing. In pairs, one partner can quietly point out things that he or she finds interesting. The first time children are taken to a place in nature, they may need other prompts to look purposefully—they may never have been asked to just take a close look. With multiple opportunities, however, they gradually feel comfortable observing intently and then the writing flows.

It is acceptable to have children write in sentence fragments. This helps them write observations faster, and these sentence fragments are easily incorporated into haiku. In as few as fifteen minutes, children can produce a good list of observations.

4. Interesting Observations. The process so far has been somewhat like brainstorming—getting as many ideas as possible, but at this point, the writers must select the most interesting observation from their lists. We find it helpful to ask each writer to get input from other children. The ultimate evaluation of interest, however, is up to the writer.

5. Three Lines. The third line of a haiku should contain the most interest; it should amaze, startle, or make the reader think—but it should be an observation. This helps ensure that the poem builds to a powerful, observation-based ending. Using a sheet of paper with three dark lines, children should

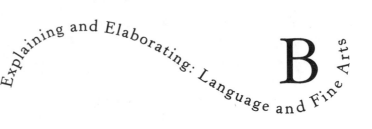

- Write their most interesting observation on the third line.
- Look at their observation lists and find two observations that build toward the third.
- Write these observations on the first and second lines.

6. Conciseness. The power of haiku flows from an economy of words. Unnecessary words, such as articles, can be deleted. Items unrelated to the central focus can be eliminated. Notice how three observations are stripped down in the following example.

~~The~~ Monarch butterfly
~~It~~ flutters to a soft stop ~~on a thin branch~~
~~It~~ closes its ~~orange and black~~ wings.

Some words are removed because they do not contribute. The writer feels that the most interesting observation is that the butterfly closes its wings when it rests. Observations that don't contribute to this are removed. The goal is to produce three short lines—the first with five syllables or fewer, the second with seven syllables or fewer, and the third with five syllables or fewer.

7. Rewrite. The final step is to rewrite the lines without the crossed-out words. Here, editing can take place. Because the third line is the most powerful, the reader pauses after the second line to set up the third line. Thus, punctuation is often included after the second line to indicate a pause.

Monarch butterfly
flutters to a soft stop;
and closes its wings.

Children's Haiku

The flavor of haiku from children is best revealed through these samples from fourth-grade students.

A small spider weaves
in and out he makes his web
it shines in the sun.

Curly seed pods grow.
They fall to the ground and wilt
and make room for more.

Spider looks at prey
a few seconds before death.
The spider ends life.

Roses are blooming.
The dew is starting to drip
as the sun rises.

Multiple flowers,
sway with gentle wind.
Violet hyacinth.

Birds high in the sky glide
down and have a good feast
on the mesquite pods.

It is up to the writer if the haiku will have a title. In most cases, haiku do not have titles. At this stage, teachers should acknowledge the accomplishment of writing haiku. Teachers praise the work of the writers, and the haiku can be shared with the class.

Haiku Assignments

After their first successful haiku experiences, children are ready for more. For example, an assignment to write five haiku in a two-week period can help them develop their observation and writing skills and learn more about the natural world. In any long-term assignment, it is generally a good idea for the teacher to check students' progress along the way. This helps children pace themselves and avoids a wait-to-the-end-rush-to-completion work habit. It also allows the teacher to make sure children are on the correct path. Thus, the teacher may decide to have children submit two haiku every few days.

It is hard to know when an exciting observation of nature will happen. Sudden thunder-

Explaining and Elaborating: Language and Fine Arts

storms, a mouse running into a hole, and a bird catching a worm are all interesting events. Haiku are usually most powerful when the observations are written immediately rather than from memories; thus in our haiku assignments, we require the observations to be current, not memories. We also encourage students to carry haiku notebooks with them so they can capture scenes in nature as they happen. Oftentimes, having the notebook is like having a camera; it helps writers observe nature in new ways.

Student Perspectives

Surveys and interviews revealed children's perspectives of haiku. On the written survey, the most common benefits volunteered were ones related to observing, understanding, and appreciating nature. One fourth-grade girl wrote, "Well, you get to look at nature in a different way. It is different than looking out your window. You look at it for a long time and you just get a picture in your head of . . . and it is so cool."

This benefit is revealed in the detail students report when asked for an interesting observation they made while writing haiku:

- "Well, I saw a little ant with fur on it. It had red fur on it. It was like somebody had stuck fur on it and dyed it red." (fourth-grade boy)
- "I looked at a seashell and it was pretty dull and then I found something about [it] and I wrote all about [it] and it turned out to be good. . . . The inside and the smoothness and the roughness on some parts." (fourth-grade girl)

These descriptions suggest that haiku helped children notice nature's exquisite details. Objects of nature that might have been stepped over or cast aside quickly became subjects of careful observation and recording in the context of composing haiku.

Extensions

A natural extension to this Japanese style of poetry is the incorporation of graphics. Children can enhance their work with black, brushstroke drawings created with paintbrushes or computer-drawing programs. These simple visual representations are a good match to poems that emphasize economy of words to convey highly focused ideas.

Frequently, children suggest writing their haiku in calligraphy or with a computer font that emulates calligraphy. Jotted notes can be transformed into pages children are eager to display. The natural result can be the creation of a class book. What pride children feel when sharing their collaborative project with family, peers, and the school library.

It's Only Natural

In the elementary years, first-hand experiences should incite children's curiosity and be a starting point for learning about nature. Haiku writing is an effective way to achieve these goals. In the haiku writing process, children observe, choose an object of interest, record, and observe more. They then reflect and write about nature. As you read their haiku, you will have the wonderful experience of seeing nature through the eyes of children.

Peter Rillero is an associate professor of science education and JoAnn V. Cleland is professor emeritus of language arts, both at Arizona State University West in Phoenix. Karen A. Conzelman is a professor of biology at Glendale (Arizona) Community College.

Resources

Print

Atwood, A. 1977. *Haiku-vision*. New York: Charles Scribner's Sons.

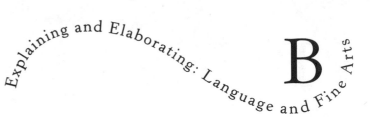
Atwood, A. 1973. *My own rhythm: An approach to haiku.* New York: Charles Scribner's Sons.

Behn, H. 1964. *Cricket songs.* New York: Harcourt, Brace, Jovanovich.

Gustafson, J. 1991. A poetry nature trail. *Nature study, 44*(4), 4–5.

Hamill, S. 1995. *The sound of water.* Boston: Shambhala.

Higginson, W. J. 1985. *Haiku handbook: How to write, share, and teach haiku.* New York: McGraw-Hill.

Huevel, C. 1974. *The haiku anthology.* Garden City, NY: Anchor Books.

National Research Council. 1996. *National Science Education Standards.* Washington, DC: National Academy Press.

Painter, A. 1988. *A coyote in the garden.* Lewiston, ID: Confluence Press.

Rillero, P. 1999. Haiku and science: Observing, reflecting, and writing about nature. *Journal of College Science Teaching, 27*(5), 345–347.

Rosenthal, V. 1987. Haiku: The process of creation. *Journal of Poetry Therapy, 1*(1), 31–37.

Ross, B. 1993. *Haiku moment: An anthology of contemporary North American haiku.* Boston: Charles E. Tuttle.

Shannon, G. 1996. *Spring: A haiku story.* New York: Greenwillow.

Strickland, D., and M. Strickland 1997. Language and literacy: The poetry connection. *Language Arts 74*(3), 201–205.

Internet

Adams, P. A haiku homepage. *http://home. clara.net/ pka/haiku/haiku.htm*

Warner, G. Haiku in the schools. *glwarner. narrowgate. net/haiku/8/viii.html*

Yotsuya, R. History of haiku. *www.big.or. jp/~loupe/ links/ehisto/ehisinx.shtml*

B

Drawing on Student Understanding

By Mary Stein, Shannan McNair, and Jan Butcher

Visitors are delighted and amazed when they come upon beautifully detailed drawings of a wide variety of insects in the halls of Upland Hills School. More intriguing is that these beautiful drawings were created by students ages 7 through 12. At the Lowry Center for Early Childhood Education, drawings of turtles with patterned shells adorn the kindergarten classroom walls. In the preschool classroom, drawings of ducks hatching from eggs are displayed along one wall and bees of various sizes line the hallway.

Drawing has always helped artists observe closely and reflect on their ideas, but using drawing as a tool to help students develop and document more complex understandings is not often a part of science instruction. Here we discuss reasons to use art as a tool for deepening scientific concept knowledge and some essential components for creating a successful learning experience.

The Art and Science Connection

Art and science have often been viewed as very different—even opposing—disciplines, art as creative expression and science as a fact-based discipline with a lockstep approach to solving problems. This view of science does not portray accurately the creativity inherent in science, nor does it help students think about science as a human endeavor (Stein and Power 1996).

The *National Science Education Standards* (NRC 1996) emphasize science as inquiry. The Standards also highlight science as a human endeavor and suggest ways that emphases in science teaching change as the Standards are implemented. Using artistic expression as a tool for learning supports the Standards by enhancing students' abilities to communicate their ideas to the public and to their classmates.

Integrating Drawing with Learning About Animals

As part of a semester-long science class, coauthor Jan Butcher's students were engaged in an indepth study of animals. The students ranged in age from 7 through 12 years, so she was careful to create learning experiences in which students had opportunities to further their understandings independent of developmental levels. One component of the class included the study of in-

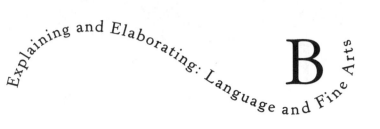
sects. Students found insects in their natural habitats, studied insects from an assortment of books and field guides, observed live catches (which were later returned to their environments) in glass jars, and examined parts of insects with magnifying lenses and microscopes. The instructional activities also included readings and discussions about insect classification, life cycles, and identification.

As one part of the study, students chose an insect about which they wanted to learn. They used resources, such as books (see Student Resources at the end of this article), living insects that had been collected, specimens from a mounted insect collection, and posters and photographs to create detailed drawings of the insects. The students became completely engaged in the assignment, and the detail and quality of their drawings were astounding. When questioned about the process, one student's comments provided insight into how drawing can help deepen understanding: "It is like when you draw it, it becomes your own. You pay attention and draw the things you are interested in."

At the Lowry Center, preschool and kindergarten children pursue project work to learn about animals. Through a variety of experiences, they gain a greater awareness of animal names, appearances, movements, sounds, and diet. The children's drawings are different, because they are representations of their individual experiences and understandings of the animals. As they learn more about animals, students reflect their increased knowledge and interest in particular animals in their drawing. The following suggestions help to successfully integrate drawing with science learning:
- promoting student ownership
- connecting drawings to specific science learning experiences

- providing resources
- providing teacher modeling.

Student Ownership

Individual students have special interests and are more likely to be engaged when they make choices to direct the learning activity. The Upland Hills students were given the opportunity to learn about and observe various insects through experiences such as field observations and exposure to literature and media before they selected which insect they would like to draw in detail.

Unlike some classroom activities in which students are all creating the same artifact, this activity was based on student interest, and the drawings and the ways students chose to represent their insects varied. Therefore, competition among students was reduced because they were all creating a unique drawing—students were not worried that a fellow student could draw a particular insect better than they could. With this variety, characteristics could be compared and contrasted.

Another component of student ownership involved students' natural interest in drawing as a means to communicate—most students love to draw. When the students were told that their drawings would be displayed in the hall outside the classroom, their enthusiasm was clear. They worked hard, paid attention to detail, and had fun in the process.

Children at the Lowry Center are encouraged to draw many things throughout the day, and a variety of materials —markers, colored pencils, paints, and crayons, and an assortment of paper—is always available for them to use. For example, they might be asked to draw their plan for the day, what they observed on a walk, an illustration of a mathematics solution, or a pictorial version of a recipe or rules to a game.

When children become excited about something they are exploring, they have a natural desire to represent that experience. For example, when a teacher brought baby ducklings into the kindergarten classroom, one boy immediately got a piece of paper and pencil and began drawing the ducklings. Students also use journals to record these experiences. Their drawings are an important part of class-created newsletters that give parents information about the children's experiences during the week. Children recall what they learned and what they liked and then illustrate this within the newsletter.

Connecting Drawing to Science

These students had spent a significant amount of time learning about insects through teacher-guided experiences. They found various insects in their natural habitats, recorded their observations in the field, and then shared their findings with other students in class discussions.

Through reading, observation, and class discussion, students learned about insect types and characteristics, habitats, and interesting facts. They also learned about the important role insects play in our world. When students were asked to select an insect to draw, their learning experiences had not only prepared them for the activity, but had also made them eager to begin. Drawing an insect was a creative way in which students could communicate their detailed understandings. Before beginning to draw, students were asked to identify the body parts they learned about. They were also asked to think about their drawings as a way to show all the details modeled by Nancy Winslow Parker and Joan Richards Wright in the book *Bugs* (1987).

The objective of the activity was to reinforce students' learning and aid younger students who knew the body parts, but could not name them: head, thorax, abdomen, six legs. The experience also provided a direct learning experience: Stu-

Safety with Insects and Animals

When handling insects and animals it is very important that the teacher use safe, humane procedures. This usually requires that the teacher have access to specific information about the animals or insects that the children will be observing. The teacher should include rules and procedures for students to follow when studying animals. For example, students should wear gloves when handling specimens and should be careful not to harm the insect or animal. Specific information about the use and care of animals in the classroom can be found at the NSTA websites: *199.0.3.5/handbook/animals.asp* and *199.0.3.5/handbook/organisms.asp*.

Children learn to look for insects outdoors during the cool mornings, when the cold-blooded creatures are moving more slowly. Stinging insects are either observed from some distance, or dead specimens are gathered and placed in magnifying boxes for closer examination. Children are told not to handle spiders until an adult has identified them as harmless. Gathering insects is done with a plastic cup and a large index card—the children scoop up the insect carefully with a cup and slide the index card underneath. Insects are observed for the day and then released outdoors.

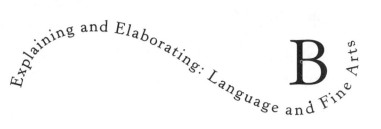
dents used their fingers, hands, and eyes to link their reading and listen to their own observations. For example, often a student had ideas about how to draw a particular insect based on field observations, but then had a desire to use additional references to check the details of their ideas.

Following special classroom presentations that exposed students to something new, children at the Lowry Center often used drawing to capture those experiences. After zoological professionals brought rain forest animals—macaw, clouded leopard, boa constrictor, gecko, frogs, and a sloth—into the classroom, allowing the children a close look at some of the animals, the children drew detailed pictures of sloths. The amount of interest in sloths was probably because they look very different from more familiar animals and because none of the children had ever seen a sloth.

Following a special presentation by an entomologist, a student drew a praying mantis. Other children drew shiny beetles with impressive pincers, while some drew dragonflies and butterflies with colorful wings. Similarly, after outdoor hikes, children used drawing to represent and revisit their experiences. After a hike to a pond, one student drew the goose she had seen. Other children drew minnows and water spiders, representing what they could see around and on the surface of the water. They drew what is underneath the surface after they looked at an aquarium filled with water and life from a pond. A piece of butcher paper taped to the table holding the aquarium made a nice "tablet" for ongoing drawings of the children's observations.

Young children can often express their understanding and concept development more effectively through drawings than verbally or in written assignments. They are often more engaged in details of their understanding when they draw. As they examine drawings, their emerging understandings become evident. For example, many young children will place a humanlike face on their animals that they eventually replace with a more accurate representation. When students draw both before and after an experience, the drawings can serve as an assessment tool for the teacher. For example, in a second drawing of the same insect, one student adds more detail, along with the features of wings, head, and antennae. He also shows much greater detail of the bee's stinger after he has learned about bees in the class. Children reflect other characteristics, such as the relative length of frog and turtle legs and the details of caterpillar legs, in representations of their animals.

Providing Resources

It is one thing to make close observations in the field and something quite different to record your observations on paper. The drawing and writing process itself encourages students to think more deeply about what they believe. It can be a way for them to continue to explore an idea or concept. Many questions begin to emerge: How many legs did an insect have? How many body sections? Were the legs hairy? Did it have antennae? What did its eyes look like?

Students need various resources to help them answer the questions that emerge. In addition to live animals and insects, students had other resources that helped them find their own answers to their inquiries. Representing something that has been observed involves recalling significant details, thinking about the relative size of body parts and background in the picture, and choosing colors or making patterns that match the model. They also used scientific tools such as hand lenses and books with photographs to help them with their work (see Resources).

Teacher Modeling

At the Lowry Center teachers modeled careful observation of detail when hiking or conducting classroom exploration. They also modeled sketching things they wanted to remember, such as a nature log recorded on hikes or a child's block construction to share with a parent.

When students were drawing their insects in the classroom, the teacher also modeled the process. She was as busy as the students in learning about her insect of choice, drawing her insect using the same information, processes, and resources that students used. The teacher's role became one of modeling through example. When students observe their teacher engaged in the same activity that they are doing, it assures them the activity is important and worthwhile. At the same time, it is a learning experience for the teacher.

Deeper Learning

These experiences show how art and drawing can be used as a tool to deepen student understanding. Just as "writing to learn" has emerged as a means to deepen understanding, drawing is another tool through which students can be encouraged to think deeply about what they know and have observed. Students' questions during this process also suggest that drawing can be used to encourage inquiry. It is important to view the drawing activity as a student-centered inquiry through which students can express their creativity and find answers to their own questions. Otherwise, integrating drawing may be no more useful than having students copy sentences out of a book.

People often compartmentalize their knowledge and strengths by saying things like "I'm a math and science person" or "My strength is in language and the arts." As educators we recognize these labels and narrow definitions can limit what our students believe they are good at and eventually what they will choose to do. Broadening students' perspectives by integrating art as a tool for scientific inquiry enables students to become more reflective and aware of their understanding.

As questions emerge, students learn how to find answers to these questions and how their artistic creations can be used to communicate what they have learned. Through artistic experiences, students experience science as a human endeavor that uses the full range of human creativity and does not promote science and art as opposite ends of a continuum. As students begin to view themselves as artists, scientists, and humans unhampered by labels, all of society will reap the benefits of artistic expression.

Mary Stein is an associate professor in the Department of Teacher Development and Educational Studies at Oakland University in Rochester, MI, and a former president of the Council for Elementary Science International (CESI). Shannan McNair is an associate professor in the Department of Human Development and Child Studies at Oakland University in Rochester, MI. Jan Butcher is an elementary teacher with a special interest in science at Upland Hills School in Oxford, MI.

Resources

Doris, E. 1991. *Doing what scientists do: Children learn to investigate their world.* Portsmouth, NH: Heinemann.

Hein, G., and Price, S. 1994. *Active assessment for active science: A guide for elementary school teachers.* Portsmouth, NH: Heinemann.

Humphryes, J. 2000. Exploring nature with children. *Young Children, 55*(2), 16–20.

National Research Council. 1996. *National Science Education Standards.* Washington DC: National Academy Press.

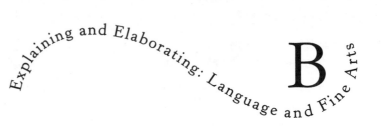

Ross, M. E. 2000. Science their way. *Young Children,*
55(2), 6–13.

Stein, M. T., and Power, B. A. 1996. Putting art on
the scientist's palette. In R. S. Hubbard and K.
Ernst, Eds. *New Entries: Learning by Writing and*
Drawing. Portsmouth, NH: Heinemann.

Student Resources

Lavies, B. 1990. *Backyard hunter: The praying mantis.*
New York: Dutton.

Mound, L. 1993. *Eyewitness junior amazing insects.*
New York: Knopf.

Parker, N. W., and Wright, J. R. 1987. *Bugs.* New
York: Greenwillow.

Ryder, J. 1989. *Where butterflies grow.* New York:
Lodestar.

Still, J. 1991. *Amazing beetles: Eyewitness juniors no. 14.*
New York: Knopf.

Suzuki, D., and Hehner, B. 1991. *Looking at insects.*
New York: John Wiley.

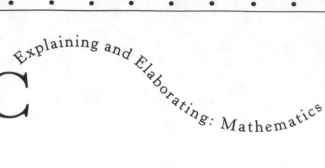
Out of Sight: Investigating Unseen Objects

By Jennifer Hoffman

Unseen objects—whether they be wrapped as birthday gifts, hidden in the dark night sky, or buried beneath the sea—intrigue learners at all grade levels. By presenting students with mysteries and encouraging them to develop their own methods and procedures for investigation, science teachers can build a learning community of enthusiastic, motivated problem solvers and critical thinkers.

In the following module, fourth-grade students measured and mapped unseen objects hidden within boxes representing the ocean floor. These instructional activities use the element of mystery to motivate student inquiry in an interdisciplinary, collaborative setting.

When participating in these investigations and activities, fourth-grade students were encouraged to ask questions about objects, organisms, and phenomena in the environment. They planned and conducted simple investigations, used equipment and tools to collect data and ex-tend the senses, used data to construct an explanation, and discussed investigations and conclusions.

These goals relate to Content Standard A of the *National Science Education Standards* (NRC 1996). Content Standard A asserts that, as a result of activities in grades K–4, all students should develop abilities necessary to do scientific inquiry and gain an understanding about scientific inquiry. By giving learners the opportunity to engage in these inquiries, teachers can also meet the requirements of Teaching Standard B, which describes how teachers of science will be able to guide and facilitate learning.

About the Module

For this module, I prepared the following materials for each group of three to four students:

- role cards for the members of each group to use on a rotating basis: leader, recorder, observer, presenter, manager (for four students, use the leader, recorder, observer, and presenter cards; for three students, use the leader, recorder, and observer/presenter cards)

- a wrapped box holding durable objects such as paper clips, metal fasteners, sealed plastic bottles filled with water, wood blocks, or any other objects that can be dropped or shaken and make a sound when handled without threatening the safety of the participants
- two metric rulers
- one platform scale and one balance scale
- a sealed empty cereal box with a grid of holes punched and numbered on top (see Figure 1). Fill each box with objects such as wood, clay, gravel, or foam; secure each object with tape or glue within the sealed box.
- a slender, smooth wooden dowel marked for each centimeter up to 13 cm, or 5 cm above the height of the tallest box. Dowels can be found at a craft store or hardware store. Reserve extra marked-up dowels in case of breakage or misplacement.

The Birthday Gift

In the first activity of this module, "The Birthday Gift," I displayed a wrapped gift box to the class. Students worked with members of their group to generate a list of ways they could discover the contents of this gift box without opening it or changing its shape. The students brainstormed various ideas for investigating the box that would rely on all of their senses. They also suggested measuring the box for its height, width, and mass.

I gave each group one wrapped box and encouraged students to conduct their own tests to discover the contents of the box and make inferences based on their trials. One student inferred there were three pencils inside one of the boxes. Another asserted there were tacks in a box that actually contained metal fasteners.

The students attempted several tests to discover the contents of the wrapped boxes. They held the boxes up to their ears and shook them to hear what kind of sound they made. They threw the boxes up in the air and caught them. They smelled the boxes and weighed the boxes. They used the balances to compare the mass of the boxes to objects they found in the science lab, such as books, beakers, magnifying glasses, chalk, and my desk supplies—paper clips, pencils, masking tape, and staplers. Students also dropped the boxes from varying heights.

As I visited each group, I asked each individual what he or she hypothesized to be hidden in the boxes. After a student told me his or her hypothesis, I would pose the following questions, "What test or tests led you to form that hypothesis? What other studies would you like to conduct so that you might test your hypothesis? What additional materials would you need?" I would also encourage the members of a group to ponder and question each other's hypotheses and ideas.

One student, reflecting upon how she had used a balance and gram masses to measure the gradual dehydration of apples during a previous investigation, requested a balance when discussing her hypothesis. Students were also asked to consider which test supplied them with the most information. They unanimously chose the "shaking and listening" test.

After this introductory lesson, I asked the students how this experiment related to ocean studies. To answer this, they investigated the science laboratory and observed the shells, ocean posters, games, preserved blowfish, and aquariums arranged at the "Things to See at the Sea" interactive center. After much discussion, they concluded that the wrapped box was like the entire ocean because its shape can't be changed and the middle and bottom aren't visible.

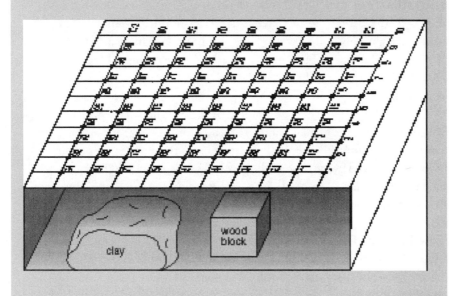

Figure 1. Cereal Box with Items Placed Throughout.

Mapping the Unknown

For the second activity, I gave students a sealed cereal box with a grid of numbered holes on top (see Figure 1). The cereal box contained objects such as wood, clay, gravel, or foam. I distributed wooden dowels that were marked at each centimeter. I asked the students to gently examine both objects and determine how they could use the dowel to discover what was inside the box without altering its shape.

When I asked the students to list ways to map the contents of the box, they were brimming with suggestions. Their ideas included poking holes, measuring height, as well as listening and feeling while probing. I explained that they would have the opportunity to carry out their procedures during the next laboratory session.

When the class arrived for their next session, they were filled with enthusiasm and curiosity. As they entered the laboratory, they began asking questions such as, "Will we get the same boxes as last time?" "Do we get to use the centimeter sticks again?" and "Can I tell you what I think is inside the box?" Curiosity played an important role in this module for maintaining motivation, enthusiasm, and continuity.

During my anticipatory set, I asked students to employ the procedures they had developed to map the unseen objects in the box (Hunter 1982). The only guideline was to use the grids in the laboratory booklets (Figure 2) to create a map and key of the floor of the box. Managers from each group eagerly searched for the boxes they previously investigated with their groups. When they returned to their stations with their materials, learners immediately began plotting and planning techniques to investigate the contents of their designated box.

Students brainstormed ways they could record each trial they conducted using the dowel as a probe. One trial involved placing the dowel into a numbered hole in the box until the probe could go no farther. Students were encouraged to examine the grid of holes numbered from 1 to 100 on the box and the two-dimensional grid of points found in their laboratory booklets. I asked students to discuss symbols they might use on the grid to show where objects were located in the box as well as where objects were not found.

I visited each group and listened to their discussions, offering guidance when necessary. I asked individuals what symbols they had decided to use and why. Some students placed an "X" through each numbered point on the grid when their probe hit the floor of the box. Other students circled each numbered point where their probe touched an object in the box. A few individuals shaded in pencil or used specific marker colors to mark where objects were or were not found in their boxes. Students made keys illustrating the symbols, patterns, or colors they used in their maps.

It was gratifying to see every student actively engaged in this activity. They first discussed how to probe and graph the unseen objects. Their experiences with group work helped them listen, express their thoughts, and plan their inquiry in an organized, supportive fashion with little outside intervention. All groups shared certain similarities in the way they carried out their investigations. Everyone decided to use the wooden centimeter dowel as a probe as well as a tool to measure the height of the box and its contents.

The students were encouraged to take risks by exploring a variety of strategies. They were given the freedom to be creative and unique in their thinking in an environment where many approaches and techniques could be employed while using scientific methodology.

Each group differed in the way its members implemented the plans they arranged. Two groups probed and graphed the numbered holes in the box in order from 1 to 100. Another group probed and graphed section by section. A fourth group immediately began probing and graphing where the object was located.

Regardless of method and individual ability, all students were able to describe the height and length of the objects they mapped. By consult-

Figure 2. Laboratory Booklet Guidelines.

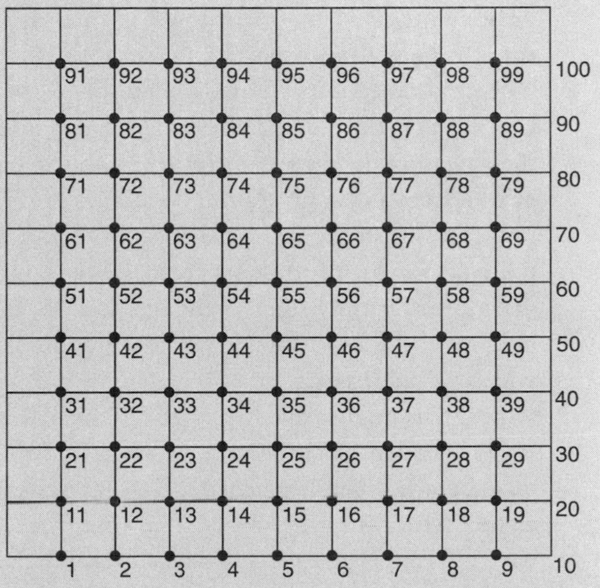

Use the above grid to map where objects are located in the box.

1. Explain why you chose this method of mapping.
2. Where were the highest objects located in the box?
3. Take some time to ponder your research and data. Form a hypothesis regarding the contents of the box. What do you hypothesize to exist on the "ocean floor" that you mapped?
4. How did you use your senses to form your hypothesis?
5. If a ship were to travel through the seas above the "ocean floor" that you mapped, what advice or directions would you give to keep the ship out of harm's way?
6. What other kind of graph or map would you create to represent the unseen objects in the box?

ing their maps, students might hypothesize that a block of wood is located in points 1, 2, 11, 12, 21, 22, 31, 32, 41, and 42.

Students could use their dowel to first measure the height of the box by measuring a point where no object was found—where the dowel could touch the floor of the box. They could then measure the distance between the top of the box and the point where the dowel hit an object. If this distance was 2 cm and the height of the box was 6 cm, students could subtract the distance from the height of the box to find the height of the unknown object at this point, which would be 4 cm.

Students might have hypothesized the object was a wooden block because of the sound the dowel made when it touched the object as well as the hardness of the object. They might also have inferred it was a wooden block because the height remained constant at 4 cm. Students were able to describe the length of the objects by combining the height measurements with the data gathered on their grid maps. Students independently formulated their conclusions. They confidently showed where they hypothesized rocks, foam, clay, and other objects to be situated. Students beamed with confidence and pride as they were praised for their research and conclusions.

Comparison with Real-Life Mapping

During the next session, students compared the depth-sounding technique used by oceanographers to the methods they employed to map the floors of their boxes. I asked the class how they could use their technique to map the actual floor of an ocean. Students quickly realized a dowel would be impractical for measuring something as deep as the ocean.

I then discussed with them how oceanographers use sound waves instead of dowels to mea-

sure the depth of an ocean floor. I asked the class to complete a chart comparing and contrasting the depth-sounding technique used by oceanographers to the methods they used to map the floors of their boxes. A sound wave was compared to a dowel, the ocean was compared to the cereal box. Students also studied maps of ocean floors on the Earth.

Other ideas were presented on the CD-ROMs *The World Book Multimedia Encyclopedia* (Gordon 1996) and *The New Grolier Multimedia Encyclopedia* (Schenck 1993). Students used various selections to learn about the tools oceanographers use to explore the sea, such as research ships that employ depth-sounding techniques, floating devices, submersibles, satellites, computers, and other technical tools.

When students were told they could open the boxes, they did so with the care and delicacy of surgeons. Jubilantly, they revealed the hidden "treasures" and compared the actual objects to the students' data and assertions. When asked to place the contents back inside the boxes, students did so with the utmost care. Their "finds" had become quite valuable to them.

The Blind Men and the Elephant

Students analyzed the skills involved in their group work while reading and discussing *The Blind Men and the Elephant* (Backstein 1992). This story tells the tale of six blind men who lived together near the palace of a rajah in India. The men had never encountered elephants before. One day, one of the blind men encouraged the others to walk with him to the palace of the rajah. An elephant happened to be standing nearby. The men each touched a different part of the elephant with their hands. One man described the elephant as being like a snake after touching the elephant's trunk. After touching its leg, a second man described the elephant as being like a tree, and so on. The blind men discussed their observations and inferences. Their discussion escalated into a heated argument, with each man trying to persuade the others that his hypothesis is the only correct one. Their arguing awakened the rajah. After listening to their discussion, the rajah explained to the men that an elephant is a large animal and that they had each touched only one part of the elephant. He encouraged them to put all the parts they had explored together to discover what an elephant is truly like.

After reading *The Blind Men and the Elephant,* students compared their research and behavior to that of the blind men (Figure 3). The children felt that their investigation was reminiscent of the men's research of the elephant because, initially, they had each taken turns probing different sections of their designated box. They believed their behavior differed from that of the men in several ways and offered advice to the men so the men could better communicate with one another and discover more things together in the future. Based on their experiences, they made a list of suggestions to help the blind men work together to best describe an elephant's appearance. Students suggested being better listeners, understanding there is not always one right answer, realizing there are often many ways to look at a problem or question, and making a list of questions regarding what can be learned about the elephant.

Student Inventions

As a culminating activity, students designed inventions for mapping the ocean floor. I asked them to think about the many techniques scientists use to investigate unseen objects hidden beneath the sea. I then asked, "What invention

Figure 3. The Science-Literature Connection.

Read the story The Blind Men and the Elephant. *After you have had time to read and reflect upon the questions below, discuss the questions with the members of your group.*

1. Why did the six blind men each share a different description of what an elephant looks like?

2. Think about the role you played in your cooperative group during the depth-sounding activity. How were you like one of the blind men in the story?

3. What advice would you give to the six blind men so that they could better describe an elephant?

would you create to map an ocean landscape?"

I encouraged them to be creative and use their imaginations. Each student had the opportunity to visit my interactive invention center that is filled with the interior devices found in music boxes, telephones, modems, batteries, and various other inventions.

One student's invention, the "Robotect Fish and Camera" first required the construction of a mechanical fish. This fish has a camera built into its fins and a tail that can videotape the ocean floor as well as deep-sea animal and plant life. Another design, the battery-operated "Insta-Mapper," is an underwater, computerized camera with a zoom lens able to take pictures of faraway objects and landscapes quickly, reminiscent of an instant camera. After the camera takes a photograph, the computer creates a map of the object or landform. The Insta-Mapper is able to tell, in a timely fashion, if there are lost ships, icebergs, or landforms hidden beneath a particular region of the ocean.

Assessment

Assessment was divided into three categories. In the first, learners were assessed according to their ability to solve problems and think critically. In the second, assessment was based on measuring and employing scientific methodology. In the third, the students had to demonstrate their creativity, inventiveness, and ability to compare and contrast. Each category sought to fairly evaluate the individual student-scientist according to his or her unique learning style.

Assessment was actually a shared endeavor. I asked students to assess their own work using a rubric. Students were asked to self-evaluate their participation in this investigation by asking themselves questions such as "Did I think of questions that helped me learn about oceanography and ways to explore unseen objects?" "Did I feel comfortable forming hypotheses during this investigation?" "Was I able to investigate the box and use tools to map the contents in the sealed cereal box?" and "Did I learn any new skills that might help me in future investigations and other disciplines?"

I also used a rubric to assess students in the following categories: problem-solving skills, use of scientific methodology, comparing and contrasting skills, and creativity. I observed and interviewed students throughout the investigation. I reviewed their laboratory booklets, which contained questions, hypotheses, observations, data, feelings, impressions, explanations, conclusions, and illustrations. I also asked students to assess my performance during this investigation.

Mystery Solved

After having participated in this teaching module—which can also be adapted to investigate unseen objects in environments other than the ocean floor—students had grown in many ways. They had a renewed appreciation for the numerous connections between mathematics, science, and literature. The children were more comfortable using scientific methodology. They felt more comfortable taking risks and forming their own hypotheses.

I gave students the encouragement to be creative and imaginative in their work while developing the skills and abilities necessary for scientific inquiry discussed in the *National Science Education Standards*. Students recognized that each person has his or her own talents and strengths. Most of all, they learned that everyone can discover, solve mysteries, and achieve in science.

Jennifer Hoffman is an elementary math and science teacher at the Gifted Child Society in Glen Rock, NJ.

Resources

Backstein, K. 1992. *The blind men and the elephant*. New York: Scholastic.

Cusick, P. 1993. *Science matters: Habitats, oceanography, planets, and technology/grade six*. Middletown, CT: Weekly Reader.

Hunter, M. 1982. *Mastery teaching*. Thousand Oaks, CA: Corwin Press.

National Research Council. 1996. *National Science Education Standards*. Washington, DC: National Academy Press.

Software

Gordon, A. L. 1996. *The World Book multimedia encyclopedia*. Chicago, IL: World Book.

Schenck, H. 1993. *The new Grolier multimedia encyclopedia*. Danbury, CT: Grolier.

Crash into Meteorite Learning

By David A. Wiley and Christine Anne Royce

"An asteroid the size of Texas is hurtling toward Earth!" Blockbuster films like *Armageddon* and *Deep Impact* have focused on catastrophic meteor impacts and captured public imagination. Why not capitalize on the excitement and investigate meteor impacts with your students? The following describes an exciting theme-based study that explores science concepts related to impacts from meteorites and integrates mathematics, language arts, and social studies. This study is adaptable for most age levels, but this article addresses students in grades three to six.

Investigating Impact Craters

After discussing the films or using available videotapes and/or the Internet, students can conduct an activity to create their own craters and examine the various structures that form upon impact. To begin, discuss students' ideas about meteor impacts and craters. Most students know what a crater is and are familiar with a variety of features on both the Earth and lunar surfaces, including mountains and valleys. But surface features also include a variety of *impact craters*.

These roughly circular features are formed when asteroids or meteoroids smash into the surface of the Earth or moon, becoming *bolides*. The explosion of material outward from the point of impact produces *ejecta*, or a blanket of rock material surrounding the impact site.

Discuss that impact craters can also have features—there are craters with and without *rays* (bright streaks that extend from the crater for a great distance), crater chains, and even craters with mountains in the center of them. Although impact craters are most obvious on the lunar surface, they also exist on Earth. Scientists believe that meteors struck Earth during and shortly after its formation. Results of these meteor impacts include the Barringer Crater, located near Flagstaff, Arizona, and a crater located in Deep Bay, Canada. The Barringer Crater spans a diameter of more than 1.2 km, is more than 150 m deep, and is believed to have formed between 20,000 and 50,000 years ago.

Conducting the Activity

Once the introductory discussion is complete, divide students into groups of three to begin the investigation. To build the crater models, each group will need

- a box top, such as that from a case of photocopy paper, filled with flour 5 cm deep (to represent the lunar surface)
- a sprinkling of colored sand or dry coffee grounds sufficient to coat the flour and provide a contrasting color (to help students see the changes that occur on the lunar surface when the marble strikes)
- a shooter marble and a golf ball (to represent the bolides)
- a wooden coffee stirrer
- a 1 m x 1 m drop cloth, such as a large plastic garbage bag that has been cut open
- a ballpoint pen
- a meter stick or ruler
- a balance

First, have students clear a one-square-meter workspace on the floor and prepare the lunar surface in the box top by filling it with flour about 5 cm deep. Each group should spread a drop cloth on the ground and place the box in the center of the workspace. Have one student smooth the surface using a ruler and another student carefully sprinkle the flour with colored sand or dry coffee grounds, making sure not to mix the two layers.

Working with group members, one student measures 30 cm above the surface with a meter stick, a second student drops the marble from that height to model the impact crater, and the third student measures the depth and diameter of the crater and the length of any rays that form. To measure the crater's depth, students stand a coffee stirrer on the low point of the crater and mark with a pen the top of the crater rim on the stirrer. They then measure the marked area on the stirrer. When all the measurements are complete, students record the information on the data sheet (see Figure 1).

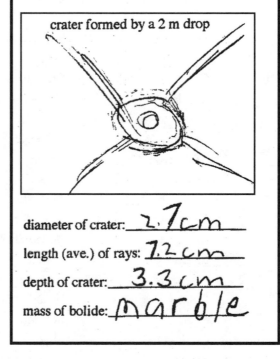

Figure 1. A student's sample data sheet.

crater formed by a 2 m drop

diameter of crater: 2.7 cm

length (ave.) of rays: 7.2 cm

depth of crater: 3.3 cm

mass of bolide: marble

Now move a chair next to each group's testing surface and have them conduct the experiment again, dropping marbles (bolides) from heights of 60 cm, 90 cm, and 2 m. Be sure to tell students to drop each marble in a different section of the box top so that the craters will not overlap. Rotate roles among the group so that each student has at least one chance to measure the drop height, drop the marble, and measure the crater. When all of the trials are complete, have the group determine the mass of the marble on a balance and record it on the data sheet.

Next, have each group conduct the activity with a golf ball, dropping it from a height of 90 cm. Record the data from this new crater on the data sheet as well.

Table 1. Some impact craters found on Earth.

Name of Crater	Country	Latitude degrees	Longitude degrees
Araguainha Dome	Brazil	16s	53w
Bosumtwi	Ghana	7n	1w
Carswell	Canada	58n	109w
Charlevox	Canada	48n	70w
Clearwater Lake	Canada	56n	74w
Decaturville	United States	38n	91w
Deep Bay	Canada	56n	103w
Dellen	Sweden	62n	17e
Gosses Bluff	Australia	24s	132e
Gow Lake	Canada	56n	104w
Kentland	United States	41n	87w
Lappa	Finland	63n	24e
Manicow	Canada	51n	69w
Manson	United States	43n	95w
Mien	Sweden	56n	15e
Oasis	Libya	25n	24e
Redwing	United States	48n	103w
Pies	Germany	49n	11e
Rochechouart	France	46n	1e
Saaksjarvi	Finland	61n	22e
Serpent Mound	United States	39n	83w
Serra de Canahala	Brazil	8s	47w
Vredefor	South Africa	27s	28 w

When the entire activity is complete, discuss the following ideas with your students:

1. Models are extremely useful for experimentation, but models are never perfect representations of natural phenomena. List three ways this model is different from actual cases of bolide impacts. (Flour is softer than the Earth or moon surface. Marbles are round, not rock-shaped. The marble comes straight down, not at an angle.) How might you create a more realistic model? (Pack down the flour to make the surface harder. Use a real rock instead of a marble. Drop the rock from a greater height.)

2. What happened to the diameter and depth

of the crater when the marble was dropped from higher altitudes? (The diameter and depth of the crater increase a little bit. Using the same size marble, there isn't a great difference in the size of the craters. Students usually comment that there is a bigger "puff" when the marble hits the flour, and they notice that more "stuff" comes out of the crater.)

3. What differences did you observe between when the marble was dropped from 90 cm and when the golf ball was dropped from the same height? (The crater from the golf ball is larger and deeper.)

4. What factors investigated in this activity influence how large an effect might occur if Earth were struck by another meteor? (The size of the meteor, its speed, and the angle at which it is moving are important factors.)

Integrating Mathematics

In addition to developing science-process skills, such as recording data, the craters activity also provides opportunities to develop students' mathematics skills. To do the activity, students must know the definition of diameter and the proper procedure to measure the diameter of a crater.

Once students have made craters with marbles and golf balls, they can extend their learning by making craters with different-sized objects, such as tennis balls and ball bearings. Not only does this give students a chance to practice their measuring skills in the metric system, but it also provides an opportunity to develop students' graphing skills. For example, using data from the craters activity, students can create a picture graph, placing a symbol that represents the diameter size of the crater formed in the appropriate column. Students can also con-

struct graphs comparing the size of the crater to the size of the object, or to the mass of the object used to create the crater.

Integrating Language Arts

There are several ways to integrate language arts into the study. For example, using information from the World Wide Web, students find and display an image of a famous crater on Earth. An image of the Barringer Crater can be found at *http://starchild.gsfc.nasa.gov/docs/StarChild/ solar_system_level2/arizona_crater.html*. After observing the photographic image, challenge students to describe in writing how the craters they formed in their activity resemble the famous crater they observed on the website.

Another language arts activity helps develop students' journalistic skills. Using the five-W format of "who, what, when, where, and why," students can write and present a news report describing one of the meteor impacts they created in the activity as if the impact had occurred in their neighborhood. In their stories, students should pay particular attention to who discovered the crater, what is believed to have caused the crater, when the impact occurred, where the crater is located, and what the crater looks like.

Linking Social Studies and Geography

A social studies extension activity can discuss how different materials, such as the metal of the meteorite, have been used by civilizations such as the Eskimos in Greenland. Metal found in meteorites might have been used for spears, arrows, and other forms of hunting equipment. Questions like "Do Eskimos live in Greenland?" "Why do they need pieces of metal?" and "What is their culture like?" will encourage further exploration.

Explaining and Elaborating: Mathematics

Geography and map skills can also be integrated into the study. If students understand the concepts of latitude and longitude, they can identify sites of craters on Earth. Table 1 lists some of the known meteorite strikes greater than 5 km in diameter. Once each student plots the locations of the craters listed in the table using a map or a globe, the class can brainstorm reasons why more meteor impact craters are found in the northern hemisphere than in the southern hemisphere. With guidance and probing questions, students usually identify the northern hemisphere as the "land" hemisphere and the southern hemisphere as primarily the "water" hemisphere based on the distribution of land and water.

When an exciting topic like meteor impacts is integrated across the curriculum, it's easy for students to see that science is connected to their lives. With a creative approach to the curriculum, a teacher can really make an impact.

David A. Wiley is a professor in the Education Department at the University of Scranton, PA. Christine Anne Royce is an assistant professor of education at Shippensburg University of Pennsylvania in Shippensburg.

Resources

Hartmann, W. K., and Cain, J. 1995. *Craters! A multiscience approach to cratering and impacts.* Arlington, VA: National Science Teachers Association.

National Research Council. 1996. *National Science Education Standards.* Washington, DC: National Academy Press.

Vogt, G. L. 1996. *Asteroids, comets, and meteors.* Brookfield, CT: The Millbrook Press.

Internet Resources

http://www.barringercrater.com/
This site provides background information about the Barringer Crater and the history behind its discovery.

http://www.meteorite.com/meteor_crater/mc_hike.htm
This site provides a virtual tour of the Barringer Crater rim.

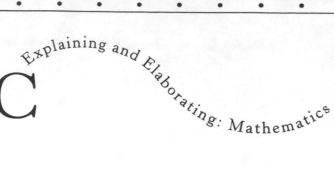
Convection Connections

By Ann M. L. Cavallo

Children are fascinated with large bodies of water, such as lakes and oceans. They feel the wind on their faces and observe lake and ocean water as it moves in waves. But do they know what makes the air and water move?

The following two investigations helped upper elementary and middle school students better understand air and water movement, or convection currents. Although the following activities aren't new, they are uniquely presented within the context of the learning cycle (Marek and Cavallo 1997).

Each learning cycle consisted of the three phases of the learning cycle inquiry model: exploration, term introduction, and concept application (Marek and Cavallo 1997). In the learning cycle, students worked in collaborative groups and engaged in active inquiry during investigations.

Learning Cycle One: Circles in the Sky

Our first learning cycle investigation examined the effects of temperature on air movement.

Exploration

Be sure to keep the classroom doors and windows closed during Parts A, B, and C of the exploration to minimize drafts.

Part A. Materials (per student) for the exploration included

- an empty clear glass bottle with an opening just big enough to hold a penny or dime (e.g., soda pop or flavored water bottles)
- a penny or dime
- a small cup of water, such as a bathroom paper cup

Students placed a bottle upright on their desks, dipped their index fingers in the water, and wet the rim around the mouth of the bottle. Students then placed the coin on the mouth of the bottle. Keeping the bottle on the desk, students wrapped their hands around the bottle and held it still.

In a few moments the students observed that the coin pops up and down on the mouth of the bottle. This observation generated much excitement and interest. I asked the students, "Why is the coin popping up and down on the bottle opening?" They thought that they were squeezing the bottle and forcing air upward, so they tried the experiment by gently holding the bottle —it still works, of course. I asked, "Can you see or hear anything as your coin pops?" Students observed a bubbling and heard a hissing sound. They noticed that air was escaping from the bottle. I asked, "What is causing the air to escape?" Students generated the theory that when their hands heat the air inside the bottle, the air moves up and out of the bottle. The coin pops up and down when the air escapes. The warm air inside the bottle is expanding and rising.

The children questioned the purpose of the water around the rim, so they tried the experiment again without coating the rim with water. The students weren't able to see the coin pop, but they concluded that the air is escaping between the glass rim and the coin—it just cannot be seen. The water serves as a seal, which makes the coin pop up.

In my experience, this activity works best if students are already familiar with conduction and heat transfer. They need to know that energy moves from hotter objects or areas to colder objects or areas. If students are having trouble explaining the popping coin, ask students how heat transfer may be taking place in this system (hands on the bottle). The students will note that heat transfer occurs from their warm hands to the cool glass bottle. The glass bottle then heats up and transfers its heat to the air inside the bottle. The class can try cooling the bottles—place them in a refrigerator, freezer, or a cooler with ice—before the experiment.

More Air Explorations

Part B. For this activity each student used
- the same bottle from Part A
- a balloon
- a marker

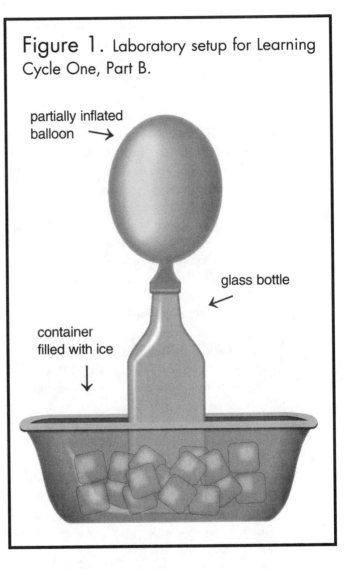

Figure 1. Laboratory setup for Learning Cycle One, Part B.

partially inflated balloon →

glass bottle

container filled with ice ↓

- and a plastic container—a small tub—filled with enough ice so that a bottle can be about two-thirds submerged.

Students drew things such as a face or their names on the uninflated balloon with their markers. Students partially blew up the balloon and attached it around the mouth of the bottle. They then placed the bottle and balloon in the container of ice (Figure 1).

After a short time, students observed that their balloons had deflated and the drawings or words on the balloon had shrunk. I asked questions such as, "What happened to the balloon? Where did the air go?" The children guessed that the air went down into the bottle. The air inside the balloon cooled (contracted) and sank down into the bottle. Because the balloon was sealed over the mouth of the bottle, students realized there is no other place for the air to go except inside the bottle.

Students then took their balloon-bottle setups out of the ice and placed them on their desks. Their balloons inflated again. As the bottle warmed to room temperature, students noticed the drawing or words on their balloon become large again. The students said, "Wow, look at mine!" and "My drawing looks normal [or big] again." I asked the children to explain what was happening to the air. They explained that the air in the bottle was warming (expanding) and rising back into the balloon.

Part C. Part C of the exploration was set up before beginning Parts A and B. Students worked in pairs. The materials included tape and two thermometers for each pair of students. Students first read their thermometers and recorded the beginning temperature. The student pairs then taped—with the help of the teacher—one of their thermometers on the walls around the classroom close to the ceiling and one on the walls close to the floor. The thermometers completely circled the room.

After students completed the investigations in Parts A and B, they found their thermometers and recorded the temperatures. Students displayed the temperature of their thermometers on the chalkboard or poster board, indicating their locations as near the floor or ceiling. The students calculated the class average tempera-

ture readings for the ceiling and the floor and noticed that both the individual and average temperature readings were higher by several degrees at the ceiling compared to those temperatures at floor level. Thus, warm air tends to rise, and cool air tends to sink.

You can integrate mathematics into this curriculum by using all of the data and asking students to graph the observed temperatures at the ceiling and floor. Graphing these data provides a dramatic illustration. A simplified line graph (Figure 2) provides a visual way to represent these temperatures. Students immediately notice the differences. "Look at this, the line showing the temperatures measured at the ceiling is above the one showing temperatures at the floor! It must be hotter at the ceiling than the floor."

Term Introduction

Working in groups, students compiled all information obtained in the exploration. They wrote a statement and drew a picture that described and summarized their observations of each part of the exploration. The students drew representations of what was happening to air in each exploration, using arrows to show air movement. Students often colored the arrows with red indicating warm air and blue indicating cool air.

For Part A, students drew their bottles showing the arrows pointing upward and moving out of the bottle. For Part B, the students drew their bottle-balloon setups with arrows pointing downward from balloon to bottle when the bottle was placed in ice, representing air moving downward. When the bottle was taken out of the ice and placed on the desktop, students drew another bottle-balloon setup with arrows showing air in the bottle moving upward into the balloon. In Part C, students drew the classroom and showed arrows representing warm air up toward the ceiling and arrows showing cool air near the floor.

In each part of the exploration, students noticed from their drawings and recollections that warm air moved upward and cool air moved downward, or that warm air was above the cool air. So their concept statement showed they had constructed the understanding that "Warm air rises and cool air sinks." The terms *contract* and *expand* mainly relate to the bottle-balloon experiment, where students observe that air from the balloon can "fit" into the space of the bottle when it is cooled with ice, so it must be taking up smaller space or contracting. The air fills the balloon back up again—expanding it—when the bottle is taken out of the ice.

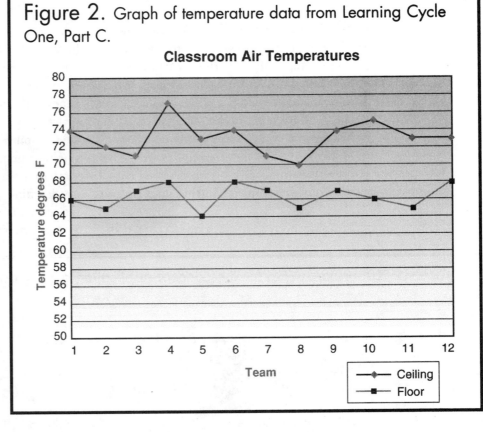

Figure 2. Graph of temperature data from Learning Cycle One, Part C.

Student groups posted their statements and drawings on the chalkboard or poster board. Students then read other groups' statements and made comparisons with their own. With the teacher facilitating the process, the students constructed a concept statement such as warm air (expands and) rises, while cool air (contracts and) sinks.

After students formulated the concept statement, the teacher introduced the term that labels the concept *convection*. Students may or may not use the terms *expands* and *contracts* during the exploration, and they may not know the meaning of these terms. Instead, students may use "spreads apart" or "comes together," which

are perfectly valid and more meaningful to them. Once students understand the meanings, you can help them substitute the terms *expand* and *contract* for these phrases.

Concept Application

Several concept application activities helped expand and enhance students' understanding of *convection*. An especially good concept application activity is a teacher demonstration using a convection box or similar apparatus that shows the complete circular motion of air in convection. The Franklin Institute Science Museum website *(www.fi.edu/tfi)* contains such an activity, called "What Is Wind?" A modified version of the activity is presented here. Materials included

- an aquarium or other large clear container
- a clamp lamp or desk lamp that can hang over the top of the aquarium with a 100-watt light bulb
- a small plastic container of ice
- one punk (or other tinder material)
- matches
- scissors
- plastic wrap
- protective clothing including goggles and gloves

Wearing protective clothing, I covered the aquarium with plastic wrap, cutting an opening at one end for the head of the lamp and at the other end for the punk (Figure 3). The lamp hung over and slightly into the covered aquarium at one end. At the opposite end I placed the container of ice on the bottom of the aquarium beneath the hole made for the punk. Using a match, I lit the end of the punk, let it burn for a few minutes, and then blew it out. I placed the smoking punk through the hole in the plastic wrap so it was suspended over the container of ice. Standing around the demonstration apparatus, students observed that the trail of smoke from the punk made a complete cycle. Students

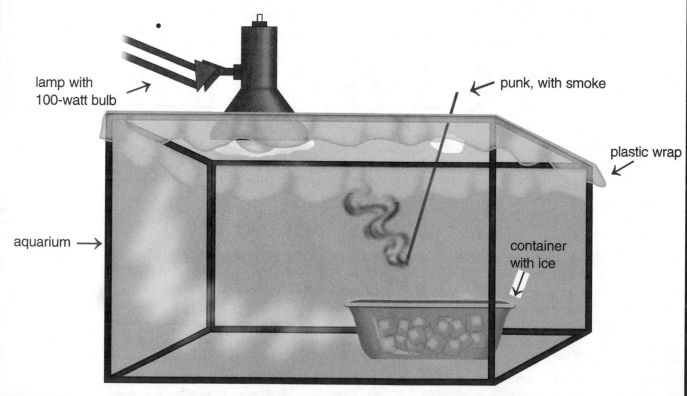

Figure 3. Laboratory setup for the concept application activity described in Learning Cycle One.

lamp with 100-watt bulb

punk, with smoke

plastic wrap

aquarium →

container with ice

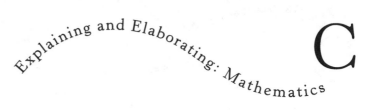

expanded their understanding of convection through the observation of the complete cycle, or *convection current*.

Another concept application involved heating the inside of a plastic trash bag with air from a blow dryer. After filling the bag with warm air and pinching the opening together, students let it go and it rose to the ceiling. Students explained the rising bag as the "warm air rising" part of the convection concept.

Other application activities include asking children how hot-air balloons "work." Students may research books or websites that discuss how hot-air balloons work, integrating science with reading and technology. Or, students could build hot-air balloons in their classrooms as art projects. Students may also read stories about the history of balloon flight or read related trade books. The students could also write a creative story about being a particle of air and describing their journey in a convection current or about taking a trip around the world in a hot-air balloon (integrating geography and social studies).

Learning Cycle Two: Circles in the Water

Exploration

The materials (per group) included:

- two clear-plastic bottles
- a shallow container with a flat bottom (to catch possible water spills)
- a source of warm water (lukewarm tap water) and cold water (water kept on ice or in a refrigerator)
- food coloring
- plastic transparencies cut into 10-cm squares. Students filled one bottle with cold water and

set it upright inside the plastic container. The students then filled the second bottle with the warmer water and placed a few drops of food coloring into the warm water. Then, placing the square of transparency firmly over the mouth of the warm-water bottle, students turned the bottle upside down and placed it on the mouth of the cold-water bottle in the plastic container (Figure 4). Working together, the students slowly removed the transparency square from between the two bottles, so the water in each bottle "touched." Students carefully let go of the bottles so they balanced on top of each other.

The students were surprised that the water within the two bottles did not mix; the warm water with food coloring stayed in the top bottle, and the clear, cold water stayed in the bottom bottle. (The water in the bottles remained separate until the water approached room temperature, which took a while—about 10 minutes for the water to start mixing, over an hour for complete mixing to take place). Students explained their observations by stating that cool water sinks or stays on the bottom, whereas warm water rises or stays above the cool water. Students almost immediately wanted to try different configurations of the bottles such as cool on top, warm on bottom).

What happened at this point in the investigation was especially exciting and fun for the students—and me. The children asked questions such as, "What would happen if the bottles were switched, with the cold water on top and the warm on the bottom? What if we put different colors of food coloring in each bottle? What if we put the cold water on the bottom with food coloring and warm on the top without food coloring? What happens if we put food coloring in the cold water only, but place the cold-water bottle on top?"

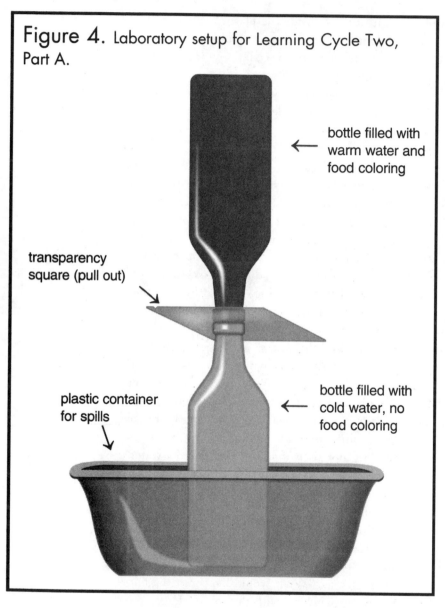

Figure 4. Laboratory setup for Learning Cycle Two, Part A.

bottle filled with warm water and food coloring

transparency square (pull out)

plastic container for spills

bottle filled with cold water, no food coloring

Students formed groups to select a question to try as an experiment. For example, one group chose placing food coloring in the cold water on the bottom and no food coloring in the warm water on top. Students drew their group's experiment on the board, then tried their selected experiment to determine the results. When the group experiments were completed, the children shared their findings with the rest of the class. They drew diagrams on the chalkboard or poster board and explained what they observed. These varied experiments again led students toward the understanding that cool water sinks or stays on the bottom, whereas warm water rises or stays above the cool water.

Term Introduction

For term introduction, students compiled the data from the exploration and discussed their observations with group members. Each group formulated a statement that described and explained their observations, which were posted on the board for discussion. The groups compared their statements with those of others in the class. With the teacher facilitating the discussion, the students constructed one statement that summarized and explained the observations made in the exploration: Warm water (expands and) rises, and cool water (contracts and) sinks. The teacher then reintroduced the term that names this concept: *convection*.

Concept Application

To apply the concept, you may use additional science experiments and also integrate the concept with subjects across the curriculum. I demonstrated an experiment that required a large rectangular container of clear, cool water—like an aquarium—and a small cup or vial of warm water colored with food coloring. Students can help with this demonstration by taking the temperature of the water, placing the food coloring in the vial, and setting the vial in the aquarium.

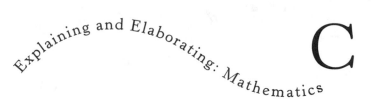

The students surrounded the desk that held the large container of water. Before beginning, the students recorded the temperature of the water in the large container and the temperature of the water in the vial. Then, a student placed the vial of warm, colored water inside the large container, standing it upright in one corner. Students observed that the colored water in the vial moved up and across the top of the cold water in the large container. Then, as the colored water cooled, it sank to the bottom of the large container, making a circle. Students could now explain their observations: The warm water (in the vial) expands and rises, and, as it cools, it contracts and sinks. The students used the term *convection* to explain their observations, and I also reintroduced the phrase *convection current*.

Other concept application activities included discussions on topics such as, "How does the bottom of the deep end of a swimming pool feel compared to water at the surface?" In addition, the children could conduct library or Internet research on ocean currents and read stories dealing with ocean currents. The students could read historical accounts of ocean currents and how they have affected ships and ocean travel through time.

Tying It All Together

The two learning cycles led into a long-term unit of study on weather and/or bodies of water, such as oceans. Our studies led to students linking air convection currents with ocean convection currents in explaining weather phenomena, such as hurricanes. The students tracked weather patterns and obtained satellite images via newspaper or television reports, the Internet, or through various other sources such as almanacs.

I assessed student learning in various authentic ways throughout these learning cycles. I mea-sured students' understanding through their verbal, diagrammatic, pictorial, and written explanations at many points throughout the investigations. I also assessed science-process and thinking skills as students solved problems and generated ideas for new experiments, as in Learning Cycle Two: Circles in the Water. I evaluated students' technical writing through laboratory reports and creative story writing. These assessment techniques helped me observe and measure student learning and progress as it was occurring throughout the learning cycles (Marek and Cavallo 1997).

Engaging students in these investigations fulfilled the *National Science Education Standards'* Content Standard A: Science as Inquiry for grades 5–8 (National Research Council 1996). These activities helped students develop thinking skills through inquiry and helped them relate concepts learned in science with everyday life. The learning cycles also provided an opportunity for scientific discussion and debate, which is another valued emphasis of our national Standards in science education. The next time these students feel wind on their faces or see ocean waves, they will better understand the underlying science processes that make it all happen.

Ann M. L. Cavallo is an associate professor of science education in the College of Education, Wayne State University, Detroit.

Resources

Marek, E. A. and A. M. L. Cavallo. 1997. *The Learning Cycle: Elementary School Science and Beyond.* Portsmouth, NH: Heinemann.

National Research Council. 1996. *National Science Education Standards.* Washington, DC: National Academy Press.

The Franklin Institute Science Museum, 222 North 20th Street, Philadelphia, PA 19103. 215-448-1200; *www.fi.edu/tfi.*

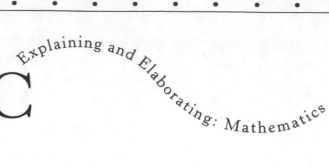
Mission to Mars:
A Classroom Simulation

By Katie Rommel-Esham and Christopher Souhrada

From NASA Headquarters, Washington, DC

Dear Students:

Here at NASA we are currently observing possible evidence of life on the planet Mars. Pictures taken from the Mars Global Surveyor have revealed what seems to be a colony of organisms gathered at the northern base of Olympus Mons (24° N latitude and 132° W longitude).

In an attempt to involve the public in current missions, we're seeking students' input in the development of an exploration procedure. Our goal is to sample all possible species identified within the target area.

To assist us in our efforts, we are asking that students create a scale model of the target area (actual dimensions, 5 km × 3 km). Further research on Mars should be completed before attempting this mission.

Your help researching and determining the population of the target area using sampling procedures is greatly appreciated. Unfortunately, due to the confidential nature of our mission, there will be no further communication with NASA. Please submit your verified results to NASA Headquarters, Mars Exploration Program, 300 E St. SW, Washington, D.C. 20546–0001.

Topic: exploring Mars
Go to: www.scilinks.org
Code: MIX96

So began a Martian simulation activity that took place in our fourth-grade classroom. During a unit on the Earth, students studied habitats and discussed with us items needed for life to exist, such as food, shelter, and water. The discussion led students to wonder whether life existed on other planets such as Mars. Students felt that life on Mars also required food, shelter, and water, although they did not believe that any of these things were present on Mars.

The Mars discussion generated student interest and presented an opportunity for further exploration. In their habitat studies, students had begun considering population issues and relationships among species, so we thought a Mars simulation activity would be a great way to incorporate population issues and have students learn about estimation and data extrapolation. In addition, we thought it would be beneficial for students to work as if they were the astronauts or scientists actually completing a mission so they could practice their research, observation, inference, and other science-process skills.

A "Classified" Assignment

When I presented students with "official" materials from the National Aeronautics and Space Administration, they were intrigued but intimidated. Some thought the letter was genuine, some were not sure, and some were certain the letter was false. We let them carry the discussion and come to a consensus on their own: The letter probably was not real, but they should take it seriously just in case. Students enjoyed the idea that they were working on something important.

As we discussed the letter with the class in detail, we set the mission goals below:

- *Create a scale model of the target area.* Students had learned about scale models in previous lessons, where they had examined the scale-model relationship of the Sun, Moon, and Earth in the classroom and worked with scales on maps in atlases and other sources. We discussed how we might create a model of a Martian habitat: make a salt-dough model, make some kind of model outside on the grass, or make a model with manipulatives in the classroom. We finally decided to make our scale model in the classroom using Legos®—we chose to use these blocks because they were readily available in our classroom and came in various sizes and colors that we felt lent themselves to different model scenarios—the different sizes of red blocks could represent various generations of a particular species.

- *Estimate the total number of each species in the sampling area.* At first, students expressed some confusion on how to sample. As we introduced this goal, however, we talked about what students already knew about sampling. (They understood sampling as something related to the United States census and as a way the government "gets estimates of our coun-

try's population.") We discussed the difficulties of finding out the number of a particular group of people in a population, such as finding the percentage of people in the general population who are left-handed, and how, because no one could actually count all those people, population samples are used to approximate the information. Finally, we talked about how the sample numbers are related to the population estimates and how those numbers are computed (by *extrapolation*). I defined *extrapolation* as using data from a sample to get information about the overall population. In a sense, the data is expanded from the sample to the whole group.

- *Communicate completed sampling procedure and conclusions to NASA in writing.* (Visit *www.nsta.org/elementaryschool* to see an example of a student-written report from this mission.)

Researching the Mission

Once the project's goals were introduced, students set to work. As the letter directed, students spent the next several days using the Internet and other resources to research Mars (see References). Through their research they discovered several critical areas to take into account: geography, lack of a breathable atmosphere, and comparisons between Mars and Earth.

For example, students discovered the geography of the Martian site would impact where a rover could venture or how easy or difficult it would be to get around on foot. Also, the necessary use of oxygen tanks with a finite amount of oxygen would impact the time spent on the surface.

Students' research showed them that both Mars and Earth shared landforms, such as mountains, seabeds, and deserts, but there were differences as well. One of the differences students observed was that the terrain on Mars was very stark due to the lack of vegetation. Although there are also rocky places on the Earth, those places also have trees and other types of flora. Another difference students noted was a lack of bodies of water. The stark nature of the pictures they saw made a big impression, and this was perhaps what students perceived to be the greatest difference between Mars and Earth.

After noting what they found and recording these facts and other information in their science notebooks, students shared such discoveries as

- Mars is about half the size of Earth.
- It is impossible for water to exist as a liquid on the surface of Mars because the atmosphere is too thin and the temperatures are too low.
- Many features on the surface of Mars appear to have been created by liquid in the past; if there had been liquid, then there could have been life.
- Some craters on Mars look like craters on the moon.

We also showed the class a PowerPoint computer slide show of actual images of Olympus Mons, where students would be doing their sampling, and Mars that I had culled from various Internet resources.

The Mission Begins

With their body of Mars knowledge growing, students now felt ready to construct a scale model of the Martian terrain on the floor in the classroom. The letter had indicated that the "real" target area was 5 km × 3 km in size, so we scaled our model at 5 m × 3 m to fit in the classroom. (If space is limited in your classroom, a gym, auditorium stage, or other large, open area also works.) The students measured the area with a meter stick and taped the boundaries with masking tape.

Later, when students were out of the room, we introduced "organisms" into the habitat by randomly scattering multisize, multicolor Legos® inside the habitat to represent the various species of life on the surface of Mars. The Legos® did not represent "real" organisms; instead, students referred to each organism by its color—the "blues," the "reds," and the "yellows."

When students returned to the classroom after a lunch break, we asked them to observe the model closely. We asked, "Are the species distributed evenly? Do they cover every inch of the surface?" Students observed that the organisms were not uniformly distributed over the 5 m × 3 m rectangle and that there were clustered areas, empty areas, and areas where the distribution was somewhat uniform.

"Reading" the Model

After their initial observations and questions, students realized it was necessary to assemble a coordinate/grid system over the model so that general areas of the habitat could be referenced and recorded.

Connecting to the Standards

This activity relates to the following *National Science Education Standards*:

- Content Standard A: Science as Inquiry;
- Content Standard C: Physical Science (grades K–4: characteristics of organisms, life cycles of organisms, organisms and environments; grades 5–8: populations and ecosystems; and diversity and adaptations of organisms);
- Content Standard D: Earth and Space Science (grades K–4: objects in the sky; and grades 5–8: Earth in the solar system); and
- Content Standard E: Science and Technology.

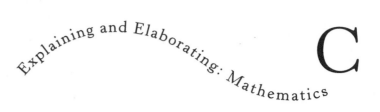

Figure 1. The "Mars terrain" sampling grid.

The letter had indicated that the "real" target area was 5 km × 3 km in size, so we scaled our model at 5 m × 3 m to fit in the classroom.

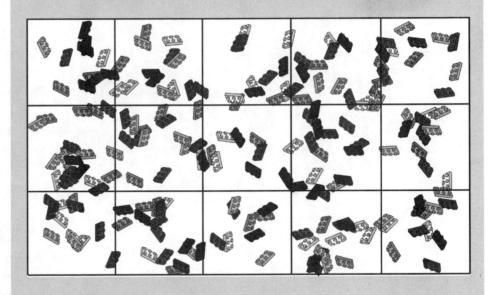

Because the model was simulating a terrain in which humans need oxygen to function and cannot wander about freely, students felt it would not be practical or possible to count all the organisms in the area. We discussed different ways to count only a sample, such as picking a corner and counting the organisms in that corner, but the students quickly realized this method would not be any type of standard, but an "eyeball" measurement from which they could not extrapolate. Eventually, one student suggested making a map of the area, which eventually led the class to the idea of laying a grid.

We discussed how counting the various species within a reasonable number of smaller grid squares would make it possible to estimate and extrapolate the entire population in the target area. In addition, we talked about the fact that there was no "perfect" number of grids to use, and that a subjective decision might have to be made (as is often the case in statistics). If the grid was not fine enough, then the estimates might under- or over-represent the total population because the distribution of organisms was not uniform. Eventually, the class decided to make a grid with a total of 15 squares, each 1 m × 1 m in size.

To make the grid, students sectioned off the rectangular area into the 1 m × 1 m square units with string, taping the string to the floor both vertically and horizontally, across the model (Figure 1).

Next, students divided into teams of five to sample the population using the established grid.

We drew random numbers for each group and used those numbers to assign the squares. There were five groups of students, and they sampled 5 of the 15 squares. (Teachers need to make sure only some of the grid squares are counted to ensure a useful sampling method.) Each team was responsible for taking a complete census of its assigned square. Each group counted the number of each type of organism in its square and recorded the data in a data table, reporting the results to the entire class.

Calculating the "Species"

Once each assigned square was counted, the groups combined their data to find the "species" totals in the sampled grid squares. The class data table is shown in Figure 2.

Next, students calculated the averages for each species using the data collected. This num-

Figure 2. Class data table.

	Red	White	Yellow	Green	Blue	Gray
Team Alpha	2	8	1	6	3	5
Team Beta	5	1	3	4	2	4
Team Gamma	1	3	6	1	4	1
Team Delta	6	3	4	5	7	8
Team Epsilon	2	4	1	2	5	2
Averages	3.2	3.8	3	3.6	4.2	4
Estimated totals	48	57	45	54	63	60
Actual	50	50	50	50	50	50
Difference	-2	7	-5	6	13	10

ber represented the average population of each species per grid square. Students then multiplied the average number for each species by the total number of grid squares (15) in the habitat to project the entire population. This final number provided an estimate of each species' population throughout the Martian habitat.

For example, the table shows that the average number of white organisms per square is 3.8 based on the data collected. If there were 3.8 white organisms in each of the 15 grid squares, the total number of white organisms would be $3.8 \times 15 = 57$. Similarly, the average number of red organisms per sampled square is 3.2, which yields an overall population estimate of $3.2 \times 15 = 48$ red organisms. In the case of the white organisms, the average provided an estimate that was too large, while the average number of red organisms provided an estimate that was too small. (I had scattered 50 of each type of organism.) Still, both were reasonably close.

The students completed their initial population calculations without the computer but used a calculator. Some teachers, however, may want to use a spreadsheet program in which students do the calculations. They can practice their computer skills as they work with cell formatting and formulas to perform the calculations.

Measuring Student Learning

The assessment for this lesson was both ongoing and formal. We evaluated student understanding at each step of the mission. Using a checklist, we determined the stages of the mission completed by each student/team. For example, before students could move to the mission's planning stage, they needed to use a variety of sources and gather information about geographical features, atmospheric features, and terrain in the research phase.

Formal assessment measures included quizzes and written materials that were to be "sent back" to NASA. Students wrote a report outlining how each of the mission goals were met and described the step-by-step procedure of the experiment. They also completed a data table with calculations. We evaluated each student's set of materials. The documents enabled us to assess students' writing abilities, procedural organization, comprehension, computation skills, and problem-solving abilities.

An Interdisciplinary Success

Building a scale model of the Martian terrain not only provided students with an interactive way to explore the idea of completing a census and interpreting its results, but it also involved many learning disciplines, making the experience a valuable curricular tool.

More Mars Learning

Once the students have established basic population data from a scale model, they can create new and varied scenarios.

- By changing the distribution of species, the teacher can model environment or habitat changes in the future. This would allow the class to address more specific habitat objectives. For example, the entire collection of one of the original "inhabitants" could be removed to represent the extinction of a particular organism.

- The teacher could remove most of a certain color and then ask the students to make inferences based on this new distribution. Using prior knowledge of predator/prey relationships, interdependencies among species, and geography, students should then predict future stages of species interaction. For example, the population of one species could be dramatically increased to represent the extinction of a predator for that species. If a predator of one species is severely diminished or eliminated, that species may grow uncontrolled until available resources are depleted and the food chain is adversely affected. In another example, if geographical/climate changes occur (say a pond dries up during a drought), water sources will become scarce and the local inhabitants will be forced to move, creating a change and perhaps an imbalance in the local habitat.

- The teacher could redistribute the organisms to model the seasonal migration of species or change in the ecosystem that required movement on the part of the inhabitants (such as flood, drought, and volcanic eruption).

Building a scale-model habitat with upper elementary students links science-process skills and mathematics in an original way.

In science, students developed process skills throughout the investigation. They conducted research using the Internet; constructed a model; and collected and evaluated data, making inferences based on that data.

In mathematics, students used multiplication and division in order to average and extrapolate the data collected. Simple, beginning-level statistics were addressed with the organization of data and through our discussions about whether students' calculations were "reasonable" based on the scale model.

In language arts, students developed skills as they read to conduct research; orally communicated procedures and results to their peers; and followed the writing process while documenting their results for NASA.

The sampling procedure students modeled in this Mars simulation could easily be adapted to other uses in science class. For example, students could use the sampling technique they practiced to determine the number of insects in an area of the schoolyard. Or, they might use the technique to investigate mealworm/pupa/beetle populations to determine the total number of each stage of beetle development in a given population, or perhaps to estimate the number of fish in a pond.

When studying genetic traits, students could use the procedure to determine the approximate number of students with a particular trait, such as left-handedness. Because this data may actually be "collectable" from the entire school population, students would be able to test the accuracy of the sampling process.

Whether used as an investigative "mission" or as a data-gathering tool in another capacity—however you choose to implement the sampling procedure in your science classroom—you're likely to find it a successful learning experience for students.

Katie Rommel-Esham is an assistant professor of mathematics and science education in the Shear School of Education at SUNY College at Geneseo, NY. Christopher Souhrada teaches fourth grade at Horizon Elementary School in Sterling, VA.

References

Dyson, M. J. 1999. *Space station science: Life in free fall.* New York: Scholastic.

Johnstone, M. 1999. *The history news in space.* New York: Scholastic.

Miles, L., and A. Smith. 1998. *The Usborne complete book of astronomy and space.* New York: Scholastic.

Mitton, J., and S. Mitton. 1998. *Scholastic encyclopedia of space.* New York: Scholastic.

Ride, S., and T. O'Shaughnessy. 1999. *The mystery of Mars.* New York: Scholastic.

Simon, S. 1990. *Mars.* UK: Mulberry Books.

Internet

Check out the following websites for pictures of Mars:

NASA. NASA Center for Mars Exploration. *cmex-www.arc.nasa.gov/CMEX/index.html*

NASA. Mars Orbiter camera pictures. *mars.jpl.nasa.gov/mgs/msss/camera/images/*

Students for the Exploration and Development of Space. Mars. *www.seds.org/nineplanets/nineplanets/mars.html*

Students for the Exploration and Development of Space. Mars Exploration Page. *www.seds.org/~spider/mars/mars.html*

Section

2

School and Community
Connections

A

Schoolwide Themes

Diving into a Schoolwide Science Theme

By Michele Lee, Maria Lostoski, and Kathy Williams

Science learning can happen anywhere. Using initiative and creativity, teachers of various subjects can create interdisciplinary learning opportunities. Elementary students at our school begin each year with a science theme. The theme encourages faculty to make innovative curriculum ties and unifies students through their common learning experiences. In and out of the science classroom, all kindergarten through sixth-grade students have opportunities to expand their scientific knowledge.

This year the theme was "Dive into Oceans." Because oceans play a universal role in our understanding and appreciation of Earth's beauty and diversity, teachers could incorporate this topic into various classroom activities. Other examples of themes from past years include waste management/recycling, nutrition, computers, and the Chesapeake Bay. This article presents interdisciplinary lessons developed for an all-school theme and used in science, art, and music classes.

Science Connections

The curricula in science classes encompassed an overview of physical, biological, and geological aspects of oceanography through hands-on, interdisciplinary experiences. One of the first topics included the location and number of oceans. We modified the "Oceans All Around Us" activity found in *NatureScope* (National Wildlife Federation 1988). Early elementary students found and labeled with numbers the major oceans on a globe. We actually taught the five oceans (the *NatureScope* activity refers to only four), though teachers disputed the existence of the Antarctic Ocean. This was a good point of discussion with students regarding how scientists do not necessarily agree all the time.

For the activity students had laminated pictures of the globe. After they had labeled all of the oceans, students were asked if they thought it was possible to travel around the globe while riding in a boat. They used wet-erase markers to trace on their world map the watery path that their imaginary ship might take. Students could

also trace with their fingers an imaginary path around a three-dimensional globe. Through this exercise, we emphasized that, though different parts of water have different names, Earth has essentially one connected ocean.

With the aid of world maps and globes, older students reviewed geography by labeling continents and oceans on a world map. To compare the amount of land with the amount of ocean, students played a game with a "huggable," plush Earth ball. As the ball was tossed from student to student in a circle, students chanted "Land or sea? Which will it be? I'll toss it up and we will see!" The teacher recorded how often students' left thumbs rested on land or ocean. By the end of the game students drew the conclusion that there was more ocean than land.

A parallel was made between the diversity of terrestrial habitats and the diversity of oceanic habitats. If deserts and rainforests have different animals and plants and environmental conditions, it made sense that kelp forests, tidal pools, and coral reefs are just as diverse. To better understand the workings of these ecosystems, students in first through third grades focused on a given habitat—kelp forest, tidal pools, coral reefs—for which they created a three-dimensional diorama in the school hallways (National Wildlife Federation 1988). The kelp forest is given as an example here, but the method is applicable to other marine ecosystems.

Second-grade students made the analogy of kelp plants being like the trees of a land forest. The children learned about plant parts as they cut paper blades (leaves) with floats and attached them to green-streamer stems (floats are the air-filled bladders at the base of each blade of a kelp plant; these help buoy the plant toward the ocean surface and sunlight). The tops of the kelp plants "floated" to the ceiling (ocean surface) to-

ward the sun. "Sunlight" shone into the ocean from a ceiling light covered with blue cellophane paper. Holdfasts (the part by which a plant clings to a flat surface) made of green streamers anchored the kelp plants to rocks on the ocean floor. Students created rocks by wrapping paper around crumpled paper found in the recycle bin.

Many students knew that sea otters live in the kelp forest. When the otters, created from construction paper and a basic pattern, were placed in their habitat, the students wondered what the otters might eat. Thus, in the holdfast area, paper circles with long, spiny pipe-cleaner legs (brittle stars), cut-out foam meat trays and pipe-cleaner legs (crabs), and foam balls with tooth-pick spines (sea urchins) were placed at the bottom of the forest as a food source for the otters. Students found out these were good food sources after watching the National Geographic Kids video, *Really Wild Animals: Deep Sea Dive* (1994). The video shows footage of various habitats including the kelp forest and how/what the otter eats. Students also used Norbert Wu's *Life in the Oceans* (1991), which has a section on kelp forests' flora and fauna.

With the introduction of new animals to the diorama, students wondered what these new arrivals would eat. By using *Life in the Oceans*, *Exploring Saltwater Habitats* (Smith 1994), and *The Great Undersea Search* (Usbourne 1995), students determined how the flora and fauna were interconnected. They learned that brittle stars clung to kelp, filtering seawater for food. Sea urchins and crabs consumed the kelp. The teacher introduced giant kelpfish to control the crab population. As students made the various animals and kelp, the teacher added and displayed them in the hallway diorama. Given the limited space on the "ocean floor," the kelp forest was soon crowded by the 100-plus sea urchins and crabs. Thus, introducing the kelpfish to control the population seemed appropriate.

At first the students complained about the limited choice of paper colors for the fish (green and brown); however, when the idea of adding a bird to the habitat was introduced, the students realized the importance of camouflage. Many more animals could have been added to this ecosystem, but, even with a select number of animals in the watery forest, a diorama introduced basic components of a marine habitat and generated conversation about the interconnection between plants, animals, and the environment.

Art Integration

Both science and art use the powerful tools of observation and imagination. The more carefully students observe their subject, the better they can capture its essence in a drawing. Learning

National Science Education Standards

Teaching Standards

Standard A

Adapt and design curricula to meet the interests, knowledge, understanding, abilities, and experiences of students. Select teaching strategies that support the development of student understanding and nurture a community of science learners. Work together as colleagues within and across disciplines and grade levels.

Standard E

Display and demand respect for the diverse ideas, skills, and experiences of all students. Enable students to have a significant voice in decisions about the content and context of their work and require students to take responsibility for the learning of all members of the community. Nurture collaboration among students.

Standard F

Teachers of science actively participate in the ongoing planning and development of the school science program. In doing this, teachers plan and develop the school science program.

Content Standards

Life Science Content Standard C

Characteristics of organisms (K–4)

Organisms and environments (K–4)

Diversity and adaptation of organisms (5–8)

to feel the uplifting experience of sensory enrichment and enjoy the simple power of nature to delight us are worthy goals of our teaching and as essential as factual information.

Artists worldwide have explored the subjects of oceans and seas, and it is easy to find reproductions of their work. Mythology of many cultures is rich with stories of the sea; for example, Poseidon and Dionysus from the Greeks, and Urashima Taro from Japanese folklore. Claude Monet's water lilies, Henri Matisse's sea-inspired paper cuts, Georgia O'Keeffe's shells, and Winslow Homer's watercolor seascapes all offer exciting inspiration for students.

Fish and oceans are always an appealing theme for art students. The opportunity to work on the theme "Dive into Oceans" set the stage for much synergetic learning that enriched students across grade levels and subject areas. The more information and interest students bring to the subject of a project, the richer their art becomes.

Kindergarten students used tempera paint to capture the rhythm of water at peace or in a storm, observed the many colors of blue and green that made up the watery part of their painting, learned vocabulary such as *seascape* and *horizon line,* and added the sky above the water.

The children also drew pictures of the three art-room goldfish. Students were sent back many times to carefully observe the goldfish (shape, how many fins, etc.) while drawing. After students drew the goldfish, they made collage fish in colors and shapes of their own choosing, using what they had learned. Torn paper "seaweed" completed these bold, colorful works. A classroom collection of a variety of sea stars was an excellent beginning for clay projects with kindergarten students. Broken pieces of coral were perfect for adding texture to the clay.

The opportunity to work on the theme "Dive into Oceans" set the stage for much synergetic learning across grade levels and subject areas.

The creation of sea stars prompted discussion about body parts, what sea stars eat, and how they move.

First-grade students named their homerooms: the Sharks, the Whales, and the Penguins; these sea creatures were perfect for use in mural work. The penguin mural was quite inventive: Cut paper was used to make penguins that were placed on a painted background. The shark and whale murals involved drawing the many kinds of whales in crayon and collaborating to paint a beautiful blue-and-green sea.

Gyotaku, a Japanese method of making a print from a real fish, was an exciting introduction to the second-grade unit on printmaking. Ink or tempera paint is simply brushed onto the fish (fish were bought gutted but whole from the grocery store) and tissue or rice paper is placed over the fish to make an impression. Third-grade students made "stuffed fish" with two identical outlines of fish cut from construction paper, stapled together, and stuffed with newspaper. The imaginative yet anatomically correct fish were proudly hung in a coral reef display.

In fourth grade the medium was watercolor

and the subject was real and imaginary colorful fish. Models of wooden and plastic fish, pictures, and a collection of shells and sea stars were available for students to observe and use in their drawings. With the theme in science classes well under way, students added many details to their art using their increased knowledge about sea life.

Extending to Music

The science theme was also a natural choice for creative activities in music. Second-grade music students created a rap as a way of more intimately appreciating the rhythmic and rhyming elements essential to a rap's success. After listening to various rap songs and analyzing how the lyrics were derived, students decided to create a rap song. But what would the rap be about? Writing on a particular subject is one thing, but trying to incorporate rhythm and rhyme into the writing was a tall order for second-grade students. They needed a subject that was immediately accessible so they could concentrate on fitting lyrics to the rap beat.

The students delighted in the opportunity to display their knowledge of ocean life. With this knowledge and a bit of creative license, they brainstormed fanciful and factual ideas for their rap. The children very proudly performed the final draft for the teachers in science class and clearly enjoyed the connection made between science and music. The rap also incorporated a review of short vowel sounds; it was a language arts lesson as well.

Third- and fourth-grade music students took a different approach to applying the science theme. They began with the question: How have the human cultures that have flourished around and on the sea expressed the meaning the sea has had for them? Students then dis-

cussed various ways music provides this means of expression from legends to funny stories to epics and ballads. The sea chantey is one genre that third- and fourth-grade students performed in a choral concert. For example, children in third grade sang a sea chantey from the time of Henry VIII called "Haul the Bowline." Children in fourth grade learned "Blow the Man Down," "Fire Down Below," and "The Herring." Thus, music students were able to explore the important relationship between oceans and human beings.

Working Together

Oceans cover about 72 percent of our planet, yet people are just beginning to understand the importance of these vast interconnected bodies of water. Teachers want students to develop a greater understanding and respect for the oceans. The beauty of the yearly science theme, including "Dive into Oceans," is that we are not teaching each other's subject area but rather complementing and connecting through shared themes while retaining the integrity of each curriculum. Focusing on a theme builds the school's sense of community and encourages learning in various disciplines.

Michele Lee is a science coordinator and teacher, Kathy Williams is an art teacher, and Maria Lostoski is a music teacher, all at the Lower School at Norwood School in Bethesda, MD.

Resources

Science Books

Center for Marine Conservation. 1989. *The ocean book: Aquarium and seaside activities and ideas for all ages.* New York: John Wiley.

Delafosse, C., and Gallimard, J. 1999. *Under the sea.* New York: Schlolastic.

Gibbons, G. 1999. *Exploring the deep, dark sea*. Hong Kong: Little, Brown.

National Geographic Society. 1994. *Really wild animals: Deep sea dive* [video]. Burbank, CA: Warner Home Video.

National Research Council. 1996. *National Science Education Standards*. Washington, DC: National Academy Press.

National Wildlife Federation. 1988. *Diving into oceans*. Washington, DC: Ranger Rick's NatureScope.

Reader's Digest Association. 1992. *Underwater nature search*. Malaysia: Victoria House.

Scarborough, K. 1997. *Watch it grow coral reef*. London: Time-Life, Marshall Editions Development.

Smith, S. 1994. *Exploring saltwater habitats*. Greenvale, NY: Mondo.

Time-Life Books. 1996. *Under the sea*. Hong Kong: Orpheus Books.

Usbourne Publishing 1995. *The great undersea search*. Tulsa, OK: EDC Publishing.

Wildlife Education. 1996. *Whales: Zoobooks, 13*(12), 1–17.

Wildlife Education. 1990. *Seabirds: Zoobooks, 7*(10), 1–17.

Wu, N. 1991. *Life in the oceans*. New York: Little, Brown.

Art Books

Adams, G. E. 1993. *Fish, fish, fish*. New York: Dial Books.

Ehlert, L. 1990. *Fish eyes: A book you can count on*. New York: Harcourt Brace Jovanovich.

Lionni, L. 1970. *Fish is fish*. New York: Pantheon.

The Metropolitan Museum of Art. 1980. *Hiroshige: A shoal of fishes*. New York: Viking.

Munthe, N. 1983. *Meet Matisse*. Boston: Little, Brown.

Peppin, A., and H. Williams. 1991. *Looking at art*. Chippenham Wiltshire, Great Britain: Merlion.

Roalf, P. 1992. *Looking at paintings: Seascapes*. New York: Hyperion Books for Children.

CD-ROMs

Topex/Poseidon: Perspectives on an Ocean Planet
Interactive CD-ROM with Quick Time movies that narrate written information.

Topex/Poseidon: Visit to an Ocean Planet
Interactive, educational CD-ROM that reveals the importance of oceans to global climate and life.

(Both CD-ROMs available from Jet Propulsion Laboratory, Educator Resource Center, Village at Indian Hill, Suite 200, 1460 East Holt Blvd., Pomona, CA 91767; 909-397-4420.)

Our Crowded Shores
Data on coastal population and development, coastal management, and developmental impacts animations.

Marine Mammals Ashore: A Field Guide for Strandings
Stranding response and investigation guidelines, information on marine mammal biology and behavior, identification guidelines, and illustrated procedures.

(Both CD-ROMs available from the Office of Public and Constituent Affairs/Outreach Unit, National Oceanic and Atmospheric Administration, 1305 East-West Highway, Station 1W514, Silver Spring, MD 20910.)

Testing the Waters

By Roberta J. Aram, Mary Brake, David Smith, Gina Wood, and Pat Hamilton

Apples, oceans, rainforests, and space. What do these topics have in common? They are themes around which elementary teachers have built interdisciplinary units as a way to meet *National Science Education Standards* goals (NRC 1996). "Student achievement in science and in other school subjects such as social studies, language arts, and technology is enhanced by coordination between and among the science program and other programs. Furthermore, such coordination can make maximal use of time in a crowded school schedule" (Program Standard B). In addition to possibilities for cross-curricular coordination, thematic units have the potential to facilitate cross–grade level and even intergenerational educational opportunities (Brophy and Alleman 1996).

In our small rural school in southwest Missouri, coordination of a schoolwide water theme provided students with science learning experiences with a Science-Technology-Society orientation reflecting many of the Standards. Water was chosen as the theme for the following reasons:

- Water is a central element of the natural world that is a familiar and easily accessible resource (Teaching Standard D) that interests young and old alike and of which all have prior experience and knowledge (Teaching Standard A, Program Standard B).
- An inquiry-oriented exploration of water's physical and chemical properties, life-giving attributes, and connections with technology and the environment easily links school science disciplines (Program Standard B) and encourages student collaboration across grade levels (Teaching Standard E).
- Water is a foundation block of the economic livelihood in our region as well as many parts of the world, and the abundance or scarcity of clean water is both a personal and social concern (Content Standard F).
- Water is a frequent subject in literature, art, music, and history, from "Jack and Jill went up the hill to fetch a pail of water," to the dependence on water in the 19th and 20th century U.S. westward expansion, providing plentiful opportunities to link science, the arts, and humanities (Program Standard B; Teaching Standard A).
- The water theme provided common ground by which Standards could help us shift emphases in our school science programs (see Figure 1).

Ready, Set, Get Wet

Our collaborative exploration of water began in 1996 when the high school biology/environmental science teacher participated in a summer professional development course designed to help teachers develop Standards-based thematic units using local water studies as the central theme (Aram and Roy 1994). The high school teacher created his first water unit, the centerpiece of which involved his environmental science students in collecting, analyzing, and reporting water quality data (e.g., macroinvertebrate counts, flow rate, dissolved oxygen level) for their local stream. He subsequently encouraged faculty schoolwide to form a team and participate in further summer professional development (Teaching Standard F; Professional Development Standard A) designed to assist interdisciplinary teams of teachers in developing and aligning locally situated water units with the Standards (Annenberg 1998).

A five-person team consisting of teachers of first grade, high school biology, middle school science, and high school mathematics as well as the campus librarian, willingly volunteered. Over a two-year period, this team worked closely with the science and education college faculty and local water experts (Professional Development Standard D)—both in the classroom and on local waterways—to develop thematic units that met the interests and developmental needs of students and provided for intergenerational shared learning experiences (Professional Development Standard B). Collaborative opportunities for water studies throughout our small district were implemented across the campus.

Grade One Takes the Plunge

In collaboration with the high school biology/environmental science teacher, the first-grade teacher developed a stream unit emphasizing Content Standards D (Life Science) and F (Science and Technology). Early in the unit, the first-grade teacher led her students in a discussion of how they could use their five senses in exploring their stream. Prior to their stream field trip, high school environmental science students and their teacher visited first grade and held a "show and tell" to introduce first-grade students to common water insect species they might find in their stream. High school students guided the young children as they examined preserved specimens and compared them with photograph enlargements provided in the professional development workshop by Missouri's Volunteer Water Quality Monitoring Program. First-grade students and their teacher, with the high school students and their teacher, were then ready to take a field trip to the stream to collect and study "water critters."

As soon as they got off the bus, first-grade students were instructed to sit down and use their senses to listen, see, smell, and touch the stream environment. Later, back in the classroom, they would individually record these sensations in an accordion book.

Four first-grade students were grouped with a high school student who guided students in safely wading into the creek, collecting macroinvertebrates using a kick net, then sorting and identifying the indicator species using a pictorial identification key from Missouri's Volunteer Water Quality Monitoring Manual (1998). High school students helped the younger students recognize unique characteristics of each species, such as size, shape, and movement. Finally, first-grade students observed the older students performing tests on stream water to measure amounts of dissolved oxygen, nitrates, pH, and water temperature. High school students

Aschoolwide Themes

Figure 1. Standards help shift emphases in our school science programs.

Standards	Less emphasis on:	More emphasis on:	Our program put emphasis on:
PROGRAM	Independent grade-level programs	Coordinated programs across grade levels	Water theme coordinates elementary through high school
	Textbook and lecture-driven curriculum	Variety of components, such as inquiry-oriented laboratories and field trips	Inquiry-oriented field and classroom investigations of local waterways
	Broad coverage of unconnected facts	Science related to social issues students encounter in everyday life	Science related to local water quality, conservation, and usage
	Science isolated from other subjects	Connecting science to other school subjects	Water studies including mathematics, social studies, and communication arts
TEACHING	Rigidly following curriculum	Selecting and adapting curriculum	Developing and implementing water-themed curriculum
	Lecture, text, and demonstration	Active and extended scientific inquiry	Active and prolonged inquiry into local water-quality issues
	Recitation of acquired knowledge	Opportunities for scientific discussion and debate	Intergenerational opportunities for discussion of ideas related to water-inquiry studies
	Maintaining responsibility and authority	Sharing responsibility for learning with students	Sharing responsibility for water-inquiry studies with students
	Supporting competition	Supporting a classroom community with cooperation, shared responsibility, and respect	Supporting a schoolwide community of water investigators through cooperation, shared responsibility, and respect
	Working alone	Working with other teachers to enhance science programs	Elementary, middle, and high school teachers and support staff working together in water studies
CONTENT	Studying subject disciplines for their own sake	Learning content in the context of inquiry and science in personal and social perspectives	Learning content through local water inquiry
	Separating science knowledge and processes	Integrating all aspects of science content	Integrating science content and processes through water inquiry
	Activities that demonstrate or verify science content	Activities that investigate and analyze science questions	Water studies that investigate local water quality
	Investigations confined to one class period	Investigations over extended periods of time	Water studies that contribute to an ongoing local database
	Emphasis on individual process skills	Using multiple process skills—manipulative, cognitive, and procedural	Using integrated process skills and technical field procedures to gather water-quality data
	Private communication of students' ideas and conclusions to teacher	Public communication of students' ideas and work to classmates	Reporting findings from water studies to local media, senior citizens, and stream bank landowners

Standards	Less emphasis on:	More emphasis on:	Our program put emphasis on
PROFESSIONAL DEVELOPMENT	Learning science by lecture and reading	Learning science through investigating and inquiry	Teachers increasing their science knowledge base through local water investigations
	Separation of science and teaching knowledge	Integration of science and teaching knowledge	Teachers improving their practice as they learn science through local water investigations
	Fragmented sessions	Long-term coherent plans	Teaching teams working with university science and education faculty for several years
	Teacher as an individual based in a classroom	Teacher as a member of a collegial professional community	Teachers as members of a collegial professional team facilitating cross-grade level water studies
	Teachers as targets of change	Teacher as source and facilitator	Teachers implementing change

explained each test in simplified terms, why it was being performed, and what the results meant.

Upon returning to the classroom, first-grade students each made an accordion book showing how they used their five senses during the field trip. (To make a 2″ x 3″ four-page accordion book: Take a sheet of paper and fold in half lengthwise, then fold in half widthwise. Now fold top flap back to the crease and turn the book over, then fold the top flap back to the crease on the other side.)

Students contributed to a class "Big Book" by drawing a picture and writing a sentence about what they saw, smelled, heard, or felt on their trip to the creek. They drew and wrote about their encounters with crayfish, water pennies and worms, their school bus ride, and the pungent smell of rotting leaves.

During three subsequent visits, high school students used photographs, illustrations, and information from the *Missouri Conservationist* (Trial 1992) to tell first-grade students the "life stories" of the aquatic macroinvertebrates first-grade students discovered in their stream. High school students also taught the younger students which aquatic macroinvertebrates were pollution tolerant, somewhat tolerant, or pollution

sensitive. First-grade students then understood how sampling aquatic macroinvertebrates helps determine whether the water in which many of them play is clean and safe. They admired their high school mentors, encouraging the mentors to assume their best behavior when working with their young fellow science investigators.

The first-grade students continued to study local aquatic macroinvertebrates by examining photograph enlargements and discussing characteristics of each including its shape; presence or absence of gills; and number and placement of legs, antennae, and tails. All students selected a macroinvertebrate, made drawings, wrote several descriptive sentences about the characteristics of their "water critter," and shared their work with the class.

Senior Citizens Provide History

Later in the semester, the first-grade students invited longtime community residents to talk to their class about changes the seniors had seen in the stream over the years. Students enjoyed listening to the older residents talk about changes in the appearance and uses of the creek. The children found out that the stream covered about the same area it had 50 years ago, but it had once had deep swimming holes and was deeper and colder. One 80-year-old neighbor told wonderful stories of catching really big fish when he was a boy growing up along the stream.

Through class discussion with their teacher and guests, first-grade students realized that fertilizer, insecticide, and weed killer spread on lawns, gardens, and farm fields; residue from cars in parking lots; and litter from streets, sidewalks, and playgrounds could run off into their stream. They learned about the hazards of throwing picnic leftovers or litter into the water while boating or fishing.

A sense of community was strengthened as students and seniors shared mutual concern for and increased resolve to take care of their shared natural resource. Students reminded their parents to be careful about chemicals applied to the lawn and to never use their stream as a trash can. Children picked up bags of litter from their playground to prevent the litter from running off toward their stream less than a mile away. Children wrote and drew pictures in their journals about these experiences, showing what they had learned (Assessment Standard C).

Science Club Dives In

Our school has one academic extracurricular club—the elementary science club. Club members in fourth through sixth grades adopted the water theme with the goal of monitoring and keeping our creek clean (Content Standard F). The club met once a month with the middle school science teacher and the librarian who has a background in water studies.

Initially, club members learned how to measure water quality through chemical testing, macroinvertebrate sampling, observing and recording the features of the stream bank and riparian corridor, and measuring stream flow.

The club regularly performed stream-monitoring activities, such as collecting and reporting water-quality data and cleaning up litter along the waterway. Students reported club activities and findings by mailing data to a state agency database that contains baseline water-quality data from across the state.

High school students often provided extra help to the elementary club by offering streamside assistance. One high school student was grouped with each team of three fifth-grade club members to supervise chemical water testing procedures for accuracy, record water-quality data, and help collect and identify macroinvertebrates for a reference collection. High school students and elementary club members worked side by side in litter cleanup as a community service. Local and regional newspapers printed feature stories showing club members at work on the creek and reported on students' pursuits to find out more about the local water cycle through visits to a drinking water treatment plant, wastewater treatment plant, and power plant.

Making a Splash with Book Bags

The school librarian contributed to the water theme in several ways. Her unique combination of professional development in water studies and her role as librarian made her instrumental in assisting with student fieldwork. Her field training gained while participating in water activities with the schoolwide team enabled her to provide supervision for all field data collection activities, and her flexible schedule allowed her to accompany elementary, middle, and high school students to the stream. Therefore, she served as a leader when teachers took students to the streamside "classroom."

In addition, the librarian greatly increased our collection of library resource materials related to the water theme by reading reviews from library professional journals and browsing bookstores to select fiction and nonfiction reference books for all grade levels. Students at all levels were able to research water topics using a wide range of current print and other resources. Kindergarten students in particular benefited from her efforts. The librarian incorporated the water theme into a Pond and River book bag program that encouraged parents and students to spend time reading and interacting with each other.

Initially, literature for our book bags and age-appropriate activities related to the literature were identified. Each bag, made of heavy fabric printed in a fish or water motif, contained one to three water theme–related books, an introductory letter, a list of the contents in each bag, and activity pages. The bags contained all materials necessary for completing the activities, such as crayons, blunt scissors, and glue sticks. Items to be returned were marked with return labels. Also, a brief evaluation form was included for parents to provide feedback about the book bags.

Families were encouraged to spend 15 to 20 minutes several times a week reading the books and completing the activities included in the bags. Kindergarten students could check out book bags once a week. When books, nonconsumable supplies, and the evaluation form were returned to the school the following week, other students eagerly checked out the book bags. The Pond and Stream book bags allowed kindergarten students and their families to learn more about natural water in general and our stream in particular.

Standards Saturate Water Theme

Teachers reported that the schoolwide water theme helped them implement the science Standards as well as mathematics and communication arts standards by providing a local, real-life, easily accessible focus for curriculum development efforts across grade levels and disciplines. Together, teachers incorporated Standards-aligned science content in an inquiry format. More importantly, the group developed a synergistic sense of cooperation and collegiality across grade levels and disciplines.

The water theme is an ongoing process as the original team and university faculty invite current and new faculty to work alongside them in designing and implementing water studies. Team members and their students share their time, expertise, and materials and have fun as they encourage faculty to improve education across the disciplines through Standards-aligned water studies. Teachers agree they are more accountable to each other and welcome the opportunity to model respect, cooperation, and collaboration among each other for their students. They are proud to be successfully shifting their teaching from traditional to contemporary models of science education by saturating their curriculum with a water theme.

Roberta Aram is an associate professor in an elementary teacher preparation program and teaches science methods courses at Southwest Missouri State University in Springfield; Mary Brake teaches second grade at Billings (Missouri) Elementary School; and David Smith teaches biology, chemistry, and environmental science at Billings High School. Gina Wood is the middle school science teacher and Pat Hamilton is the librarian in the Billings School District.

Funding for this project was provided by Missouri's Eisenhower Funds for Professional Development, Missouri's Department of Conservation, Missouri's Department of Natural Resources, The Watershed Committee of the Ozarks, City Utilities of Springfield, Drury College, and participating school districts.

Resources

Andrews, E. 1995. *Educating young people about water: A guide to goals and resources.* ERIC Clearinghouse for Science and Mathematics and Environmental Education. Columbus, OH.

Aquatic Project WILD: Aquatic education activity guide. 1995. Bethesda, MD: Council for Environmental Education.

Aram, R. J., and Roy, P. 1994. *Increasing science literacy through watershed monitoring.* Grant proposal submitted to the Missouri Coordinating Board for Higher Education. Jefferson City, MO.

Brophy, J., and Alleman, J. 1996. *Powerful social studies for elementary students.* New York: Harcourt Brace.

Edelstein, K. 1996. *Pond and stream safari.* Ithaca, NY: Cornell University Media Services Resource Center.

Missouri's Volunteer Water Quality Monitoring Manual. 1998. Jefferson City, MO: Department of Natural Resources.

National Research Council. 1996. *National Science Education Standards.* Washington, DC: National Academy Press.

Reid, G.K. 1967. *The golden guide to pond life.* New York: Golden Press.

Trial, L. 1992. Life within the water. *Missouri Conservationist, 52*(9), 12–17.

Watercourse and Western Regional Environmental Education Council. 1995. Project WET: Water Education for Teachers Curriculum Activity Guide. Bozeman, MT: Montana State University.

Internet

Annenberg/CPB Math and Science Project. 1998. Increasing Elementary Science Literacy through Water Education in *The guide to math & science reform,* an online resource for the education community.
www.learner.org/theguide

Project-Based and Interdisciplinary Science Units

B

Our Growing Planet

By Elizabeth Lener

Perhaps no one issue affects us all so directly as human population growth. No person in this country is immune to longer lines at the grocery store, to traffic jams, or to the heightened pressures on the natural environment that surrounds us. However, these impacts are trivial compared to those felt by people in other parts of our planet.

The United States in the year 2000 had a population of 270 million and is expected to grow to 335 million by the year 2025 (Population Reference Bureau). This is equivalent to adding a New York City to the world every month of every year. Although the U.S. growth rate of 0.9 percent is below the world's growth rate of 1.5 percent, it is higher than that of most industrialized nations.

Resources usage is phenomenal in the United States. For example, Americans constitute less than 5 percent of the world's population, but they use nearly 25 percent of the world's resources. We are responsible for 23 percent of the world's carbon dioxide emissions, and we own 25 percent of the world's cars. The facts all seem to point to the same conclusion. To ensure a safe and happy future for ourselves and our neighbors around the world, we need to examine the choices we make and evaluate their impact on our natural environment and the people in it.

What better time to introduce these ideas than in elementary school? Children are naturally curious and passionate about taking care of the world around them. Our science department chose to use this topic as the focal point of our schoolwide theme entitled People and the Planet (Wasserman 1996). I put the unit together, and each teacher modified activities slightly for his or her own classroom. Approximately 360 first-through sixth-grade students participated in the unit. First- and second-grade students met twice a week for 40 minutes, and third- through sixth-grade students met four times a week for 40 minutes. Students conducted activities culled from various resources.

The unique blending of experiences was one of the reasons for the unit's success. The unit had three main parts: human population growth over time; the impact of population growth on Earth and its people; and projects aimed at making positive changes within the local community.

Human Population Growth

We began the unit by figuring the population growth over the last 500 years. Fourth- through sixth-grade students did an AIMS activity called Global Gains (Weibe 1996). The activity dealt with the concept of doubling time. Students used actual population data from the years 1500 through 2000 to make projections about when

they thought the population might double again. As they graphed the population growth, they were able to see the pattern of exponential growth, as well as predict the time it would take our population to double.

Third-grade students created a wall-sized population graph. They put a timeline on the wall outside of the science classroom. They were shocked to see that the world population grew from 500 million people (five squares) in 1500 to 6 billion people (60 squares) by the year 2000.

Many students had difficulty understanding the size of numbers like millions and billions, so we had students participate in activities to help them grasp the magnitude of these numbers. Measuring a Million (Wasserman 1996) taught fourth- through sixth-grade students how to use their measuring skills to solve the problem of how tall a stack of 1,000,000 and 1,000,000,000 sheets of paper would be. Students were amazed to learn that a billion sheets of paper would stand 130 km high.

First- through third-grade students did an activity that allowed children to visualize big numbers like millions and billions (see box, "Seeing a Million Stars"). These activities provided a way for students to imagine how much space 1,000,000 people need.

What a Crowd!

Learning about how the population has grown would be meaningless unless we also talk about how those growing numbers affect everyday activities.

The population unit also included several activities dealing with crowding. In the "Population Circle" (Wasserman and Scullard 1994), students explored how crowded the world is becoming. After marking a circle on the classroom floor with masking tape, two students—each representing 250,000,000 people—stand in the circle. Each second the game is played represents one year. The data for the population numbers are found in "Population Circle," in *Counting on People*. The activity continues until 24 very crowded people are standing in the circle.

The "Crowding Can Be Seedy" (Wasserman and Scullard 1994) activity allowed students to conduct experiments with radish seeds. The class divided into three groups. Group one planted five radish seeds in a dirt-filled cup; group two planted 25 seeds in their cup; and group three planted 50 seeds in their cup. After observing the seeds' growth over several weeks, the effects of overcrowding were quite evident. Students observed that the cups with the most seeds did not support healthy plants.

Food Facts

Populations cannot grow indefinitely without consequences; however, the topic of carrying capacity proved to be a sobering one for our stu-

---

Seeing a Million Stars
(Wasserman 1996)

First- through third-grade students

- Draw 10 stars on a piece of paper and make 100 copies.

- Have students tape these sheets all around the room to see what 1,000 stars look like.

- Discuss how many rooms would be needed for a 1,000,000 and 1,000,000,000 stars.

Hunger Banquet (Wasserman and Scullard 1994)

Fourth- through sixth-grade students

- Buy a myriad of tasty foods that students will enjoy—anything from donuts to chips.

- Set the food on the counter in front of the room.

- Put a menu on the board listing food prices.

- Set up two large tables in the room: on one table represent a first-world country by placing a tablecloth and vase of flowers; leave the other table plain to represent a second-world country.

- Hand students envelopes with fake money and an identity card as they come into class.

- Inform students that they each represent one of three places: a first-, second-, or third-world country.

- Instruct third-world country students (the majority of students) to sit on the floor in the back of the room, while allowing their first- and second-world neighbors to sit at the two tables.

- Give first-world country students $40 to spend on food.

- Give second-world country students $8 to spend.

- Give third-world students $3 to spend on food.

- Make false visas to sell at the food market as well.

- Charge second-world students $1 per visa, and charge third-world students $7 per visa to the second world and $9 per visa to the first world.

First- through third-grade students

- Have each student choose a colored piece of paper as they come into class.

- Inform students that each color represents a different type of country.

- Separate students based on the colors of the papers they are holding.

- Give first-world students an opportunity to eat a tremendous variety of foods.

- Offer second-world students the same foods, but allow them only a certain amount.

- Provide third-world students saltine crackers only.

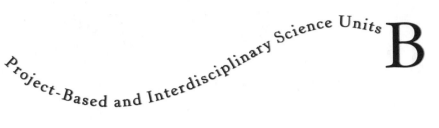

dents. Project WILD, an interdisciplinary, supplementary environment and conservation education program for K–12 educators, has an activity that deals with this topic in an active way. In "How Many Bears" (Project WILD 1992) students compete for an important limited resource—food. The goal of the game is survival—"bears" should try to collect as much "food" (construction paper squares) as they can in each round. As students conduct the activity, they soon realize that the amount of food cannot support all of the bears. Some bears do not make it past the first round. After each round, we discussed what happened and how it is similar to what happens naturally to animal populations.

Without a doubt, the most fascinating part of our unit was a "Hunger Banquet"(Wasserman and Scullard 1994) that focused on the unequal distribution of wealth and resources in the world today (see box, "Hunger Banquet"). There was much uproar as fourth- through sixth-grade students realized how the activity would work. Some of our classes figured out ways to send people to the first world to get food and others did not. Some of the third-world groups pooled their money to buy a visa for one student. The student with the visa would travel to the first world and ask for money and food. That student would then bring back the money and food to share. All of our classes had heartfelt discussions about the importance of sharing with others and responsibly using resources. These discussions continued at home, in carpools, and in classrooms during the days that followed.

We modified the Hunger Banquet for third- and fourth-grade students. The third-world students were given saltines only, while the first-world students received a variety of foods (see box, "Hunger Banquet"). Second-world students

Although children can't make choices that affect population numbers, they can do a great deal to lessen the environmental impact. We worked hard to find activities that would allow students to feel empowered.

received smaller amounts, but they still had more than enough. This is an extremely emotional activity for students, especially when they realize that they are not going to get food at the end of the class. The learning that comes from the activity, however, is immeasurable. This activity generated a great deal of frustration and sometimes jealousy. Many students felt the activity was not fair. We used these feelings as a springboard for discussion on the distribution of wealth and goods and how this distribution is not fair.

If we were not born in the United States, how would our lives be different? The students who were in the first world did not feel the same suffering as their classmates, but they were often uncomfortable with their status. They often tried to help their classmates in need. When we

Timber (Wasserman 1996)

- Divide students into groups of four.

- Give each group 120 wooden craft sticks in a coffee can to represent trees.

- Assign students to be: the forest manager, the logger, the forest, and the timer.

- Give the forest manager 32 wooden craft sticks and give the forest the coffee can of 120 sticks.

- Tell the timer to begin. Every 15 seconds, have the forest manager give the forest a tree.

- Have the loggers take away trees at the end of each minute, according to the population size. For example, at the end of the first minute, the logger takes one tree; at the end of the second minute, the logger takes two trees; at the end of the third minute, the logger takes four trees. After eight minutes, there will not be enough trees to keep up with the population's demand.

- Provide students with new exponentially growing population numbers throughout the activity.

- Discuss how many trees are needed and how they need to be planted exponentially to keep up with the population growth.

- Discuss the different use of trees.

- Brainstorm ways to cut down on the number of trees needed.

discussed everyone's feelings, it helped everyone to see different viewpoints.

Our Natural Resources

We then focused on how the increased population has an impact on the natural environment. By studying endangered species in our state, we learned that habitat destruction is one of the leading causes of this problem. Students played a game called "Timber" (Wasserman 1996) in which they acted as loggers and forest managers and discovered what happened to a forest over time as human population grew (see box, "Timber"). At the end they realized that the forest cannot support the demand and watched as the trees disappeared.

For homework, students also tabulated their daily water usage and were amazed to learn the quantity of water they consumed, both directly and indirectly. We gave students handouts from the "Water, Water Everywhere" activity (Wasserman 1996). It listed the amount of water used for many household functions and goods. For example, brushing teeth used on average 19 liters of water per day. Students used a tally sheet to list their water usage for a day. We evaluated students based on their level of detail and the accuracy of their mathematical calculations.

Working Toward Positive Change

After studying this topic for several weeks, students were ready to do something that would work toward positive change. Although children can't make choices that affect population numbers, they can do a great deal to lessen the environmental impact. As teachers, we worked hard to find activities that would allow students to be active and feel empowered. We also wanted to concentrate on local issues that affected our children. For example, we focused on cutting down the amount of garbage we produced at lunch. We called it "Pollution Prevention Lunch." Our first- through fourth-grade students brought lunches to school. Together, we looked at ways to bring lunches to school that would produce the least amount of waste possible. Students were encouraged to bring in reusable food and beverage containers and silverware. To cut down on nonreusable items such as paper napkins, we recycled some fabric scraps and turned them into cloth napkins by cutting them into squares with pinking shears. Students used fabric crayons to design environmental pictures on their napkins, which they brought in with their lunches each day. Students took home their cloth napkins each day and laundered them. Making the cloth napkin encouraged them to bring other cloth napkins from home as well. All of the science teachers went to each class and tallied the total number of positive items each class brought in for their Pollution Prevention Lunch. Two of our teachers made trophies out of old Tupperware containers. The trophies were then presented to the winning class.

Students conducted other conservation efforts as well. Third- and fourth-grade students made cards to remind people to turn off all of the light switches and faucets in the building. As a class, fifth- and sixth-grade students chose issues to focus on. One class wanted to educate everyone about using less paper, so the students wrote reminder cards for all of the paper towel dispensers in the bathrooms. They also wrote an article about saving and recycling paper that went home to each family.

Several students even wrote a short play to perform for the lower school. The play dramatized a situation in which two students were washing their hands in the bathroom and used many extra paper towels. Another student came in and announced that she was the "paper towel patrol" and that people should only use one towel. The students then related facts about the amount of paper Americans use and the impacts that using less and recycling can have on the environment.

Another class created an informative webpage for our school website instructing the school community about saving fuel by properly inflating automobile tires. Another class started a "stop junk mail" campaign. The students provided the address for stopping junk mail on our website as well as facts about paper use in the United States and recycling. Students also made "stop junk mail" posters for our school.

Assessment and Beyond

Students were evaluated throughout the unit based on their participation in the activities and their level of input in class discussions that followed. Fourth- through sixth-grade students were given several quizzes on the concepts we covered throughout the unit including exponential growth, carrying capacity, and the impacts of population growth. Fifth- and sixth-grade students received a grade based on the level of detail and accuracy of mathematical calculations on their water-usage homework assignment. The posters and signs for light switches were not formally graded for younger students, but they were graded based on their level of quality and detail for fifth- and sixth-grade students.

We knew the project had greatly affected students when, several weeks after we finished the theme and returned to the regular curriculum, students began participating in a new project. A Brownie Girl Scout troop began collecting coats for people who did not have enough clothes to stay warm during the winter. All of the science teachers were heartened when the students said that the idea had come from what they had learned during our population study. Even one person can make the difference in our ever-growing world. In addition to the learning that took place, this unit helped students become more conscious of their decisions and to feel that they could be active participants in determining the future of their planet.

Elizabeth Lener is a science teacher at Norwood School in Bethesda, MD.

Resources

Print

Wasserman, P., and A. Scullard. 1994. *Counting on people*. Washington, DC: Zero Population Growth.

Wasserman, P. 1996. *People and the planet*. Washington, DC: Zero Population Growth.

How Many Bears? *Project WILD*. 1992. Boulder, CO: Western Regional Environmental Education Council.

Weibe, A. 1996. Global gains. *AIMS*. September: p. 10–13.

Internet

Population Reference Bureau
www.prb.org/
Alliance to Save Energy
www.ase.org/

To write for information about stopping junk mail: DMA Mail Preference Service, P.O. Box 9008, Farmingdale, NY 11735-9008.

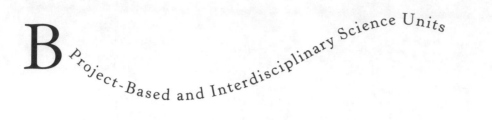

Curriculum with a Common Thread

By Maureen M. McMahon, Susan P. O'Hara, William G. Holliday, Bernadette B. McCormack, and Elizabeth M. Gibson

Imagine studying the history and technology of the Civil War through photographs taken at that time and learning about the chemistry and mathematics of photography by building cameras. That's what fifth-grade students do as a part of Project WRITE (World Resources for Integrated Thematic Education), a science-based integrated curriculum their teachers built especially for them. In four two-hour sessions each week, Project WRITE engages students in project-based collaborative learning opportunities. Science is at the heart of each unit, but literacy skills are central to each unit's outcome.

The Jigsaw-Expert Approach

As a team of enthusiastic fifth-grade teachers at a rural northern California elementary school, we were concerned with the growing emphasis on standards-based accountability for students and teachers and the increasing focus on language arts and mathematics in our school day. Certainly reading, writing, and mathematics skills are important components of a student's success, but how does science fit into our children's school life? What if you could meet literacy requirements while engaging students in quality science learning?

We wanted to create integrated project-based units where science was central for learning across the disciplines. There was one possible problem—none of us had an extensive science background. Our team was composed of fifth-grade teachers with varying skills, teaching practices, and experience. There were two new teachers, three teachers with 7 to 10 years of experience, and one teacher with more than 15 years experience in the classroom.

However, as creative elementary teachers, we compensated for what any one teacher lacked individually by using a jigsaw-expert approach in developing and implementing the curriculum. Each of us selected a science grade-level expectation from the district-mandated science curriculum standards and built a five-week integrated unit around our chosen science topic while weaving in fifth-grade social studies, mathematics, and language arts curricula. We felt comfortable knowing we would be responsible for learning and teaching only one area of science throughout the year because it allowed us to select and design highly creative and engaging learning environments and activities.

We all selected district standards according to our interests. Everyone on the team was committed to inclusion of all district standards within the total of the six integrated units. The only other requirements were that each unit must include all content areas, a fifth-grade core literature book, and a unique writing challenge. Following the initial planning, the units were also aligned with the *National Science Education Standards* (NRC 1996) (See boxes).

Figure 1 shows how Project WRITE is organized and how each unit integrated science, mathematics, social studies, and language arts. The ovals in the center indicate the science-content base of each unit; projecting from each are the integrated topics from other disciplines.

Each unit was taught for five weeks. After one five-week unit ended, each class of 30 children moved to the next fifth-grade teacher until the students experienced all six units. All of the fifth-grade students experienced complex, motivational, integrated units throughout the school year.

The following chronicles the adventure the

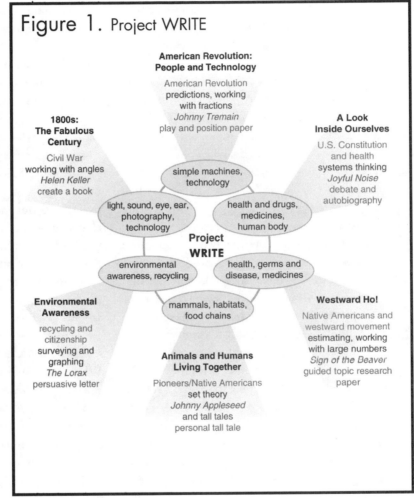

Figure 1. Project WRITE

fifth-grade children experienced as they journeyed through each of the six integrated science-based units.

American Revolution: People and Technology

In this unit students enter a classroom littered with toaster parts, old typewriters, and computer components. The teacher tells them they will be studying the American Revolution, a war in which simple technologies and machines had a great impact. Students' faces light up when they realize they will be able to tinker with real gadgets as they study the physics of simple machines and the mathematics of fractions.

Playing with pulleys and inclined planes, students learn that simple machines are machines with few or no moving parts and that they help make tasks easier. Students discuss the six simple machines—lever, pulley, wheel and axle, inclined plane, wedge, and screw. As they drag plastic bags full of sand across different surfaces and at different angles, they learn about gravity, force, friction, and cause and effect. Groups of students build a wedge using a wooden wedge and a rectangular block and discover that the wedge makes physical work much easier. The children also construct a lever from a ruler and a pencil. They then compare lifting an object by hand to lifting it using a lever.

In small groups students disassemble toasters, typewriters, computers, and printers into the parts that constitute a simple machine. The students take a large sheet of paper with the names of all simple machines written on it and tape the corresponding parts to the appropriate headings. Sometimes students must determine how something works before being able to categorize it as a simple machine. Then each group shares the information with the class explaining its reasoning. Discussions arise about the number of parts that make up a whole.

As part of this unit, students read *Johnny Tremain* (Forbes 1962), a fictional account of a young boy during the American Revolution. They also read *My Brother Sam Is Dead* (Collier and Collier 1989), the story of a boy whose family is divided, with his brother fighting on the Patriot side and his father taking the Loyalist side. Students engage in an activity called "question the author," a literacy technique used to ensure students are comprehending the story. In addition, students read different historical accounts of the American Revolution. Students view the structure of war through the technology of simple machines and examine both the positive and negative effects of technology.

The unit culminates as teams of students write and perform a play that showcases science, history, mathematics, and language arts content and processes. For example, one group of students wrote a play about a family who lived during the American Revolution. The central character was a young boy fascinated with gadgets and whose brother had to fight in the war. Because of his interest in gadgets such as cannons, the boy wanted to fight in the war with his brother, yet was afraid that his brother would die.

A Look Inside Ourselves

When students move to the next unit, they investigate the health issues surrounding drug use and abuse. Students study the positive and negative effects of drugs on the human body, how drugs are produced, how drugs are controlled, and issues surrounding drug abuse in society.

The project begins when students interview their parents, grandparents, guardians, or other significant older adults, such as aunts and uncles, about notable times in their young lives. With this information the students meld their own memories of their parents and grandparents with their own personal events through a journal-writing exercise. This information-gathering phase leads to rich student discussions of self-image, peer relations, stereotypes, and societal problems, all based on student anecdotes.

Students first learn about themselves as individuals and then begin a journey into thinking of themselves as citizens of their local commu-

Project-Based and Interdisciplinary Science Units

nity and then as citizens of the United States. This provides a natural link to social studies. The Bill of Rights is studied and students look critically at controversial issues. From here, students investigate laws regarding personal freedoms and choices. The teacher facilitates examination of complex legal and scientific issues surrounding drug use and abuse. More science and social studies mesh as students research the legalization of drugs currently banned by the Food and Drug Administration. Students begin to realize that complex knowledge of science, society, and the law is necessary to truly understand many citizens' rights and responsibilities issues.

Mathematics is then integrated into the unit as students study the concepts of *systems thinking,* which refers to the notion that nothing exists alone. All knowledge is relative to other knowledge and processes.

Joyful Noise: Poems for Two Voices (Fleischman 1992) is included in the unit as a base from which to discuss insects' important role in the production of many medicines. It may seem odd to study insects when studying drugs and the law, but the lives of many insects, the foods they eat, and their digestive enzymes are fundamental in the production of many important medicines. Additionally, the complicated rhyming patterns and entrances and exits of the poems' two voices are used to highlight alertness and dexterity issues that arise with drug use and abuse. Students match cadences, coordinate the time they enter the reading, and bring rhythmic beauty to poetry. The teacher then leads a discussion about the difficulties in achieving success with multiple readers of *Joyful Noise,* even under normal circumstances.

The culminating group event is a student-managed debate on the legalization for medicinal use of certain FDA-banned drugs. Students form teams and have a position from which to argue. They gather their own information, write argument statements based on cited research, and practice debating skills and strategies.

Westward Ho!

The teacher begins this unit by asking students to brainstorm all the diseases they have heard about. They excitedly list more than 50 diseases ranging from scurvy to a rare blood disease that one student's brother has been fighting since birth.

With teacher guidance, students talk about diseases based on whether they were historically a threat or are still a threat. The teacher asks questions such as "What diseases seem to be most prevalent today?" "Do you know of any diseases that threatened people's lives in the past, but are no longer a threat?" This introduces the topic of American Indians and the many diseases that thinned their populations—some almost to extinction—during the westward expansion in the United States beginning in the mid-1800s.

As the unit progresses, science, social studies, mathematics, and language arts are woven into one unit. Diseases and germs are the science core. The social studies content enters this unit through the book *The Sign of the Beaver* (Speare 1983); through historical accounts and diaries of the pioneers' crossing of the American West; and through American Indian stories of these trying times, which are presented by guest speakers from the Native American Museum in Sacramento. So many new angles from which to view life in America as pioneers moved west.

After much reading and discussion students choose a topic within the scope of the American westward movement about which to write a final research paper. The paper must have a science theme. Some of the topics students have selected are "A Single Disease Wreaked Havoc on an American Indian Tribe," "Health and the Westward Movement," "American Indian Medicines," and "Smoking and the Preservation of Food."

While students work on research papers, they study alternative medicines commonly used by American Indians, diseases, germs, and medicines. Teams of students research medicinal ceremonies from American Indian tribes and design and create medicine masks. The students share their research with each other while watching a videotape of ceremonial events of an Apache tribe in the Southwest. Videotapes like these are available through the Bureau of Indian Affairs, 1849 C St., NW, Washington, DC 20240-0001.

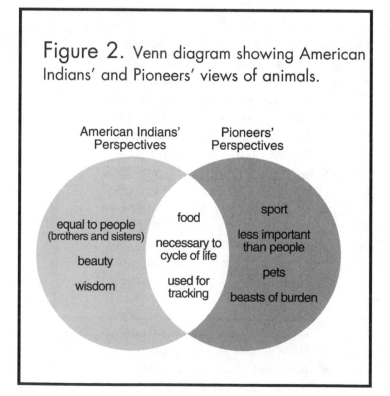

Figure 2. Venn diagram showing American Indians' and Pioneers' views of animals.

American Indians' Perspectives

Pioneers' Perspectives

equal to people (brothers and sisters)

beauty

wisdom

food

necessary to cycle of life

used for tracking

sport

less important than people

pets

beasts of burden

Animals and Humans Living Together

The cohabitation of humans and animals forms the basis of another unit. Students study animal classification and explore the similarities and differences between humans and other animals. Students discuss early American pioneers, comparing American Indians' perceptions of nature and animals to those of European settlers. As cultural similarities and differences are identified, students use mathematical techniques of Venn diagrams and set theory to discuss and display their understandings of the complex relationships (see Figure 2).

In this unit teams of four or five students choose to study an animal or group of animals that lives in the continental United States. Using defining characteristics chosen by the class, each team researches and draws pictures of their animal. Students share information and resources to better understand their animal's characteristics, habitat, eating habits, and basic survival traits.

To add a language arts component to this science-based unit, children read folk tales and tall tales from both European and American Indian authors that help build a cultural understanding of the people involved in the westward movement in the 1880s.

Near the end of the unit students create and refine their personal tall tale. Some students have written tall tales about events that happened in their lives, while other students have used a Paul Bunyan model and invented larger-than-life characters and feats.

Finally, in the tradition of oral storytelling, students relate their tall tales to their peers.

Environmental Awareness

Environmental issues within the community are the central focus of the next unit. To begin, the teacher reads *The Lorax* (1971) by Dr. Seuss to

Using the science-based integrated units addresses the following National Science Education Standards' teaching standards:

- B—Teachers of science guide and facilitate learning.
- C—Teachers of science engage in ongoing assessment of their teaching and students' learning.
- D—Teachers of science design and manage learning environments that provide students the time, space, and resources needed for learning science.
- E—Teachers of science develop communities of science learners that reflect the intellectual rigor of scientific inquiry and the attitudes and social values conducive to science learning.
- F—Teachers of science actively participate in the ongoing planning and development of the school science program.

introduce students to environmental issues. She also invites the town's recycling coordinator to class to familiarize students with issues and vocabulary surrounding the environment. The volunteer talks about recycling and the importance of maintaining a healthy environment. He discusses what materials are biodegradable and asks students to think about what they throw away and whether any of those things are biodegradable.

Mathematics enters the learning setting as students design and conduct recycling surveys of people living around them. The results of their survey are then included in a persuasive letter that students write to a company regarding the company's recycling habits. The students get the following directions for the project:

"You are to choose one question to ask 25 people. The question must relate to the topic of your persuasive letter. When you have completed your survey, graph your results showing each answer in a different color. Then write at least five true statements based on your results. These will be included in your persuasive letter."

Students can survey 25 people of their choice—friends, relatives, and other community members. Students collect, collate, record, graph, and analyze all survey results. One group of students wrote to a fast-food chain about their plastic containers. Their survey question was "When you go to this restaurant do you always put your plastic containers in a recycling bin?" Another group wrote to a jelly bean company regarding the dyes they use in making the candy.

With their new environmental knowledge, small groups of students choose a topic and then prepare and teach a mini-lesson to second-grade students. Peer teaching leads students to greater understanding of the science and social studies behind environmental laws, citizens' feelings about the environment, and individuals' responsibilities for care of the environment.

During the unit students also build and maintain a class worm bin, which is set up in the classroom as a focal point for environmental discussions. This project demonstrates how simple it is to compost organic matter rather than throw it away.

To build a worm bin we use

- a sturdy, shallow plastic box with drainage holes and a tight-fitting lid (use a utility knife to make the holes)
- four (10 cm × 20 cm × 2.5 cm) wooden blocks

Relevant National Science Education Standards' content standards for each science-based unit.

American Revolution
B—Physical Science
F—Science in Personal and Social Perspectives
G—History and Nature of Science

A Look Inside Ourselves
C—Life Science
F—Science in Personal and Social Perspectives

Westward Ho!
C—Life Science
F—Science in Personal and Social Perspectives
G—History and Nature of Science

Animals and Humans Living Together
C—Life Science
G—History and Nature of Science

Environmental Awareness
C—Life Science
F—Science in Personal and Social Perspectives

1800s: The Fabulous Century
B—Physical Science
E—Science and Technology
F—Science in Personal and Social Perspectives
G—History and Nature of Science

- newspaper
- red worms (available at bait and tackle stores and garden or landscaping stores)

The teacher explains that the box is shallow because the worms need to live near the surface in order to breathe and that the bedding used must provide the worms with a balanced diet and a damp place to live. To engage the stu-dents, the teacher leads them in a discussion by asking "What do you think we might use as bedding?" Students usually suggest leaves because they are damp and would provide food. In reality, we use moistened newspaper that is torn into 2.5–5 cm strips.

The students place the box on the wooden blocks to allow air circulation and then fill it three-quarters full of damp news-paper strips. The teacher places the red worms on top of the fresh bedding. Then the teacher asks the students what they think the worms should be fed. As the students make suggestions, the teacher writes a list on the board. Students generally list vegetable scraps, grains, fruit rinds and seeds, bread, coffee grinds, and tea bags.

Once each week, students dig a shallow hole in the bedding, dump food waste in it, and bury the waste. Students bury the food in a different spot each time to encourage the worms to move around. At the end of five weeks the volume of the bin has decreased and the bedding looks more like compost.

1800s: The Fabulous Century

In the next unit students learn about the be-ginnings of photography, read about the his-tory of the period, and look at pictures from the Civil War—the first major war from which photographs exist. Discussions of pho-tography bring students to ask questions about light, sound, and the eye and ear.

In the initial demonstration, the teacher cov-ers the classroom windows with cardboard. He draws a camera and an eye on the board and la-bels their parts while explaining how the two items are similar. The teacher discusses the pro-gression of photography technology and tells students that the word _camera_ comes from the

French *camera obscura,* or dark room. Then he says a Spanish sentence using the word "room," which is *recamera,* and asks the class why they think this is. One student answered "Because a camera is like a room and the window is like the lens."

The teacher then draws a diagram on the board of a cube representing a room and a hole representing a window (see Figure 3). Adjacent to the cube he draws a school. He then draws lines that come from the top, middle, and center of the school through the small hole and onto the opposite side of the cube. The line from the top of the school goes to the bottom of the wall and the line from the bottom of the school goes to the top of the wall. The teacher explains that these lines represent light beams and that this is how a dark room can be used to create an image.

Next, the teacher turns off the lights and pulls down a white screen in the center of the room. He removes a piece of cloth from a small opening in the cardboard. A blurred, upside-down image of the school courtyard appears on the screen. The students gasp with surprise and excitement, "That is so cool! I didn't realize that that would happen."

Students are then asked what they notice about the image. The students generally point out that it is blurry and upside-down. The teacher demonstrates that as the opening is made smaller, the image becomes clearer. The class discusses how this works. The teacher explains that it works like the shutter-aperture technology of a camera—as the hole is made smaller, less light comes through which makes the image clearer.

Mathematics is integrated when students measure angles of reflection and refraction and estimate the speed of light and sound. Groups

Books for Science-Based Integrated Units

Davidson, M. 1997. *Helen Keller.* New York: Scholastic Paperbacks. ISBN 0590-42-4041.

Demuth, P. *Johnny Appleseed.* 1996. New York: Grosset and Dunlap. ISBN 0448-41-130X.

Fleischman, P. 1992. *Joyful noise: Poems for two voices.* New York: HarperCollins Children's Books. ISBN 0060-21-8533.

Forbes, E. 1962. *Johnny Tremain.* New York: Bantam Books. ISBN 0440-22-8271.

Seuss Geisel, T. 1971. *The Lorax.* New York: Random House. ISBN 0394-82-3370.

Speare, E.G. 1983. *The sign of the beaver.* New York: Bantam Books. ISBN 0440-22-8301.

of students perform various 15-minute experiments at workstations. In one experiment students look at their eyes in the mirror and sketch and label both the external and internal parts of the eye. They then look at a light while covering one eye with their hand for a few seconds. They pull their hand away quickly and look at each other's pupils and record any changes. Students also color a simple flag and stare at it for one minute. They then stare at a white piece of paper and note what happens and try to explain it.

Sound is also explored throughout the unit. The teacher asks students to think of something that happens in weather where you see something and then hear the sound later. The students come up with thunder and lightning. The students are guided through the discussion by questions such as "Why do you see the lightning and hear the thunder later?" Students eventually begin to discuss how fast sound and light travel. By the end, they understand that light

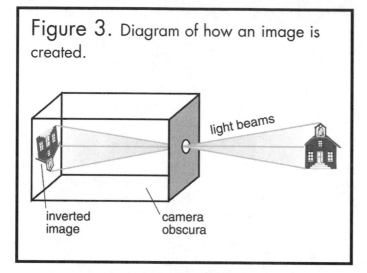

Figure 3. Diagram of how an image is created.

travels faster than sound so you can see it before you can hear it.

Students read *Helen Keller* (Davidson 1997) to learn about what it is like to be blind and deaf. This leads to a discussion of the senses and how we rely on them and ties into what students have learned about the eye and ear. While discussing the book, the teacher invites a blind middle school student to visit the class to talk about his daily life. Students ask him questions like "Do other kids tease you?" "How did it feel to be born blind?" "Can you read Braille?" When the student leaves, the class discusses what they have learned.

As light and sound are investigated in more detail, other inventions of the late 1800s are showcased, such as the phonograph, telegraph, and telephone. The teacher uses student excitement to springboard into a challenge project where each student researches an invention, event, or interesting person from the 19th century. Then, with teacher and peer guidance and the use of classroom computers, each student creates a book from his or her research. Students

have produced books on topics such as a biography of Abraham Lincoln, electromagnetism, and the beginnings of the Civil War. A class database is used for the students to log in their work and retrieve teacher feedback.

Assessment

Each unit is project based and every project has a performance and writing components that are assessed. The students are highly engaged throughout each five-week unit, but not every piece of student work is collected. The students are encouraged to build on what they learn and collect what they need to meet the unit's project goals.

What a learning adventure each student experienced by the end of the year. With Project WRITE every fifth-grade student received quality, meaningful science learning opportunities integrated into project-based challenges throughout the year. How simple a model, how great a success!

Maureen M. McMahon is an associate professor of science education at California State University, Long Beach; Susan P. O'Hara is an assistant professor of technology education at California State University, Sacramento; William G. Holliday is a professor of science education at the University of Maryland; Bernadette B. McCormack is at the University of Georgia; and Elizabeth M. Gibson is at the University of California Davis. All authors were members of the Science Teaching and Research Center at the University of California Davis at the time of this project.

Resources

American Association for the Advancement of Science. 1993. *Benchmarks for science literacy.* New York: Oxford University Press.

Beane, J. (1991). The middle school: The natural home of the integrated curriculum. *Educational Leadership, 49*(2), 9–13.

National Research Council. 1996. *National Science Education Standards.* Washington, DC: National Academy Press.

Rev Up Your Veggies!

By Melissa DiGennaro King

Elementary students are perpetually inquisitive about force and motion: What forces act on everyday objects? What makes them move? Why do they stop? How does mass affect speed? Movement in the physical world around us is a fascinating display of interacting forces. Children can easily see objects in motion, but they cannot see the "invisible forces" that act on these objects.

Activities that encourage young scientists to investigate the principles of physics capture their interest naturally. As teachers we continually ask, "What will grab students' attention, stimulate their curiosity, and hook them into learning?" After receiving a letter from the Washington Apple Commission announcing the Lunch Box Derby, I guessed that my fourth-grade students would take up this unique challenge enthusiastically. Intended as a contest to promote teamwork and encourage innovative thinking with a focus on nutrition, the Lunch Box Derby challenges fourth- and fifth-grade students to design, build, and race cars made from fresh produce. Each class is allowed one entry, with the best entries from each region competing at the national level.

At the time, I was planning a unit on force, motion, and energy (Virginia Standards of Learning, see Figure 1). I realized that some of these physical science concepts could be developed through the Lunch Box Derby. The *National Science Education Standards* (NRC 1996) present a vision for scientific inquiry that encourages students to ask questions, plan and conduct investigations, use tools to gather data, and think critically and logically about relationships between evidence and explanations. This contest offered a creative opportunity to reinforce physical science concepts, such as design and the laws of motion, through active discovery and inquiry-based learning.

Capture the Enthusiasm

The Lunch Box Derby Web site, *http://www.bestapples.com*, supplies official entry forms, important details about the competition, and participant guidelines (see The Rules). I carefully outlined the steps needed to complete the project and estimated a two-week time commitment. Then, I secured permission to proceed from my principal, scheduled a date for the race, and explained the Lunch Box Derby to the school staff.

To present the derby concept to students, I displayed some produce and asked, "What could we do with this? Could we make something original? Could we construct movable objects?

Could we put fruits and vegetables together to make vehicles? Could we get them moving like cars?" At first, students were skeptical, but then the novelty intrigued them. Their initial laughter transformed into a resounding, "Yeah, let's do it!"

Design and Construction

From the outset, the derby project fostered student cooperation and collaboration, one aspect of the recommendations in the Standards (Teaching Standard E: Teachers of science develop communities of learners that reflect the intellectual rigor of scientific inquiry and the attitudes and social values conducive to science learning.) Each team of four students had at least one potential leader. Designated student roles for group success included a 1) leader, 2) materials manager, 3) graphic designer and recorder, and 4) chief builder. Our initial focus on a collaborative work ethic reaped untold benefits and contributed significantly to the overall success of the Lunch Box Derby.

For vehicle design and construction, students collected assorted fruits and vegetables, including kiwi fruit, radishes, acorn squash, lemons, bananas, eggplant, cucumbers, brussels sprouts, potatoes, limes, apples, turnips, oranges, and onions. Students discussed why certain choices might be better than others for car bodies, wheels, or other specific parts. For example, students recognized that limes made reliable wheels because of their spherical shape. Other students who were determined to use an acorn squash for the body discovered that they needed help pushing the bamboo skewers (axles) all the way through. Early on, they had to deal with design trade-offs such as these.

As students discussed design constraints, they began to imagine what their finished cars might

Figure 1. Standards addressed in the Lunch Box Derby.

Virginia Standards of Learning

Grades 4 and 5 (4.1, 5.1)

  Scientific investigation, reasoning, and logic

Grade 4 (4.2)

  Force, motion, and energy

  Potential/kinetic energy, friction, inertia

National Science Education Standards

Content Standard A: Science as inquiry

Content Standard B: Physical science

  Position, motion, and speed of objects; inertia

  Effect of forces on speed and direction of objects

Content Standard E: Science and technology

  Identify problem, propose solution, design a product, communicate the process

  Design constraints and trade-offs

look like. They shared ideas, conceptualized possibilities through drawings, and made specific plans for vehicle construction. The motivation to create a winning car kept everyone on task. This application of scientific thinking to create a real design solution also captures the spirit of the Standards.

Teams submitted final design plans to the teacher for approval and assessment of the feasibility of proposed designs. Derby teams worked together making group decisions and testing various suggestions for practicality and reliability. The teams explored questions such as: "Will mushrooms hold their shape if used as wheels? Should we use something hard like rad-

The Rules

The Lunch Box Derby allows maximum flexibility in vehicle design, but there are a few established rules:

- The car that travels the farthest distance down an inclined plane is the winner. All vehicle parts must work well together, just as a healthy diet helps students "go the distance" in their own lives.

- At least five different kinds of fruits and vegetables must be used on each vehicle, reinforcing the nutritional concept of "five a day" for fruit and vegetable servings.

- Other materials allowed include: three bamboo skewers, four toothpicks, one rubber band (per vehicle).

- Wheels and axles must rotate (vehicle must roll, not slide).

- Vehicle body must not touch the floor.

The contest rules provide structure, but they also mandate creativity in working within specific restraints. The Lunch Box Derby disqualifies any student teams who fail to abide by the established rules. One team learned the hard way. Their car outperformed all the others, but close inspection revealed two rubber bands, instead of just one. The team was disqualified from the contest.

on tabletops and ramps, they made notes about what did or did not work well. Then, they modified accordingly. Each vehicle also had an original name, such as Cucumber Glider, The Squasher, and Go the Distance.

During construction, students were absorbed in learning as they tried ideas and revised their original design plans. For example, one team discovered that bananas are too soft to maintain car body integrity. Another team found out that apples are too uneven for a balanced set of four wheels. While observing, I noticed English-as-a-Second-Language students working confidently, learning-disabled students clarifying ideas, artistic students adding creative finishing touches, and student leaders communicating support for both individual and team efforts.

On Your Mark, Get Set, Go!

For the Lunch Box Derby we used a large wooden panel (1 m x 2 m) for the ramp, positioned at a 60° angle. We started out with a smaller angle (about 30°), but students found that when they placed their vehicles on the ramp, the vehicles were unable to roll spontaneously. With a steeper incline, the pull of gravity allowed all cars to roll unassisted. Some cars traveled quite a distance beyond the bottom of the ramp; students noticed the difference between heavier cars that rolled faster down the ramp and lightweight cars that traveled farther on the level flooring at the

ishes to hold wheels in place on the axles? Do the front and back wheels need to be the same? What will happen if we try limes in front and oranges in back? Should we put a big carrot on top of the car body to add more weight for rolling down the ramp?" All planning notes, drawings, and design discoveries were kept in team folders as the work proceeded. As students sketched different possibilities for derby vehicles, they added these drawings to the team folders. As they experimented with various designs bottom of the ramp. Again, they had to think in terms of design trade-offs.

The ramp was set on tile flooring to minimize friction and maximize traveling distance. A pit stop was set up in one corner for malfunctioning cars. Here, teams could make minor alterations, but design changes or complete part replacements were not allowed. The school principal served as the official judge for the contest, and parents were encouraged to come watch the event.

"On your mark, get set, go!" Teams made predictions about their car's performance, then let their inventions roll down the ramp. Three trials were allowed, with careful recording on large chart paper of distances traveled. Before racing, most teams were very optimistic about the performance of their own derby vehicles. After observing what happened during actual racing, they became much more realistic. Teams began to assess more than individual vehicle component parts, looking at how well these parts functioned in an integrated system.

After each team's trials, students compared their predictions with the distance traveled by each car in the derby. The best run for each entry was accepted as the "official" distance. As a class, we exchanged ideas about why certain cars did not go as far as expected. Was it too much rolling resistance in the wheels? Was it an operating problem with moving parts? Was it insufficient mass to build up vehicle speed on the downhill ramp? Was it too much mass to keep the car going on the level straightaway?

For the cars that wobbled excessively or went off the ramp, students discussed what design changes might correct those problems. We also talked about why some cars rolled so smoothly and traveled farther than expected. Was it due to the choice of wheels or car body? Or was it

Students shared ideas, conceptualized possibilities through drawings, and made specific plans for vehicle construction.

good overall construction? This questioning motivated students to search for relevant explanations. When one student did not have an answer, another one often did:

- The heavier cars went faster on the ramp because of gravity.
- Onions made great wheels because they're so hard.
- The axles on that car moved around and made the car go crooked.
- Once it came off the ramp, the cucumber car went really far because it's lightweight.
- The carrot car looks super streamlined!

Through concrete experiences and observations, students began to build better conceptual understanding of forces like inertia, gravity, and friction. Going beyond textual definitions, they developed an appreciation for how and why these forces acted on objects.

Reflective Analysis

Reflection is an essential ingredient of successful learning experiences. The day after the Lunch Box Derby, student teams gathered for

Figure 2. Rubrics.

Scale: (1 = not observed, 3 = observed somewhat, 5 = observed often)

Assessment: Teamwork

Stayed on task	1	2	3	4	5
Listened to each other	1	2	3	4	5
Followed directions	1	2	3	4	5
Used resources appropriately	1	2	3	4	5
Worked as a team	1	2	3	4	5
Completed work on time	1	2	3	4	5
Acted responsibly	1	2	3	4	5
Organized efforts	1	2	3	4	5

Assessment: Individual Students

Worked cooperatively	1	2	3	4	5
Participated in constructive dialogue	1	2	3	4	5
Listened to teammates	1	2	3	4	5
Approached the task seriously	1	2	3	4	5
Remembered assigned role in team	1	2	3	4	5
Assisted in design plans	1	2	3	4	5
Helped in vehicle construction	1	2	3	4	5
Used materials carefully	1	2	3	4	5

Assessment: Science Concepts

Demonstrated understanding of concepts of force and motion	1	2	3	4	5
Applied knowledge of physical science in vehicle design	1	2	3	4	5
Used available technology in vehicle design and construction	1	2	3	4	5
Showed ability to make design changes based on observations	1	2	3	4	5
Communicated conceptual understanding, verbally and in writing	1	2	3	4	5

small group discussion. They discussed what they would change to improve vehicle performance, recording the revised plans. Once again, trade-offs had to be considered and group consensus was required. For example, students recognized that appropriate wheels were a key element for racing success.

After watching the derby, most had a better idea of which fruit or vegetable choices were more reliable for a Lunch Box Derby vehicle. They learned that rolling resistance made a big difference. Denser produce with smoother surface area proved to be best as wheels because these fruits and vegetables created less friction as cars traveled down the ramp. Only one derby team had chosen onions for wheels in their derby car. Once other teams saw how well this car rolled down the ramp, some wanted to include onion wheels in their revised plans. Although less visually appealing than their initial citrus choices, students began to realize that vehicle performance was more important than looks.

That night, the homework was to draw a "dream derby car." Each student independently sketched and labeled his/her ideal derby vehicle. Students were encouraged to be realistic as well as creative. In Writers' Workshop students wrote about what they learned from participation in the Lunch Box Derby. In their writing, several dominant themes emerged. Most of the students stressed how much they had learned about teamwork and cooperation during the Lunch Box Derby. They noted the importance of listening to other people's ideas. Some recognized they should have paid more attention to trial runs for their vehicles to detect design flaws before the actual competition began.

Many students wrote about the importance of careful observation, and quite a few had discovered that persistence and patience are critical aspects of the design process. One student said, "Even though things might not turn out as you expect them to, you can always try again." This follow-up helped assess student-learning outcomes and provided valuable student practice with written communication skills.

Assessment

During Lunch Box Derby activities, assessment data came from multiple sources. As students worked in teams, I used a rubric to evaluate team performance; I used a second rubric to assess the work and efforts of individual students and a third to assess the science concepts learned (see Figure 2 for rubrics). The Lunch Box Derby folder from each team contained initial sketches, final design plans, vehicle performance notes, and a page of reflections. The contents of these folders became part of the assessment package for each team.

In the computer lab, students created graphical representations of racing data. Working in pairs, the children entered names of individual vehicles and the distances the vehicles had traveled in the derby. Next, students made bar graphs to show how performance compared. Some students entered data from all three trials so they could show how much the distance traveled varied for each derby entrant.

This task highlighted the effectiveness of visual displays in illustrating numerical data. For example, students noticed that one derby car had performed consistently well in all three trials, whereas others had widely varying distances in each trial.

Students also wrote summary statements of the data, which helped me determine whether they understood what the graphical information told us about our Lunch Box Derby. This technology application was another tool for me to use in student assessment.

Crossing the Finish Line

The culminating activity for students was sharing the Lunch Box Derby adventure with a wider audience. Students were excited and wanted to spread the word. Near the school's front entrance, we displayed photographs of the "veggie cars," colorful graphs of vehicle performance, samples of student writing, and drawings of dream derby cars. The wall display stimulated lots of conversation and even more questions for the students. This unique experience captured the community's attention, and the positive feedback showed that people do notice those who dare to be different.

Melissa DiGennaro King is the investigation station teacher at the Arlington Science Focus School in Arlington, VA. She formerly taught fourth grade at Barrett Elementary School in Arlington.

Resources

Board of Education, Commonwealth of Virginia. 1995. *Standards of Learning for Virginia Public Schools.* Richmond, VA: State Board of Education.

Lunch Box Derby. Washington Apple Commission, P.O. Box 550, Wenatchee, WA 98807.

National Research Council. 1996. *National Science Education Standards.* Washington, DC: National Academy Press.

Internet

The Internet offers fascinating sites that build on what students learned about force and motion during the derby project.

Car and Ramp, www.arborsci.com (#P2-8020). Arbor Scientific, P.O. Box 2750, Ann Arbor, MI 48106-2750. 800-367-6695; (Arbor Scientific features the "Car and Ramp," a hands-on laboratory with ramp, pulleys, a spring scale, a wooden protractor, and a plumb bob. In the kit, a small car with ball-bearing wheels and rubber tires can carry loads of up to 600 g. Used with an accurate timer, these materials would further develop concepts of force and motion introduced in the Lunch Box Derby. My students were very enthusiastic about the Lunch Box Derby experience. I wanted to spend another two weeks exploring concepts of force and motion through these extension activities. In the future, I will allocate more time for them.)

Project Reptile!

By Deborah Diffily

Good teachers continually plan learning experiences to help young children make connections within and among areas of study (Zemelman, Daniels, and Hyde 1998). Integrating curriculum is important in helping children make these connections. Class projects offer an effective child-centered approach that helps organize and integrate curriculum. Class projects differ from other methods of integrating curriculum in that projects are:

• studies of children-selected topics
• research based
• directed by children with guidance from the teacher
• conducted over a period of weeks
• concluded with the children sharing what they learned

One successful class project conducted by a group of my kindergarten students—building a reptile exhibit—came out of the students' great interest in reptiles.

The school where I taught is a public school with a mission of challenging traditional assumptions of education. Applied-learning projects were encouraged there, and individual teachers facilitated child-directed projects. By definition, students involved in an applied-learning project must share what they learned

with a specific audience. The reptile exhibit project motivated students to learn above grade-level expectations and addressed standards identified by the *National Science Education Standards* (NRC 1996). In planning and implementing the reptile exhibit, I addressed Teaching Standards A, B, C, D, and E, and students met Content Standards A, C, E, and G (See box, "Standards Addressed").

Throughout the eight weeks of planning, working on different components of the exhibit and giving tours, the children continued their typical daily schedule minus a few minutes from each activity. The time taken from the other routines totaled almost one hour, so the last hour of the day was dedicated to project time. See box "Timeline for Reptiles Exhibit Project" for more details about what the class did each week.

How It All Started

The kindergarten students already knew quite a bit about reptiles. They had observed and cared for classroom pets—a rat snake and two box turtles—for several months. The classroom's science center was full of books about reptiles and the children returned to these books week after week. What really set the project in motion, however, was a student's birthday party held at the local zoo. Everyone in the class had been invited, and talk of the party filled the class

Topic: reptiles
Go to: www.scilinks.org
Code: MIX146

for days before and after the event. The herpetarium was the children's favorite exhibit. Conversations about the reptiles dominated the classroom. During a class meeting the week after the party, two students persuaded their classmates that they needed to know "more, much more" about reptiles.

Research, Research, Research

Learning about reptiles involved many activities over the next several days, and students' knowledge and skills were enhanced in various content areas. For example, students compared the eating habits of our class' box turtles; every afternoon they fed the two turtles the same type and amount of food. They then drew pictures of the food, and each day they marked off with an *X* the food that had been eaten. By testing different foods listed in a book on turtles' diets, students tried to determine which foods our turtles preferred. They also tested situations that make turtles retreat into their shells.

Conducting research strengthened the children's literacy development in multiple ways. Students listened to books read aloud and responded to them by drawing pictures. They learned to read words, such as *turtle, tortoise, snake, lizard, alligator,* and *crocodile,* from the labels in the science center where they sorted and posted photographs of reptiles. Older students often read parts of books to the kindergartners to help them understand the pictures.

During their research, students collected reptile facts for about two weeks. Students dictated facts they had learned and identified whether they learned the information from a book or from observation. The students sorted the facts by source. Then, using published animal fact cards as models, the children rewrote the fact in their best handwriting and sketched reptiles to

create their own fact cards. Some students compiled the fact cards into their own reptile books.

Several students wrote letters to administrators and families to coordinate field trips to view reptile exhibits. Others wrote letters to personnel at a science museum and at the zoo to schedule class visits. The students wrote all of the letters themselves, using the level of developmental spelling they were capable of. I included a transcription of the letter, so the adult receiving it did not have to struggle to read it.

Students learned to seek help from topic experts through my prompting, asking question such as "Can you think of anyone we met on our field trips who might know a lot about lizards?" Students also e-mailed questions to reptile experts in several cities. One student, Drew, had a sister who was taking a biology class at college in Austin. When Drew wondered why horned toads squirt blood from their eyes, we could not find the answer in any book we had. Drew wanted his sister to help. She explained the situation to her professor, and he agreed to accept e-mails from Drew. Drew posed the questions: "Wut do raptils eeyt? How dus a horn tod spit blud owt of his eye?" I also contacted the professor before Drew wrote.

Building the Reptile Exhibit

After field trips to a local science and history museum, students decided that they wanted to create their own exhibit on reptiles. Convinced that they knew more about reptiles than any other class in the school and confident that they could do just about anything, the children decided they could create this exhibit in "just a few days."

Applied learning projects require students to make decisions about project work, but kindergarten students have few experiences that

Timeline for Reptiles Exhibit Project

Week 1:

- Vote to study reptiles.
- As a class, read books about reptiles.
- Start listing possible resources.
- Begin collecting documentation about what is learned and storing it in pocket folders.
- Write facts.
- Draw pictures of reptiles.
- Write letters to experts.

Week 2:

- As a class, begin reading downloaded information from Internet sites.
- Continue writing facts about reptiles and drawing pictures.
- Write more letters to experts.
- Mark pages of books and articles to be photocopied for project folders.

Week 3:

- Plan field trips to see reptiles at the zoo and museum.
- Continue writing facts about reptiles and marking pages of books and articles to be photocopied for project folders.
- Create reptile pictures in different media.
- Write reptile stories, books, and poems.

Week 4:

- Take field trips to zoo and science museum.
- Do group research.

Week 5:

- Measure the room to be used for the exhibit.
- Make floor plans and arrange furniture.
- Discuss and make lists of what should be included in the exhibit.
- Decide how items in the exhibit should be displayed.

Week 6:

- Write letters to borrow reptile specimens from the science museum.
- Create more pictures of reptiles using various media.
- Hang these pictures for the entrance to the exhibit.
- Create and send out invitations to exhibit opening.
- Create and distribute a memo inviting classes in school to tour the exhibit.
- Discuss criteria for a good brochure.
- Draft exhibit brochure copy.
- Finalize and make copies of the brochure.

Week 7:

- Finish hanging facts and pictures.
- Set up specimens with labels.
- Hold museum opening for families and special friends of the class.

Week 8:

- Give tours to other classes and visitors to the school.

prepare them for this. I used a pondering approach to lead the students into considering certain ideas (e.g., "I was thinking last night that we are learning a lot about reptiles. I wonder if we could make an exhibit like they have at the zoo?"). If the students did not accept the suggestion, then I let it drop. After making leading suggestions, I followed and supported the students' decisions regarding planning the exhibit.

The first planning step was to hold a class meeting and brainstorm ideas. We decided to include in the exhibit pictures they had drawn, books they had made, books we had read, and our class snake and turtles.

The students had seen a photograph essay at the museum, so they decided to make their own photograph display as part of their exhibit. Several children had taken photographs of the animals on the field trip using the class camera. Students chose photographs from the field trip and wrote labels to describe each photograph. The students used the writing process to write the label copy. They drafted, edited, and revised their labels. I helped them stretch out the words verbally so they could more easily hear the sounds in those words. I did not spell for them, nor did I type their labels.

Once students had decided on the words to include on the picture label, they conferred with their classmates to make sure the copy explained the photograph and to ensure that others would understand what they had written. Many of the students could read each other's labels. Because many of the families had become familiar with the children's developmental spelling from examples I had been sending home all year, they were adept at reading the student's efforts.

Then students typed the copy in final form on the class computer and mounted the photograph and label copy onto poster board cut to a standard size. The students used glue sticks to attach the photographs and labels.

It's Almost Showtime

Students worked on the exhibit items for three weeks while continuing their research. As the exhibit date drew nearer, the class asked the custodian to bring tables to the basement so they could set up the exhibit. Students placed a few items on the tables:

- the turtles and snake from the class's science center
- books children had written about different reptiles

On the floor they taped lizard, turtle, and alligator footprints to indicate which way visitors should walk through the exhibit.

The students and I met in the basement to evaluate their efforts. The children approved the walls and the floor, but they decided they needed more live reptiles to put on the tables—two live specimens were not enough for the exhibit. With my help, students successfully e-mailed a museum staff member and asked to borrow specimens from the museum's teaching collection.

Students also chose other items to hang on the museum walls including:

- their original reptile drawings and paintings
- labeled photographs from nature magazines and field trips
- the fact cards

The children displayed different orders of reptiles on different-colored posterboard (snakes and lizards—blue; turtles and tortoises—red; alligators and crocodiles—green). The fact cards were glued on the same color poster board as the specimens.

At this point the children worked in groups finishing last-minute details. We kept running lists of things to do for the exhibit opening. The groups formed as students volunteered to do things. I did not assign students to work together. If there was a task no one volunteered for, I might ask one or two students to volunteer.

In one group the children examined brochures they had collected at the museum. Students discussed the criteria for good brochures and created their own exhibit brochure guided by their list of characteristics. According to their criteria, a good brochure:

- has lots of words
- tells what is in the exhibit
- has pictures with lots of details
- is folded

Another group of students made promotional signs and posters about the exhibit.

The class designed a museum opening invitation for parents, grandparents, friends, and volunteers. With help from older students they looked up addresses in the telephone book and in the school directory and addressed their own envelopes. Some students worked on a note to all the teachers in the school inviting all classes to schedule a tour of the exhibit. They kept track of the tours on our large class calendar after I modeled for them how I keep track of my meetings.

Exhibit Day

On the day of the exhibit opening, more than 60 adults crowded into the museum exhibit space. The opening was two hours long and was invitation-only for family and friends of the class. The tour wasn't scripted, and the excitement of the kindergarten students was evident as they acted as docents for those who came to the opening. The rest of the week was spent giving tours to other students in the school and visitors to the building.

Project Lessons

Through this project students learned important lessons they might not have learned in more traditional science-related instruction (Manning, Manning, and Long 1994). Students learned that they could find fascinating facts about reptiles through multiple resources. For example, students dictated to me that they had learned:

- A turtle is a reptile.
- A snake is a reptile.
- Reptiles shed their skin.
- Some snakes eat eggs.
- Our snake eats dead mice.
- Snakes don't chew.

Some higher-ability students, who were particularly engaged in finding unusual facts, dictated such facts:

- King snakes eat other snakes.
- Horned toads squirt blood from their eyes.
- Frilled lizards puff up their frills to scare enemies.

The students learned that they could record these facts and read them to other people. They learned they could write letters and have adults write back to them. They learned about working as a team member and finding solutions while making group decisions. And through the reactions of the visitors to their museum exhibit, they learned that they could create important products that adults took seriously. Through their involvement in researching reptiles and creating a museum exhibit that people came to tour, students learned that they could do important work.

In any given project, the topic will vary and the specific topic will drive the type of research that is conducted (Wolk 1998). Based on their knowledge and skills, different groups of children will determine various ways to organize the information they discover. Not every group

The National Science Education Standards Addressed in Project Reptile

Teaching Standard A:

Teachers of science plan an inquiry-based science program for their students.

Teaching Standard B:

Teachers of science guide and facilitate learning.

Teaching Standard C:

Teachers of science engage in ongoing assessment of their teaching and of student learning.

Teaching Standard D:

Teachers of science design and manage learning environments that provide students with the time, space, and resources needed for learning science.

Teaching Standard E:

Teachers of science develop communities of science learners that reflect the intellectual rigor of scientific inquiry and the attitudes and social values conducive to science learning.

Content Standard A:

As a result of activities in grades K–4, all students should develop understanding of:

• abilities necessary to do scientific inquiry

• understanding about scientific inquiry

Content Standard C:

As a result of activities in grades K–4, all students should develop understanding of:

• the characteristics of organisms
• life cycles of organisms
• organisms and environments

Content Standard E:

As a result of activities in grades K–4, all students should develop

• abilities of techonological design
• understanding of science and technology

• abilities to distinguish between natural objects and objects made by humans.

Content Standard G:

As a result of activities in grades K–4, all students should develop understanding of science as a human endeavor.

of children will choose a museum exhibit to demonstrate what they have learned. They may decide to create a brochure, write a book, or produce an informational video.

Virtually any science topic can become the focus for a class project. Any group of elementary students can learn to come to consensus about a topic to study, conduct research, make day-to-day decisions about locating resources, organize what is being learned, and select a way of sharing with others what they have learned. Any group can genuinely learn through science projects.

Deborah Diffily is an assistant professor of early childhood education at Southern Methodist University in Dallas, TX.

Resources

American Association for the Advancement of Science. 1993. *Benchmarks for science literacy*. New York: Oxford University.

Dewey, J. 1938. *Experience and education*. New York: Collier.

Edwards, C., L. Gandini, and G. Forman. 1998. *The hundred languages of children: The Reggio Emilia approach—advanced reflections*. Greenwich, CT.: Ablex.

Katz, L., and S. Chard. 2000. *Engaging children's minds: The project approach* (2nd ed.). Norwood, NJ: Ablex.

Kilpatrick, W. H. 1918. The project method. *Teachers College Record*, *19*(4), 319–325.

Manning, M., G. Manning, and R. Long. 1994. *Theme immersion: Inquiry-based curriculum in elementary and middle schools*. Portsmouth, NH: Heinemann.

National Research Council. 1996. *National Science Education Standards*. Washington, DC: National Academy Press.

Tanner, L. N. 1990. *Dewey's laboratory school: Lessons for today*. New York: Teachers College.

Wolk, S. 1998. *A democratic classroom*. Portsmouth, NH: Heinemann.

Zemelman, S., H. Daniels, and A. A. Hyde. 1998. *Best practice: New standards for teaching and learning in America's schools* (2nd ed.). Portsmouth, NH: Heinemann.

Box Up Your Habitat

By Lynn Astarita Gatto and Reeda Stamper Hart

"Is Kentucky bluegrass blue? Will Hawaiian coral soften in salt water? Which conifer has a five-needle leaf?" These are a few of the questions students asked and investigated after receiving their envirobox environmental samples from all over the United States. It was as though the children had visited five diverse states. For the past two years the authors (two teachers of a rural Kentucky elementary class of first- and second-grade students and an urban fourth-grade class in western New York) have had their classes exchange enviroboxes with classrooms in Hawaii, Alaska, Maine, California, and New Mexico. Exchanging environmental samples from diverse regions of the United States proved to be the impetus for true inquiry amongst students.

The Envirobox Project involved a total of six classes (first through fifth grades) from around the United States sending each other a shoebox containing six to 10 environmental samples. The boxes contained items such as pressed leaves and flowers, rocks, water samples, feathers, soil samples, pieces of bark, snake skins, acorns, pinecones, shells, lobster claws, and maple syrup. Once each class received their five enviroboxes, the children began their investigations to identify the samples. Initially, the project was to be research based; however, the unique samples became the impetus for many interesting and student-focused questions and investigations and provided many opportunities for interdisciplinary activities.

Planning and Preparation

To prepare for the project, we compiled a list of possible participants from environmentally different states by networking with friends, searching the Internet, and going through address books—you meet a lot of people when you go to NSTA conferences!. We sent letters to each candidate explaining and inviting four other teachers to join the project. Every teacher quickly and positively responded to the opportunity.

Next, we sent to the participating teachers a letter that included all participants' school addresses and e-mail addresses and a set of guidelines to maintain consistency within the project. The guidelines instructed each teacher to send identical samples to participating classes and place every sample in a container or plastic bag. Six to 10 samples were recommended for each envirobox. To make communication easier for the children, the samples also needed to be identically labeled with the same number and the state's name. Each class also kept a box that included all samples it had sent to other schools. This proved very useful when trying to answer questions from the other classes.

What to Include

When students learned of the project, they eagerly gathered samples from their schoolyards and backyards. (Due to federal regulations, all living materials must be preserved. Participants did not exchange live materials, however, one enclosed a color photocopy of a brightly colored maple leaf.)

Many classroom discussions helped determine the "best" samples to send. When the Kentucky students found a snakeskin in their school garden, they really wanted to include it in their envirobox, so they decided to cut it into six pieces. The New York students felt their urban schoolyard offered only a few interesting samples, so they took a neighborhood field trip. Under a highway bridge near their school, they found many pigeon feathers—they immediately agreed these would be a "tricky" sample to include in their envirobox.

Every class wrote an introductory letter to include in its envirobox explaining things such as class makeup and a few clues about the location of our schools. In addition, the Kentucky class included a class book of autobiographies. We packaged the samples in shoeboxes, added newspaper stuffing if needed, and then taped them up and sent them via first-class U.S. mail. All six boxes were mailed for less than $20.

Predicting State Habitats

Once the classes mailed their enviroboxes to the other states, the children began predicting what might be in the boxes sent to them. The first- and second-grade students from Kentucky used a simple computer software program to draw what they thought each state's habitat looked like. The fourth-grade students from New York used detailed geographic maps, encyclopedias, nonfiction books, interview notes, and the Internet to chart their predictions of what might be mailed in each state's envirobox.

The written predictions and a large U.S. map that hung on the hallway bulletin board created interest in our Envirobox Project among colleagues, parents, and students in other classes. To indicate the places that were sending an envirobox, students pinned a piece of yarn to the state and extended it to the matching chart.

Each day someone would stop in our classroom and ask if any of the boxes had arrived. Their interest in the project was motivating to students, and classroom anticipation was high.

Arrival of the Enviroboxes

When the first boxes arrived, the response was the same in all classrooms—the children were full of conversation and urged the teacher to open it immediately. On one occasion the New York class arrived to lunch late because the children refused to go until the box was opened.

As the children pulled each sample from the box, they immediately asked questions, made identifications, and developed inferences. They were not satisfied with just looking at the samples. They begged to explore the samples with their senses: "Shake it!" "Does it make a noise?" "What does it smell like?" "Are those sharp?" We struggled to chart everything that was said and asked as each sample was pulled from the boxes. We continued this until every box had arrived.

Study Groups

Once all the boxes had arrived, the classes formed state study groups. Children chose which state samples they wanted to investigate, often based on having relatives in that particular state or having visited the state. Each group gathered the necessary tools and reference sources. Children selected from many tools including microscopes, tape measures, hand lenses, coping saws, hammers, toothpicks, probes, potting soil, pots, assorted dishes and bottles, taxonomy keys, and reference books. Each group created journals for recording its process of inquiry.

Initially, some children were satisfied to describe samples in general terms. For example, the class from New York identified the white, hard branchlike sample from Hawaii as coral. When the teacher commented that there were many kinds of coral, students then spent days researching coral trying to identify the exact type. They finally found a picture of the coral at an Internet site on Pacific Ocean animals.

After seeing the picture of the coral in its habitat, one of the children in that group said, "I bet the coral gets soft in water." When invited to try it, he put the coral in a plastic glass and then asked for salt. When the student spotted a container of sea salt on the shelf, he insisted he needed the sea salt for his experiment to be "real." He recorded his prediction and his results daily for three weeks until he concluded that the coral would not soften as he had originally hypothesized.

Once children began to see what other groups were doing, they would settle for no less than detailed identifications, and their own investigations followed as well. A hard, dried moose scat sample from Alaska proved to be very interesting! Initially, the children in the Kentucky class thought it was a rock, but when they broke

it apart (wearing gloves) and found stalk parts and tiny seeds, they realized it was scat from an herbivore. Their research led them to conclude it was from a caribou or a moose, a conclusion they based on looking in encyclopedias and on the Internet to research animals living in Alaska. Students also decided to plant the sample to see if the seeds would produce a plant, but nothing germinated.

The white crystal sample in Hawaii's envirobox ironically produced the same actions in two classes. The first-, second-, and fourth-grade students identified the sample as salt "because it looked just like the salt we put on our roads when it snows." "But, how do you know for sure?" asked the teachers. The students knew they couldn't taste it, so they decided to put commercial samples of salt and sugar under the microscope. They carefully drew detailed illustrations of both crystal structures. Then, they looked at the Hawaii sample under the microscope and immediately knew their first identification was incorrect, and the sample was really sugar; students made this determination by comparing the cubic and rounded crystal formations of the salt and sugar samples.

The New York children knew from their own experiences that the seeds sent from Kentucky looked like grass seed. But when asked for a specific kind of grass, their research from books led them to believe that it must be bluegrass. They sent an e-mail to the Kentucky class to verify it. As they sat at the computer, one of the children mentioned that they thought the grass "must be a bluish color when it grows." The others agreed with her and decided to plant it. As the seeds sprouted and grew, students were shocked to find out that the grass was not blue, but instead it was green.

The round, dark brown sample included in

the Kentucky envirobox was also interesting. The New York students immediately identified it as some kind of nut because one of the boys in the class said he had a tree with that kind of nuts. But, when asked to identify the tree, he didn't know its name. Wearing goggles, they hammered the hard shell to crack it and discover what was inside. Once students found the small, white nut inside, they began to search the tree guide. In their journal students wrote, "It must be a black walnut because on the little map it shows that black walnuts grow in Kentucky. The book says if you try to crack it open it will be very hard and it was. So, we are sure that it's a black walnut."

But some children in the group were not entirely convinced. They had also read that the pioneers used the black walnut shell husk to make brown dye. So, they decided to make a final determination by testing the "dye-ability" of their husk shell samples. After three days the cloth they had saturated in their shell-and-water concoction had turned deep brown. They definitely concluded that the sample was a black walnut.

Through prompting and questioning, the teachers were able to guide the children's investigations. Teachers encouraged the children to probe thoroughly and assisted them in developing "fair test" experiments of their own choosing. When the water sample from California was examined, some of the children in the New York class talked about the salt crystals they "saw." Debate ensued over whether it was salt water from the Pacific Ocean or fresh water from the Los Angeles Aqueduct. One group of children obtained water from the sink and compared the two samples under the microscope. Another child compared the two by feeling the water. He was quite sure he could "feel" the salt: "It feels sandy" was his conclusion. Another

group let the salt water evaporate and proved their point when the salt remained after the water had evaporated. However, one of the groups challenged them by proposing: "Maybe the regular water would have the same results." So, the test was repeated this time with a control. With this last experiment, everyone was finally convinced that the water sample was from the ocean.

Results of the Activity

The children had many experiences identifying rocks, crustaceans, nuts, plants, animal covering, seeds, leaves, flowers, and water, rock, and soil samples. The activities had children researching and inquiring. Throughout the entire project children authentically hypothesized, communicated, recorded, collected and interpreted data, and drew conclusions. Within each classroom small groups of children were constantly reporting findings or problems from their scien-

National Science Education Standards

Content Standards

As a result of the Envirobox Project, children "will develop the abilities necessary to do scientific inquiry" by asking questions, planning and conducting simple experiments, using tools to gather data and then interpreting it. In addition, scientific communication is an ongoing component to this project (Standard A). As children observe and research the environmental objects from the various habitats in the United States, they will focus on the characteristics of living things and earth materials (Standard C and D). (National Research Council 1996).

Figure 1. Letter confirming contents of the envirobox from New York.

Dear classes that sent enviroboxes,

This is to let you know what was in our envirobox. We thought it was funny that every envirobox that was sent to us had a pinecone. But we noticed that they were all different.

1. *We found the cattails by Ellison Park's Creek.*
2. *We found the pigeon feathers under a roadway bridge as we walked through the city to the park. We found a broken pigeon egg near the curb under the bridge.*
3. *We found the pinecones under a conifer tree near the baseball diamond on the road we took to the park.*
4. *The sand samples were collected by the bank of the Ellison Park Creek.*
5. *The tree fungus was scraped off a conifer tree in the park.*
6. *The needles were from the white pine tree. We chose that one especially because the white pine is the Peace Tree from our upstate New York Native American tribe, the Iroquois.*
7. *The acorn was found under a deciduous oak tree.*

We liked doing the Envirobox Project because it was like going to places all over the United States. It was exciting to get mail and guess what was going to be in them before we opened them. We really had to look for stuff to send to you. But, it was hard to do the research of what you sent. We think we did pretty well though. Let us know if we were right. We look forward to hearing from you again.

Sincerely,

The fourth-grade class in Rochester, New York

tific research or investigations. The class discussions included suggestions for problem solving, questions of doubt, and offers of congratulations.

There were also cross-class conversations and questions via the Internet. The children from Kentucky kept on their computer an ongoing database that they refined and changed as they conducted their research and investigations. They concluded the envirobox project by sending every class the database of their findings and the other classes sent letters to one another confirming the samples (Figure 1).

A final hallway bulletin board centered on the large U.S. map and displayed the samples from each state. All of the samples hung on the bulletin board in their plastic bags next to the original predictions. The samples that generated investigations, such as growing the grass seed, were placed on a table underneath the bulletin board.

Lists of final identifications, pictures of children conducting investigations, and copies of student journals and e-mail communications filled the hallways. In both the New York and Kentucky classes, every time a group of children or an individual walked by, comments, questions, and conversation were always generated. Parents and teachers could be heard saying, "I didn't know that!" or children would ask, "How did you find out all that stuff?" or "Where did you meet so many people from other states?" People were always stopping in both classrooms to comment on their own experiences in one of the states, ask a question, or compliment the students.

Interdisciplinary Connections

The Envirobox Project not only provided an authentic, scientific inquiry for our students but also allowed us to make connections between science and other disciplines in a meaningful and comprehensive way (see box, "Envirobox Project Interdisciplinary Connections"). Reading comprehension of nonfiction literature was used extensively. The children also practiced note-taking skills, recorded the processes, and made deductions. They read many reference books about the states that coincided with the samples from the boxes.

Many social studies and mathematics concepts were also an important outcome of this project. As the students researched each envirobox sample, the geography, economy, weather, and agriculture of each state became part of their knowledge base. The Kentucky students created a spreadsheet using data (city populations, distances, and longitudes and latitudes) to compare each state in the Envirobox Project. Using the spreadsheet, the children created formulas to compare the large numbers and developed algebraic equations to understand their differences.

The children's work throughout this project was easily used for embedded assessments. Their journal entries were evaluated for writing ability and for evidence and level of process skills. The children's comments and questions were observed during discussions for concept understanding. Group presentations clearly defined the children's research and investigation abilities as well as speaking competence. For a social studies assessment, the Kentucky class compared their first illustrations to their final illustrations of their states' habitats.

Truly, the Envirobox Project was a means of traveling throughout the United States to discover its wonderfully diverse environments without ever leaving the classroom. The children could vividly visualize the different

Envirobox Project Interdisciplinary Connections

Language Arts/English
- Write friendly letters to each site participating in the exchange.
- Research nonfiction books, encyclopedias, and the Internet to find information on each of the cities and/or states. Report on findings.

Technology
- Make a spreadsheet to average populations of cities, distance from our site, etc.
- Word process all communications.
- Communicate through e-mail.

Social Studies/Geography/History
- Find longitude and latitude of each city.
- Map directions from each city to our site.

Science
- Classify items in enviroboxes.
- Use the process of inquiry to identify items in boxes.

Art
- Make a drawing to predict what the biome might look like at the beginning of the unit. Experiment with different media (chalk, water colors, etc.).
- Make a drawing of your conclusions after seeing the enviroboxes.

Mathematics
- Compare size and weight of items in the enviroboxes.
- Graph weather and precipitation from each city and/or state.

habitats for each state as if they had traveled there.

Begin your own envirobox exchange by

- asking friends who may know teachers in other states
- exchanging business cards at conferences
- posting your idea in a teacher chat room

Won't you join us as we travel on our next cross-country trip?

Lynn Astarita Gatto is a second- looping to fourth-grade teacher at Henry Hudson No. 28 School in Rochester, NY, and Reeda Stamper Hart is a multi-age primary teacher at Grant's Lick Elementary School in the Campbell County School District in Kentucky. They are both recipients of the Presidential Award for Excellence in Science Teaching.

Resources

Print

Abbot, R. T. 1994. *Science nature guides.* San Diego, CA: Thunder Bay.

Burnie, D. 1988. *Eyewitness books, nature series.* New York: Alfred A. Knopf.

Carpenter, A. 1967. *Enchantment of America, state series.* Chicago: Children's Press.

Coulombe, S. 1984. *The seaside naturalist.* New York: Prentice Hall.

Fradin, D. 1981. *State series in words and pictures.* Chicago: Children's Press.

Ganlin, L. 1993. *Eyewitness explorers series.* New York: Dorling Kindersley.

National Research Council. 1996. *National Science Education Standards.* Washington, DC: National Academy Press.

Pondendorf, I. 1981. *A new true book series.* Chicago: Children's Press.

Reder, H. A. 1988. *The Audubon Society pocket guide series.* New York: Alfred A. Knopf.

Software

Kid Pix (Borderbund)
  Easy-to-use draw program.
Microsoft Works
  Easy-to-use word processing, spreadsheet, and database.
Student Writing Center
  (The Learning Company)
First Encyclopedia (Golden Books)

Internet

www.indo.com/distance
  Easy-to-use website for determining the distance from your city to any city in the world. It also provides a map route from your city to another designated city.
www.infoplease.com
  Easy-to-use website for gathering factual data about cities in the United States. Data includes state flower, bird, tree, population, weather, and latitude and longitude.

Outdoor Projects: C Authentic Science and Environmental Citizenship

Lessons from a Lake

By Susan Goethals

Much has been written about science opportunities for children at the seashore, and many schools take advantage of this kind of study. For many students, however, marine studies are not possible—the ocean is just too far away. Yet almost every school has a lake or pond nearby, and these aquatic areas can provide many of the same opportunities for students.

The fourth- and fifth-grade teachers at our school were interested in engaging students in a study that would integrate biological and physical science with a study of our state, Connecticut. As the science coordinator, I designed a study that included classroom lessons on hydroelectric power, the history and construction of a nearby lake, data recording, the use of field guides, and methods of counting natural populations. The preparation and planning activities were incorporated into the regular class schedule over a period of six weeks. The study would culminate in a field trip to the lake in the spring. Located only about five kilometers from our school is Candlewood Lake, a constructed body of water with an interesting history and a wealth of opportunities for scientific discovery. In March, students began the study of Candlewood Lake by investigating its history. Students learned that the Connecticut Light and Power Company constructed the lake in 1928 to create a reliable source of waterpower to provide electricity to the area.

An Elevation Revelation

The students had spent some class time studying two-dimensional maps, but the idea of elevation above sea level gave their studies a third dimension. We learned that this lake is situated at an elevation of less than 129 meters above sea level. When the area was surveyed before flooding, the power company purchased all land in the area around the Rocky River that was less than 132 meters above sea level. The idea of elevation determining the boundaries was intriguing to the students, so the children learned how to use a simple elevation meter by practicing in the schoolyard.

The elevation meter was constructed using the following materials, available at local hardware stores:
- a meter stick
- four pieces of wood approximately the same size as the meter stick (2.5 cm x 1.25 cm x 100 cm)
- five nuts and bolts
- 10 washers
- a small level
- masking tape

To construct the elevation meter, lay out the meter stick and three of the wood pieces in a rectangle (see Figure 1) and bolt together at the corners. Bolt the last wood strip in the center of the strip opposite the meter stick, so that it can move freely along the meter stick. Attach the level to the middle of the movable wood strip using masking tape.

To use the elevation meter, students placed the two vertical bars in an upright position with the edges of the wood flush with the ground. They then moved the cross bar up or down until the bubble in the level was in the center. The students read the number of centimeters above or below the center of the meter stick (50 cm) to determine the change in elevation between the two uprights.

With this skill mastered, the students were prepared to duplicate some of the work done by the lake's surveyors almost 70 years ago. We planned to use the elevation meter at the lake to verify that the elevation from the water's edge to the edge of the lake property was, in fact, 10 meters. To do this, we would follow a transect line from the water's edge to the property line, placing the left upright of the elevation meter exactly where the right upright had been, moving along the line in 1-m increments and adding up all of these measurements.

Measuring a Lake

During our study, the students discovered that Candlewood Lake has an unusual long, thin shape. Some of the children were interested in how to determine the actual size of a lake. In class, we discussed the geometric concepts needed to measure a body of water and decided to test these concepts. Using a large, semi-permanent puddle, a result of the sinking of our parking lot/playground, as a model lake, students tried two different methods to measure the puddle-lake.

First, we used a trundle wheel to measure the length and width of the puddle. We chose a warm afternoon, so a few of the children could remove their shoes and socks to wade into the

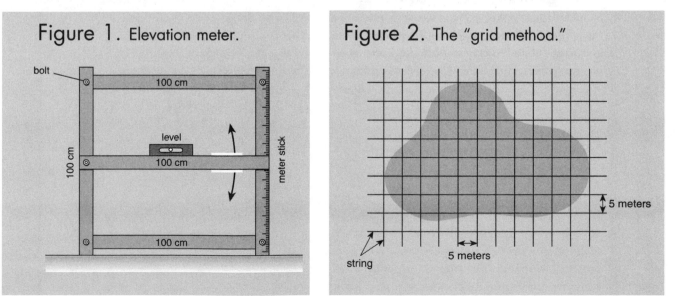

Figure 1. Elevation meter.

Figure 2. The "grid method."

puddle. We estimated the average depth by taking five depth readings from various areas of the puddle and averaging this data. To estimate the volume, we multiplied the surface area by the average depth.

The second method we used to estimate the size of the puddle-lake was the "grid method." Students constructed a string grid over the puddle, and each square of the grid measured 5 m x 5 m (see Figure 2). They constructed the grid by measuring 5-m intervals along the blacktop bordering the puddle and marking these points with chalk. We then stretched string across the puddle in both directions according to the marks.

Once the grid was constructed, the students counted each square that was more than half filled with water. Since each square contained 25 m² (250,000 cm²) of surface area, we multiplied the number of squares times 25 m² times the average depth for an estimate of the volume of the puddle.

We discussed how the grid method could be used to measure a real lake using the scale of a map and a known average depth. Since our "lake" was quite small, both methods produced results within 10 cm³. However, the students realized that because the margin of a real lake is not straight, the grid method would produce more reliable measurements.

Life in the Lake

We were very interested in studying the life in and around Candlewood Lake. Before our visit to the lake, the children spent class time preparing to measure the kinds and amount of life we would find at the lake. We constructed Secchi disks to measure the approximate abundance of material suspended in the water column. To construct the Secchi disks, we used large coffee can lids with white stripes painted on them (see Figure 3). We attached a string to each disk through a hole in the middle, and the string was knotted at 20-cm intervals.

Students learned about some of the life forms that are part of the suspended matter in the lake, such as zooplankton, algae, and phytoplankton. By using a "soup analogy," students could understand that the transparency of the water would be greatly influenced by the amount of life suspended in the water.

When the Secchi disk is lowered into the water near midday, the point at which the white paint on the disk is no longer visible is the point at which the plankton in the water is scattering most of the sunlight and reducing the transparency of the water. This depth is easily measured using the attached string.

After using the Secchi disks to take readings during our lake visit, the students compared their data with published graphs of readings from two other lakes—one very productive lake with a large algae population and one lake known to have very little algae growth (Wetzel 1983).

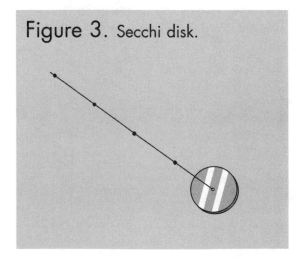

Figure 3. Secchi disk.

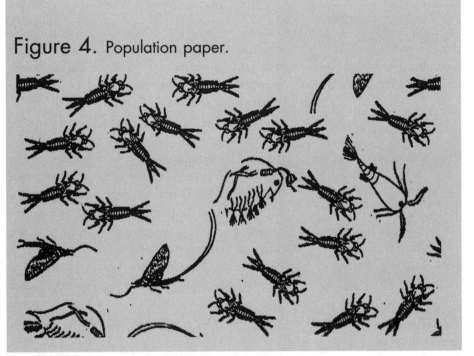

Figure 4. Population paper.

We introduced common lake algae in our area using pictures and examples. The students learned to use handheld microscopes to view samples of plankton taken from the lake. Since we had planned a spring trip, examples of zooplankton were also studied.

Students also learned how to conduct population studies at the lake. A practice study was done in class using a population consisting of the drawn outlines of mayflies, mayfly nymph, cyclopes, copepods, and daphnia (see Figure 4). Students used transparent 2-cm plastic squares (available in tangram kits) to estimate the population by placing the square randomly on the population paper and counting the number of each species contained within the square. With this data, we could then discuss relative species abundance.

Now that we were prepared to study populations, we needed a way to collect plankton. The children constructed plankton nets using the following materials:

- an old stocking
- a plastic jar
- a wide rubber band
- fishing line
- the rim of a canning jar lid or a piece of wire bent into a circle

To construct a plankton net, sew the stocking with the foot cut off to the canning jar lid or bent piece of wire (Figure 5). Attach the other end to an open plastic jar and secure using a wide rubber band wrapped twice around the jar and stocking. Attach several 30-cm strands of fishing line to the lid rim or wire to use when pulling the net through the water.

To the Lake

When the day of our visit to Candlewood Lake finally arrived in May, we were prepared to do a number of investigations. To ensure safety, students were divided into groups of six, and each group conducted the activities one at a time. Each student prepared a data collection notebook for recording information and observations about the lake. After completing an activity, a group would then sit on the grass to record its data while the other groups completed the activity. Slowing down students to record their findings made group management much easier. Four teachers and three aides supervised the activities.

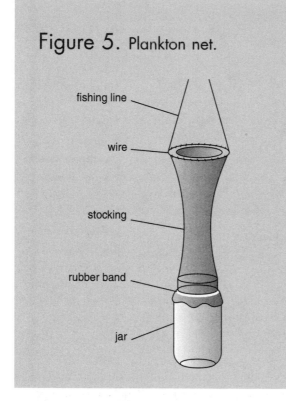

Figure 5. Plankton net.

fishing line

wire

stocking

rubber band

jar

Data to be recorded included the temperature of the air and the lake water, samples of the plants growing around the lake, elevation measurements from the water's edge to the road above the lake, and the pH of the lake water, measured with a battery-operated pH meter.

Even a very simple scientific instrument, the secchi disk, was a source of important data about conditions in our lake. Wearing their gym uniforms, students removed their shoes and socks and waded into the water, under the close supervision of the teachers. Using the Secchi disk, students found that Candlewood Lake has an abundance of plankton. In most of our readings, the white lines disappeared within the first 20 cm of depth. Later, in the classroom, students would observe the algae more closely using microscopes.

To obtain water temperatures from different depths, we attached a laboratory thermometer to a fishing pole. This thermometer could be cast out into the water and quickly reeled in to determine if the temperature of the lake water was uniform. The time needed to reel in the thermometer had some influence on the thermometer reading, yet this apparatus allowed students to determine areas of the lake where the water temperature varied. In fact, the students were surprised to find that the lake water temperature varied by more than 5°C from one area to another. This investigation showed that the physical environment of this lake was not uniform.

Students enjoyed collecting specimens, and the plankton nets were a great success. We even caught a small fish, which the children promptly named "Fred Fish," but we returned Fred to the lake. The students pressed local area plants, collected samples of the lake sediments, and even identified many mayfly nymphs in the water. Some of the specimens were brought back to school for further study. In the classroom, students spent time observing their specimens in greater detail and finishing their data collection notebooks.

A Trip to Remember

Field trips can be very costly and often result in nothing more than too much money spent in a gift shop. But with this lake investigation, students gained new insight into the history of their community, gained experience in using several scientific measurement devices, and used intermediate mathematics skills in a relevant application. The students were involved in the preparation, planning, and follow-up of this visit to Candlewood Lake, and the cost of the trip was minimal. The students have the best kind of souvenirs from this trip—scientific instruments they made themselves and the skills needed to use them.

Susan Goethals is the assistant principal at Our Lady of Lourdes School in Raleigh, NC. At the time of this study, she was a seventh-grade science teacher and principal at St. Joseph School in Danbury, CT.

Resources

Bull, J., and Farrand, J., Jr. 1977. *The Audubon Society Field Guide to North American Birds, Eastern Region.* New York: Alfred Knopf.

Fernandez, L. H. 1967. *History of Lake Candlewood, The Rocky River Project.* Unpublished master's thesis, Western Connecticut State University, Danbury, CT.

Little, E. 1980. *The Audubon Society Field Guide to North American Trees, Eastern Region.* New York: Alfred Knopf.

Milne, L., and Milne, M. 1980. *The Audubon Society Field Guide to North American Insects and Spiders.* New York: Alfred Knopf.

Western Regional Environmental Education Council. 198). *Project Wild: Aquatic.* Author.

Wetzel, R. G. 1983. *Limnology.* New York: Saunders College.

A Garden Story

By Linda Keteyian

How did a group of kindergarten through fifth-grade children realize their dream of having a little green around their urban school? With determination and a lot of enthusiasm. These children lived in Detroit, a city dominated by factories, buildings, and parking lots. Much of what surrounded their school was burned, broken, and covered in trash. There was no lush green grass or trees for shade.

The Higgins School Garden Project, an outgrowth of a science club I started in 1992, changed all that. The science club used to hold meetings Fridays after lunch to do experiments and tutor students in the lower grades in their science lessons. In 1995 the club expanded to an after-school program two days a week.

The club members and I had talked about creating a garden from the beginning of the club's formation. It seemed the natural thing for a science club to do. Students are eager and willing to learn, especially when a project captures their imaginations. That's what happened with the little school garden that grew and grew.

Beautifying the Courtyard

I asked the students which area of the school they wanted to beautify first, and the answer was unanimous: "The courtyard!" The courtyard was a barren plot, save for piles of dirt, bricks, rocks, glass, and a great deal of trash. In the past this area had been carefully tended by the entire school. During family visits to the classroom, students' grandparents would reminisce about how beautiful the courtyard used to look and how they used to plant roses there. It had been 20 years, however, since anyone had taken an interest in the neglected courtyard.

A parent of one of the club members knew a master gardener who worked with the Southwest Detroit Environment Vision (SDEV), a nonprofit community organization. I met with the gardener, a Franciscan friar who had led an urban garden project for his congregation, and told him about our club and the condition of the school grounds. He eagerly agreed to work with the students from start to finish, and through SDEV he supplied the railroad ties, wood chips, and hoses we would use to shape and lay out the garden. I contacted another organization, The Greening of Detroit, that agreed to provide the plants, trees, flowers, educational resources, and volunteer help we needed. The school also received grants from The National Wildlife Federation ($1,200); the Environmental Protection Agency ($11,800); the MEEMIC Foundation, a nonprofit organization funded by a Michigan insurance company that offers educational grants to teachers ($4,600); and New Detroit ($7,000).

SCi LINKS.
THE WORLD'S A CLICK AWAY

Topic: butterflies
Go to: www.scilinks.org
Code: MIX168

I learned about these grants through my school principal and by leafing through grant books in the state department of education grant office in Detroit. The gardener from SDEV found out about the National Wildlife Federation grant and encouraged me to apply. I applied for several grants, hoping each group would see the value of our project and the school would obtain necessary money for the garden project supplies—plants, woodchips, hoses, tools, and field trips—and various other environmental education programs at the school. And they did.

Armed with monetary support and "plant know-how" from the participating gardening organizations, I finally gave the students the green light to bring the courtyard back to life. Students glowed with excitement. "When can we bring in some plants?" "Can I plant some flowers?" "Can we have a bird fountain?"

Over the next two months, students discussed various types of gardens and began drawing possible layouts for their dream gardens. They also planted eight crab trees in front of the school. I was thrilled by their eagerness for the gardening project and responded to their questions about creating a garden with equal enthusiasm of my own: "However, before we can plant any garden, we first have to prepare the land."

By November, we were ready to begin clearing the garden site. I scheduled a Saturday for the clean-up day and sent a letter home to parents explaining the project and inviting them to help their children "level the ground." So many parents responded! They were elated at the prospect of helping their children make the community look better.

Throughout the day, students, parents, volunteers from The Greening of Detroit, and I hauled out the trash and leveled the ground with hoes and shovels supplied by The Green-

ing of Detroit, which taught the students how to use them. The work was exhausting, but no one stopped until the land was cleared. It was quite a sight to see students with wheelbarrows and shovels, their faces reflecting their determination to make a difference in this school courtyard.

The day was not without some challenges—while we worked, the water main broke, and mud piled high around the litter and rocks. The district fixed the water-main break immediately, but students weren't fazed by the disaster. Their work leveling the ground continued, business as usual. Only the mess got bigger.

During the leveling, students and I discussed how plants need nutrients such as nitrogen in the soil and that some chemicals such as lead or mercury in soil can be harmful. We also discussed that worms and decaying plant matter are helpful to plant growth. I wanted to test the soil before we planted the garden, so students collected soil into vials and sent the vials to Michigan State University for analysis.

The test results showed the soil was clean of lead and mercury and fairly high in nitrogen. We decided to add fertilizer in the form of cow manure to improve the health of the soil even more. A local conservation group donated compost, and after school one day the students spread the compost over the dirt.

The Excitement Builds

Students waited patiently throughout the fall and winter while it snowed. By this time, word had spread about the project, and more and more students and teachers were expressing an interest in lending a hand. This is how the club project turned into a schoolwide project.

During the winter months, teachers integrated age-appropriate activities on plant growth into their regular science lessons. For example, teachers had students place seeds in moist plastic bags in a classroom window to witness seed sprouting and mix vegetable peelings, soil, and water in a clean milk container to simulate composting. The Greening of Detroit volunteers also gave guest presentations about plant needs, part functions, and composting at each stage of the garden's development.

In April, the gardener I met with in the summer visited the club to meet everyone and start designing the garden. "Before we start planting, we need a plan, just like we need a blueprint for a building," he explained. The children drew diagrams of what they wanted to put in the garden, and each child was convinced his or her idea was the one that would be put into place. As you can imagine, discussion on the overall design was quite animated. The children especially wanted a fountain in the center of the garden, but we were unable to arrange a pump and an electric outlet, so students had to abandon that request.

Together, the gardener and the children created a collective plan for the new garden's design. They laid out paths and plots in marvelous symmetry on paper, with a tree nursery and a section for such native Michigan plants as daisies, tiger lilies, asters, and goldenrod. We wanted to put our own stamp on the project as well, so the master plan included a section planted with whatever the parents and children wanted to put there. I sent notes home asking for donations for this section, and we were soon inundated with all sorts of flowers, bushes, and ferns.

The gardener, his brother, and I were the ones who actually laid out the design with railroad ties and hoses the following Saturday. When students came to school on Monday and saw the plots of land, they were shocked at the courtyard's transformation. Though the plants were not yet in the ground, students knew something exciting was to come.

Shortly after the garden was laid out—at the beginning of May—another volunteer from The Greening of Detroit visited the school to show students how to plant the garden. Students followed the instructions regarding spacing and soil depth required for each particular plant. Throughout the week, each classroom took turns planting its contributions to help bring about the dream of a school garden. Many students were so excited to plant their own contribution in the garden that teachers had to restrain them from leaving class.

As the garden grew, Greening volunteers taught plant care and habitat development, such as the light requirements of certain plants in the garden. The children learned how deep to plant the trees and how wide they had to make the hole to ensure the trees' survival. We reviewed the basic plant needs of water, soil, light, and minerals (a Michigan Education Assessment Program requirement).

"What about animals?" asked a child. "How can we invite birds and squirrels to visit the garden?" The rest of the students nodded in agreement. The Greening volunteers said that to attract certain birds and squirrels, the children must set out the foods they like, such as birdseed and acorns. To this end, the gardener who had been working with us contributed two bird baths made from garbage can lids and two bird feeders made from soda bottles.

The Garden Grew!

The children could hardly wait to tend to the garden. "Does this look good?" "My plant is going to grow because I'm going to take good care of it." "Nobody better bother our garden!" and

"I can't believe we did it!" were just a few of the comments heard around the little garden as it developed. One student's artwork about the garden was incorporated into a newsletter I created and distributed to all classroom teachers. In the words of a fifth-grade student, the garden was a "garden to rule all gardens!"

To maintain the garden as it grew, I set up volunteer Saturdays where parents and their children could weed and water the garden. The science club had the primary responsibility for the garden's care, but everyone helped.

Butterfly Garden

Once the students saw the difference a garden could make in the appearance of the school and in the heart of the community, they wanted another one. In the spring of 2000 the school worked together to create the "Butterfly Garden," complete with various purple and yellow flowers—purple coneflowers, asters, and coreopsis—and bushes believed to attract butterflies. The students designed this new garden to surround the flagpole to welcome people as they first arrive to Higgins School. Volunteers from The Greening of Detroit laid out the garden design around the flagpole, and members of the science club planted the plants on their own.

Anyone visiting this school could see that its students really cared about the Earth.

In Remembrance

Students also created a third garden in front of the school to the left of the butterfly garden to honor a classmate who had died in a car accident the evening of the first day of school in August 2000. This child had helped with both the courtyard and the butterfly garden. After relating the news of his death to the club, I asked them what they would like to do in remembrance of their classmate. The children did not hesitate. Nothing but a garden would do.

The garden was rectangular in shape, surrounded by railroad ties, and filled with a variety of tulip and other bulbs designed to bloom all year. Every child in the school placed one bulb in the garden. The children helped design the layout and weeded and watered the plants. At its front, the children placed a wooden plaque for all to see that the garden had been planted in memory of their friend.

A Worthwhile Experience

Some people might consider our dedication to creating green areas a misdirection of school time. Not all learning, however, can be measured in tests. Learning also takes place when a child observes a problem that faces him or her daily, determines to change the circumstances that create that problem, and takes action on that decision. Learning occurs when children understand what other living things need and recognize that a little beauty in the world can make a difference.

These children managed to learn in spite of the odds against them. In the three years since the garden project began, the children of Higgins School have planted three major gardens and 12 trees, participated in numerous clean-up days, and learned the value of creating a clean green area in which to live and go to school. They have demonstrated a renewed interest in science class, and teachers use the gardens as outdoor classrooms when conducting lessons on plants. The children now understand the valuable role plants play in the survival of our planet: Plants clean up our air; give us oxygen; provide food for us and animals; provide our clothing and building material; and decompose and create soil, which is both a habitat for some animals and one of their basic needs.

I encourage other teachers of urban schools to start a similar project—it is possible. Sometimes all it takes is a little garden.

Linda Keteyian teaches science in grades three to five at Higgins Elementary School in Detroit, MI.

Project FLORA: Flora Love Our Revegetation Areas

By Mary Nied Phillips, Melissa Forsythe, and DJ Sanders

Down on one knee high on a rocky hillside near the Rio Grande River, with a view of the Mexican Sierra del Carmen mountains across the river boundary, a fourth-grade student examines several species of cacti growing nearby before selecting those he wants to photograph and sketch in his journal.

What a picturesque setting to learn science. Since the fall of 1998, third- through eighth-grade students living in the middle of the 1,979 square kilometers of Big Bend National Park (BBNP) in southwestern Texas have become active scientific members of their community through involvement with Project FLORA: Flora Love Our Revegetation Areas.

In this project students collected native seed, built a greenhouse to propagate native plants from this seed, learned to identify disturbed areas within the park, and revegetated those areas to restore them to pristine habitat. Throughout the project the students worked closely with their teachers, Sul Ross State University (SRSU) personnel who specialized in the local region's desert ecology, and BBNP scientists and volunteers.

A Living Laboratory

The students' living laboratory was the vast Chihuahuan Desert, which extends from northern Mexico to southern Texas and New Mexico. One of four deserts within the United States, the Chihuahuan is the youngest, highest, and wettest of the North American deserts.

The National Park Service administers both BBNP and 392 km of the Rio Grande Wild and Scenic River that forms the border between Texas and Mexico. Elevations within the park vary from 564 m to 2,233 m above sea level, and a growing need exists to preserve the great biodiversity of plants and animals within these contrasting elevations and their varied microclimates. More than 1,200 species of plants and nearly 450 species of birds have been found in BBNP—which is part of the Rio Grande migratory corridor, making it a hotspot for wildlife watchers. Mosquito fish live there, including the rare *Gambusia gaigei,* an endangered species found nowhere else in the world. Some plant species, such as the Chisos Oak, are also unique to the park. In addition to trees and shrubs, a wide variety of succulents, yuccas, agaves, and more than 65 species of cacti—surpassing the number found in any other national park—are native to the area.

Within the vast park, the San Vicente Independent School District (San Vicente ISD) is located at Panther Junction, home to the park headquarters and residences of many park employees. The majority of the district's K–8 children walk only a short distance from home to school. The entire school consists of approximately 23 students and four teachers plus a superintendent/principal, secretary, and business manager, thereby making it one of the smallest school districts in Texas.

Building a Dream

The project was conceived by two teachers who had lived and taught in the BBNP region for more than 10 years and were interested in developing activities for their students that taught not only mathematics and science content but also ways to give back to the community.

After establishing an action plan with the district superintendent and a BBNP botanist, the two teachers realized they would need external funding to accomplish their goals. A $250 grant from a BBNP project, along with a $750 grant from the H. E. Butt Foundation Environmental Challenge Program coordinated by the Texas General Land Office, was enough to start the program. Although the original project called for building a simple shaded structure called a lath house for plant propagation, the project was

broadened to include a real greenhouse when a 1999 Toyota Tapestry grant of $9,800 was awarded. The grant also allowed hiring an SRSU botany consultant to work with the children throughout the project.

Program Mission

Despite their isolation deep within the national park boundaries—the nearest hospital is located 176 km away—the staff and parents of San Vicente wanted to ensure that their students and children had long-term learning experiences in science inquiry. A community meeting with the new superintendent revealed that parents were concerned whether their children would be ready to make the transition to a larger, more populous school when parents transferred to different parks. Parents were particularly concerned that their children have a strong background in mathematics and science.

Project FLORA addressed not only science content but also community involvement, career exposure, and work ethics. Project objectives included:

1. Providing facilities and staff for developing and improving the efficiency of a native plant propagation program among SRSU (Alpine, Texas), BBNP, and San Vicente ISD.
2. Re-vegetating and restoring disturbed parklands.
3. Instilling in students a love and respect for science and their environment.
4. Integrating a course of study involving mathematics, science, and technology.
5. Providing students exposure to various careers through their work with graduate students at SRSU and National Park Service employees.
6. Serving as a model for other schools seeking community involvement.

And We're Off!

From late February through the end of the school year in May 1999, San Vicente staff and 13 students of various ages and grade levels immersed themselves in Project FLORA. The students were divided into three multiage teams: the Chihuahuas, the Bobcats, and the Red Hot Chili Peppers. Each team was assigned to different tasks that needed to be done every Friday, the day dedicated to the project. Sample tasks included creating a project task timeline, working with an architect on the greenhouse design, assisting the business manager with budgeting the project monies, ordering materials to construct the greenhouse, preparing the groundwork for the greenhouse, and developing a webpage.

The botany consultant hired with grant monies traveled 320 km round-trip to the school each week to teach the students about basic botany, including plants' cell structures, how plants germinate and grow, and the parts of plants and their functions. Students eventually learned about the propagation conditions needed to grow their native seeds in a greenhouse. For example, they learned that one of the ideal conditions for germination was keeping the temperature inside the greenhouse from fluctuating. (The best temperature is 15° to 27° Celsius.) To keep the temperature stable, the greenhouse had to be built 90 cm underground, as explained by the greenhouse architect hired with the grants.

The greenhouse design included windows high on the north side to control the escape of excess heat. The north and south sides would have screens plus removable panels made of a durable greenhouse plastic. These panels would be removed or replaced as needed to control the temperature inside the greenhouse. We also planned to install a small fan-driven heater that would come on automatically when the temperature dropped below 15° Celsius.

Eye-Opening Field Trips

Students took a field trip in November 1998 to the SRSU campus to visit the university greenhouses and learn about the native grasses being propagated there. Before Project FLORA, all the plants needed for revegetation projects in BBNP were grown in the SRSU greenhouses from seed collected in the park. The plan was for the children to take over part of the responsibility of growing such native grasses in their own greenhouse. The native grasses they would collect included *Sporobolus airoides* (Alkali sacaton), several Andropogon species (bluestems), *Bouteloua curtipendula* (sideots gramma), and many species of shrubs and small trees.

While on the field trip students also learned why they needed to revegetate damaged lands: If left damaged, the park lands could become vulnerable to erosion and exotic plant invasion. The presence of invasive plants would in turn reduce the native vegetation and affect wildlife habitats.

The field trip to the university was just one of four field trips during that year. During other trips students traveled to disturbed park areas needing revegetation. These trips were designed to teach about the different plant zones of the park, including the high Chisos Mountains, the mid-elevation desert, and the riparian zone along the Rio Grande. Students could see for themselves that many factors had affected these areas, from man-made changes, such as channelizing natural spring water to dry up wetlands and building roads and other structures, to cattle overgrazing occurring before BBNP was established in 1944. The man-made alterations allowed exotic plant species to flourish, crowding out the native ones. During these field trips, students also collected seeds from the native species found around the disturbed areas. All of these trips were taken in the fall, when the seed heads were mature. The teachers and the botanist demonstrated how to pull the seeds from the grasses and collect them in paper bags. One day of seed collecting produced enough seeds to last the year. Students cleaned the seeds when they returned to the classroom, removing the chaff and debris and keeping only pure seeds. The seeds were then labeled and stored in a refrigerator until they were planted. Besides collecting native seeds, the students were taught how to identify and eradicate the exotic species that threatened the native plants.

Some examples of exotic plants students identified were Johnson grass, buffel grass, and Bermuda grass, all of which crowd out native grasses; tree tobacco, which competes for space; giant reed, which proliferates along the river; tamarisk, which can suck all of the water from desert springs; and Russian thistle (tumbleweed), which compete with native species for space. Students helped eradicate the exotic grasses and tree tobacco by digging them up by the roots, making sure not to spread the seeds.

A plant book was designed by the teachers and students to keep track of all the native plants and seeds collected. Students pressed specimens of native plants and researched them for the book, which has become a vital part of the record keeping and monitoring documentation of Project FLORA.

The Greenhouse

Starting in February 1999, a retired architect and park volunteer led the teachers and students in designing a special greenhouse for plant propagation that would be built partially underground

Connecting to the Standards

This article relates to the following *National Science Education Standards:*

Teaching Standards

Standard A: Teachers of science plan an inquiry-based science program for their students.

Standard B: Teachers of science guide and facilitate learning and support inquiries while interacting with students.

Standard D: Teachers structure the time available so that students are able to engage in extended investigations and create settings for student work that are flexible.

Standard E: Teachers of science develop communities of science learners that reflect the intellectual rigor of scientific inquiry and the attitudes and social values conducive to science learning.

Standard F: Teachers of science actively participate in the ongoing planning and development of the school science program.

for temperature control and wind protection.

In August 1999, students, staff, and many volunteers from the Resource Management Division of BBNP finally broke ground for the greenhouse, and over the next two weeks and during weekends, students and more than a dozen volunteers dug the foundation. National Park Service personnel also worked with students to do the archaeological clearance study for the greenhouse site; dig the trenches for drainage, electrical, and water lines; and pour the footing and lay the cinderblock foundation.

A greenhouse-raising party in November attracted students, parents, and volunteers, including the school district's superintendent. All helped put backfill around the foundation and bring in wheelbarrows of gravel for its floor. A carpenter hired with Toyota Tapestry grant funds, along with all of the students, completed the greenhouse structure by February 2000. Students helped him select and measure the lumber to be cut, screw the wooden framework together, measure and put together all screen and window frames, and attach the greenhouse plastic to the finished frame.

While the greenhouse took form outside their classrooms, students were busy throughout the fall in many indoor activities, such as preparing for planting; organizing and taking inventory of stored greenhouse supplies such as potting mediums, containers, flats, plant tags, and cleaning equipment; making a checklist of tasks to be done; designing a T-shirt to present to volunteers; planning the ribbon-cutting ceremony; and writing thank-you letters with enclosed digital photos to the volunteers.

Planting Seeds

One of the students' tasks while the greenhouse was under construction was planting the native grass seed they collected during their field trips to disturbed park areas. In January 2000, each student planted at least two flats per planting session. They used 10-cm pots for the grasses and placed 18 of these pots per flat. They filled the pots with potting medium, sprinkled approximately 30 seeds on the medium, and then added a top dressing of vermiculite.

For each flat, students filled out plant tags with the name of the plant, date planted, identification number for the seed lot, and student initials. Then they soaked the flats in tubs of water and watered them three to four days a week with a mister. Students noted the date when seeds first germinated and how long it

took for all flats to germinate. These flats were placed in the greenhouse in March, when the greenhouse finally opened.

Greenhouse Ceremony

In March 2000, the school gathered with families and all the park personnel and volunteers who contributed to the successful building of its new native plant propagation greenhouse. Each of the third- through eighth-grade students who had worked on Project FLORA gave a short speech retracing the steps of the project before cutting the dedication ribbon.

The day of the greenhouse opening was also a celebration of a new grant—the school received a GTE GIFT 2000 School Enrichment grant for $15,000, which enabled San Vicente to continue to expand Project FLORA as well as provide professional development.

Revegetation

Before planting, students, under the guidance of BBNP botanists and biologists, set up drip irrigation systems with water emitters where each new plant would be planted. Then students divided into groups to dig holes and plant each seedling next to the emitter. This irrigation system kept the plants watered for the first two to three months, after which the hoses were removed to let the plants survive naturally. Later, ditches that had previously channelized spring water were opened up to allow the revegetation area to flood seasonally. After this, the students could plant without irrigation systems, when the revegetation area still had some standing water.

A Rewarding Experience for All

After students revegetated the designated park lands, they continued to monitor the new plants during field visits. Students continue collecting native seeds from the park lands, propagating the seeds in the new greenhouse, and then planting the seedlings in the revegetation area twice each year. They work with the Resource Management Division of BBNP to learn more about optimal planting times and how many plants of different species are needed for revegetation.

The students also continue working with the SRSU botanist to experiment with different potting mediums, watering schedules, and planting times, part of their efforts to determine both the best propagation methods and promote the best plant survival rates in the revegetation sites.

"Project FLORA has allowed the students of San Vicente ISD to become an active part of their scientific community," wrote Melissa Forsythe, project director. "Living in a national park, these students have a huge science laboratory in their backyard. By growing native plants in the greenhouse they helped to build, and by revegetating disturbed areas of Big Bend National Park with these plants, the students learned about the flora of Big Bend, and they are helping to preserve and protect Big Bend National Park for generations to come."

For the San Vicente students, Project FLORA is an ongoing, real life opportunity that involves them in all aspects of their unique campus environment.

Mary Nied Phillips is an environmental studies educator and the gifted and talented lead teacher at Lake Waco Montessori Magnet School for Environmental Studies in Waco, TX. Melissa Forsythe teaches sixth–eighth grade, and DJ Sanders teaches third–fifth grade at San Vicente School in San Vicente, TX. Both Melissa and DJ are the directors of Project FLORA.

Resources

Big Bend National Division of Interpretation and Visitor Services. 1997. *Chihuahuan Desert Biosphere Reserve*. Big Bend National Park, TX: National Park Service.

Big Bend National Division of Interpretation and Visitor Services. 1997. *Junior Ranger Book Big Bend National Park*. Big Bend National Park, TX: National Park Service.

Boucher, K. 1989. *Rio Grande Village Self-Guided Nature Trail*. Big Bend National Park, TX: Big Bend Natural History Association.

Eifert, L., and N. C. Martin. 1998. *Big Bend Nature Guide*. Big Bend National Park, TX: Big Bend Natural History Association.

Forsythe, M. 1998. *San Vicente School Centennial 1898-1998*. Big Bend National Park, TX: National Park Service.

National Research Council. 1996. *National Science Education Standards*. Washington, DC: National Academy Press.

Talley, L. 1999. *San Vicente School Greenhouse: An Educational Project for Kids*. Alpine, TX: Alpine Avalanche.

http:// World Wide Weather

By Kay Berglund Newhouse

"Did we remember to calibrate the instruments?"

"Someone left the weather shelter open. Do you think that could affect our data?"

"Wait. Someone messed up. We couldn't have had a 34°C day in January."

"The water is either 23 or 24°C. I'm not sure. Could someone else check?"

Wouldn't you be careful, too, if you were recording data for scientists to use in their research? If your data could help scientists around the world figure out what is happening with global warming and other environmental issues, would you want it to be incorrect?

Students at Norwood School and more than 8,000 other schools on seven continents, including Antarctica, learned how scientific research works by participating in the GLOBE program (Global Learning and Observations to Benefit the Environment). Currently, students have many opportunities to contribute data to scientists. Involving students in actual scientific research gives them the opportunity to see how science really works. Students practice measurement skills in a context that asks them to apply these skills meaningfully, and they develop a sense of accountability for the accuracy of their data. Because global warming is measured in tenths of a degree, it really does matter whether that thermometer says 23 or 24°C.

Participating in this student/scientist partnership touches on many different curriculum areas, including but not limited to the following National Science Education Standards: Content Standard A: Science as Inquiry, Content Standard D: Structure of the Earth System, Content Standard E: Science and Technology, and Content Standard G: History and Nature of Science.

What Is GLOBE?

The GLOBE program began in the United States with support from the White House, National Science Foundation, Department of Education, State Department, NASA, Environmental Protection Agency, NOAA, and many other organizations. Then-Vice President Al Gore started GLOBE as a nonpartisan effort to simply gather and share data so that questions about global warming could be answered by scientists and the children of the world, instead of by debating politicians with liberal or conservative agendas.

Currently, this worldwide program asks teachers and students from kindergarten to the graduate level to record meaningful scientific data that professional scientists can use in studying the global environment. In this student-scientist partnership, students record environmental data about water, soil, land, and the atmosphere.

One objective of the program is to gather data at the many school sites—to use the presence of schools everywhere in the world to offer far more breadth of data than a researcher could normally access. Another goal is to involve students in actual research, so tomorrow's citizens and policymakers will better understand how data is gathered. Through this hands-on experience, young people learn to value information gathered about the world's environment in their own backyards and in faraway countries. Because this student-scientist partnership spans so many diverse countries, students have an opportunity to see the world as a whole and understand that each country does not function alone. (To learn more about the GLOBE program's opportunities for international student-scientist collaboration, visit *http://www.globe.gov*.)

Norwood's Contribution

Prior to beginning this venture, the school's science teachers attended a four-day workshop to learn how to take precise measurements. GLOBE offers these workshops free to any teachers who are interested in having their students participate in the GLOBE program. We found workshops that were offered in our area on convenient dates by looking at GLOBE's website.

During the training, we had an opportunity to practice taking measurements of land, soil, air, and water characteristics with supervision and help from the GLOBE staff and teachers already working with this program. We were given a binder with background information, activities to help teach the concepts involved in GLOBE, and detailed protocols (descriptions of how to take the data measurements). The trainers emphasized taking measurements precisely according to the printed directions we received.

We learned—and later taught our students— that a small deviation from protocol in how a school takes its measurements could skew the data from that school. We also learned that GLOBE scientists use students' data to research many topics. This data was also available on the Web, so students at other schools could study our data. Likewise, scientists who are not directly involved in GLOBE also could access this database for their research. Because our data would be used for such varied purposes, we knew we needed to take measurements as carefully as the professional scientists would if they were to visit our creek or hillside.

During previous years' weather units, we asked students to gather temperature, wind, cloud, and rain data to help them develop an understanding of units of measurement and variations in their own climate (i.e., Is 120 mm a lot of rain? What does it feel like when it's 30°C outside?). We always struggled with what to do with the data because we never gathered enough consistent data to make meaningful conclusions from our monitoring activity; we just ended up throwing away our confusing handwritten records at the end of the term. We also lacked accountability—if someone measured the rainfall incorrectly, it didn't really matter to us.

When students began measuring a huge number of environmental variables for GLOBE, such as air temperature, water pH, and tree canopy density, they learned much more than just how to record these numbers. They gained an understanding of the whole research effort, as we focused on how and why people gather these kinds of data. We looked at news stories that disputed issues about global warming and other environmental phenomena, and we put ourselves in the shoes of politicians trying to make expensive decisions about what is or is not needed to keep our environment healthy.

Students learned that more data is desperately needed. For example, estimates of the amount of global warming the Earth has experienced in recent decades would be much less debatable if the data these estimates are based on were more comprehensive. Information about the locations of different soil types and characteristics of soil around the world is even scarcer, and soil scientists want more data to help them understand this critical component of the ecosystem. Because school children are so numerous and cover every possible corner of the world, they can supply a much more comprehensive and plentiful database than is currently available.

Students also learned why it is important to gather data and standardize the methods used to take the measurements. Because all this data from so many schools and countries is compiled for a complete picture of major environmental issues, students must be sure the methods used to take the data are consistent.

Recording Data

We chose several different aspects of the GLOBE program to implement at Norwood and divided our choices by grade level. Each grade learned a bit about the GLOBE program as a whole, but then focused most carefully on one particular topic, so each grade could learn

in depth how to take these measurements and report their data.

In one of the first installments of Norwood School's real-science adventure, the fourth-grade class walked to a nearby stream to measure data about the water. Students waded into the water and measured its temperature, pH, and conductivity. We then stepped up to a grassy hill to find an area without trees so our Global Positioning Satellite (GPS) receiver would have a clear view of satellites. Our GPS, which we borrowed through GLOBE for a week, measured the latitude, longitude, and elevation at this site (near to but distinct from our school's entrance) so that others interpreting our data would know exactly where in the world we were.

GLOBE gave us a list of suppliers from which we could get all the equipment needed to participate in GLOBE. These suppliers also had packaged kits with all the needed equipment for a school starting the GLOBE project.

Students took turns submerging an environmentally friendly alcohol thermometer in the stream and recording the water's temperature. (GLOBE suggested this type of thermometer because it does not contain mercury, so it cannot poison the stream if it should break accidentally.) Measurements of the pH level of the water were also recorded with a handheld pH meter.

These fourth-grade students had not yet learned the chemistry concepts behind pH, but they could easily understand its ability to give us information about the acidity of water. Students had heard media information about acid rain, and suddenly this topic of evening newscasts became more real to their lives as they recorded the acidity for themselves. Every child wanted a chance to take a reading, and many took samples from several areas of the stream to compare the values. Conductivity, which measures how well electricity flows through the water (measure of the dissolved solids), was also easily read from a handheld meter.

Dissolved oxygen was more difficult to test and required an adult to do a titration experiment with more careful safety procedures. First, a student rinsed the collection bottle with distilled water and then with creek water three times. He or she then filled the bottle with creek water. The teacher then added drops of a few different chemicals to fix the oxygen. Young scientists wearing goggles saw spectacular color changes in the vial their teacher held. "It looks like apple juice!" was one description of the color. The teacher then transferred 10 mL of the solution to a test vial and followed the directions to do a titration experiment to determine the amount of oxygen in the sample water. We found that the amount of oxygen in the stream was much lower in the fall than later in the year. We hypothesized that the oxygen might have been used by the decaying leaves that were plentiful in the stream at that time of year. Small groups of fourth-grade students—four or five volunteers at a time—return to the stream every few weeks to gather additional data.

Another aspect of the GLOBE program involved incorporating atmosphere measurements into our fifth-grade weather unit. Each day at solar noon, a pair of fifth-grade volunteers walked to the school's white-painted weather station to take our GLOBE atmosphere reading. Even the color of the wooden weather shelter presented a learning opportunity. The students experimented with placing thermometers under different-colored paper tents and found the temperatures varied dramatically on a sunny day. Students thus understood from firsthand experience that our weather shelter must be white to reflect the sunlight like the weather shelters used all around the world; if ours were black or another color, we might get artificially higher temperature readings, and we could not accurately compare our data to other schools' data.

Using a rain gauge mounted on a pole a few feet from our weather station, students measured the amount of rain that fell each day and checked the pH of the rainfall using pH paper. With a maximum/minimum thermometer, students recorded the current temperature as well as the high and low for the previous 24 hours. (Have you ever wondered how maximum and minimum temperatures are tracked? This thermometer is easy to understand when you get accustomed to using one.)

During regular science class time, students investigated cloud types and created pictures showing what different percentages of cloud cover look like. Each day at the weather station (first as a class and then on an individual basis), students used a cloud chart supplied by GLOBE to match the visible clouds with their English names and recorded the amount of cloud cover. Five other languages appear on this chart for non-English-speaking students.

After taking data from the weather station, school grounds, or stream, students record what they have learned in a database on the Web. We accessed this site through GLOBE's main Web address after identifying ourselves as Norwood School with an ID and password given to us by GLOBE. Once the data had been processed into GLOBE's system, we could pull up graphs of the data from our school or compare what we have learned at our site to what another school had found. The data we entered were added to a growing database of more than 4 million observations from around the world. Most of the data-entry pages are available in Spanish,

French, German, and English. More languages were planned to accommodate the varied languages of the students participating in this program.

Becoming involved with a larger effort, learning how to take data accurately, and submitting data to scientists and other students via the World Wide Web hold students accountable and provide excitement. Instead of practicing their measurement skills merely for their own benefit, the children are making contributions to a growing database of knowledge about the atmosphere of the Earth.

Elissa Levine, a NASA scientist who used GLOBE student data to study soils around the world, visited our school to tell us about what she did with the data. Her "ready-for-mud" appearance, relaxed friendliness as she rolled soil between her fingers, and joy at the bare earth surrounding construction at our school shattered many students' perceptions of what a real scientist looks like and does.

We found that we can really contribute to her research by taking data at our school site. Even if you are not involved in a larger research project, asking a scientist to visit your classroom will give students an idea of what it really means to be a scientist. Chances are your visiting scientist will challenge your students' stereotypes of science and scientists.

Expansion into Other Areas

Because our participation in GLOBE was about real-life science, we could not keep our learning within the standard confines of our subject area. Gathering this type of scientific data draws on mathematics skills and strengthens geography knowledge; for instance, we could easily graph our minimum temperature curve versus that of a school in Australia.

Our school's educational technology special-ist showcased our class as an example of one of the exciting ways students can use the World Wide Web. Spanish language classes joined a GLOBE Web chat about hurricane preparedness; they submitted questions and read responses in Spanish with other participants as close as Miami and as far away as Argentina. Students' desire to understand and communicate in a foreign language skyrocketed.

At Norwood, we even extended our science efforts into community service and political awareness. We sold GLOBE stuffed animals to raise money to send scientific instruments to a school in South Africa, where schools have suffered lack of funds due to political upheaval in the last few years. We sent this equipment as a gesture of personal friendliness and to help achieve a sense of global connectedness.

Research for All

There are many opportunities for students to become involved in scientific research. Though participating in GLOBE is a terrific opportunity for any interested school, *NSTA Reports!* and other periodicals often list various requests from scientists for student assistance. Such opportunities involve students in research counting birds, measuring snowfall amounts, tracking the health of streams, or collecting data about the coming of spring. What better way to learn about the nature of science and its importance to our lives than by doing real-life science?

Kay Berglund Newhouse teaches elementary science at Norwood School in Bethesda, MD.

Resources

National Research Council. 1996. *National Science Education Standards.* Washington, DC: National Academy Press.